HEART ON FIST
Essays and Reviews 1970-2016
M. TRAVIS LANE

HEART ON FIST
Essays and Reviews 1970-2016
M. TRAVIS LANE

edited by Shane Neilson

Palimpsest Press
1171 Eastlawn Ave.
Windsor, Ontario. N8s 3J1
www.palimpsestpress.ca

Book and cover design by Dawn Kresan. Typeset in Adobe Garamond Pro.
Printed and bound at Webcom Printing in Ontario, Canada. Edited by Shane
Neilson and Carmine Starnino. Copyedited by Rhiannon Russell.

Palimpsest Press would like to thank the Canada Council for the Arts, and
the Ontario Arts Council for their support of our publishing program. We
also acknowledge the assistance of the Government of Ontario through the
Ontario Book Publishing Tax Credit.

 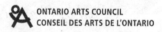

Library and Archives Canada Cataloguing in Publication

Lane, M. Travis (Millicent Travis), 1934–
[Essays. Selections]
          Heart on fist : essays and reviews, 1962-2017 / by M. Travis
          Lane ; edited by Shane Neilson.

Essays.
ISBN 978-1-926794-34-1 (paperback)

I. Neilson, Shane, 1975–, editor   II. Title.   III. Title: Essays. Selections.

PS8573.A55A6 2016B   c814'.54   C2016-903808-4

I found at Vassar two quotations that I keep with me always:

> *"I saw, also, that there was an ocean of darkness and death, but an infinite ocean of light and love, which flowed over the ocean of darkness, and in that I saw the infinite love of God."*
> —George Fox
> *"What though the longed for end be never reached and the heart itself be consumed utterly in the violence of its striving? It is enough that it burn nobly."*
> —Giordano Bruno.

M. Travis Lane

Contents

SIX: CLOSING ARGUMENTS

Crossing the Campus: Editor's Introduction

A young mother sets out from her home on Windsor Street. She crosses the University of New Brunswick campus and arrives at *The Fiddlehead* office. If anyone's in and the door's unlocked, she enters and heads straight for the "to review" shelves at the end of the hall.

On those shelves are most of the books published in Canada in a given year, arranged according to the time of their arrival at the office. The young woman considers the books, wondering if she's overlooked something; but really she's there to see if the new titles catch her eye.

For a book to have a chance with this reviewer, it shouldn't be fashionable. No—that won't do. A book's odds are better if it's written by a woman, because the reviewer is interested in how other women negotiate a life in poetry: What are their concerns? What technical choices do they make? If the book is a translation of a French Canadian, European, or Latin American poet, then the chances are also high that the reviewer will pick up that title. After all, such volumes offer her a distinct opportunity to reflect upon the nature of language. Eventually, with books in hand, the young woman leaves *The Fiddlehead* office and walks back to her home. She sits down in her den and, before her children come home from school, begins to read.

This scenario governed much of M. Travis Lane's life. Six decades after publishing her first review on Robert Frost, she has penned over 120 reviews of more than 250 books. While these numbers make Lane unique in Canadian letters—who else can claim such an impressive record?—the qualitative value of her enduring taste vaults her into the realm of "singular." Lane has an omnivorous appetite for the best, and rarest, writing she can read. This appetite has operated as a kind of lodestone for countless *Fiddlehead* readers over the decades. Because she was the journal's anchor reviewer, younger poets wanted to know what Lane might be reading, and to check their work against her insights. I know this, because I was one of them.

❁

Part of what makes Lane's reviews such a compelling minority report on Canadian poetry is her direct style. Here's how one review begins: "I do not agree with the major points of Robin Skelton's scholarly and interesting book *The Poet's Calling* (Heinemann, 1975). Because much of what Skelton says is widely believed, I think it important to quarrel with him at some length." Back then, she could be refreshingly frank about inferior work. As the years passed, her frustrations—when they came—settled into what I'll term a devastating mildness. Lane almost trotted out things before the reader as if to say, "Here they are, and they are not much, but this is what they are." For example, a poet may find herself simultaneously praised, contextualized, and diminished in the same breath, such as Mary di Michele: "[S]he has instead found the sound that suits her purposes and her audience, a delightful sound, easy to hear, a pleasure to make—and virtually indistinguishable from the sound of much contemporary prose."

We need critics to be nuanced and balanced. We also need them to acknowledge their prejudices. But how often can we expect all those qualities to work in tandem, like Lane does here when writing about Gary Dault: "When I picked up Dault's unfortunately titled collection of small, sometimes tiny, poems, two things struck me almost at once: 1) what he sees himself as doing, as his prefatory note makes clear, is something against which I have found enormous prejudices, and 2) many of these little poems are good, and some excellent." Just when you think Dault might be in for a Skelton-ing, she veers, indulging not what she finds distasteful, but indulging the poetry before her.

Yet it strikes me that, so far in this introduction, I have dwelled upon negative factors when *Heart on Fist* is overwhelmingly a collection of prose appreciations. Make no mistake: Lane loves lots of kinds and styles of poetry, and when she likes something, her enthusiasms are unmistakeable, infectious, and well argued. What better compliment can a poet get when someone of Lane's acumen writes, as she does of Catherine Owen (in an un-included review), "How I wish I had written that!"

In terms of Lane's reviewing method, she tries to provide general commentary while also providing a slightly eccentric (and often funny) personal perspective. She takes a genre and provides a mini-history about it in a paragraph or two, essential information that places the book in context so that its individual merits can be more minutely assessed. What's particularly valuable about her reviews, both to the poet under review and to her readership, is that she mostly dispenses with rhetoric and simply gets her hands deep in the engines of books, pointing out why one has such high horsepower and why another won't turn over. This strength increases exponentially when she links the pros and cons of a book's style or technique to her own preferences—we see Lane, the practising poet, come into view, and we get a better sense of the *why* of her taste. Lane's main interest is always the book at hand: whether the speaker is constructed well; whether the characters in poems have distinctive subjectivities; whether myth patterns make sense; whether described specialized activities (like sculpting, to name just one) possess the technical authority that comes from specialized language; what kinds of musical effects are employed; and, sometimes, what kind of fashionable Kool-Aid poets seem to have swallowed.

As I've already mentioned, one of Lane's favourite subjects is translation. This might come as a surprise to readers of her poetry, as she hasn't published a translated poem in any of her books (though phrases from other languages find their ways in). Translations bring the ostensible best from other cultures and keep Lane's ear attuned to new sounds. What won't be a surprise are her other big considerations, Christianity and feminism. Lane is positioned like few others to offer an opinion on the effectiveness and solidity of a poet's use of Christian iconography because of her extensive poetic practice in this area. However, the overwhelming perspective in Lane's criticism comes from a feminist, and not religious or spiritual, vantage point. Lane is a female reviewer who (unlike a lot of poets nowadays) actually does the hard work of writing well about female poets, and who has taken prominent Canlit figures to task for serial insensitivity to gender concerns.

I made sure to include less-celebrated names because Lane spent much productive time with them, ranging from lyric to avant-garde practitioners. Her erudition among the former group is obvious, but a young make-it-new-er might heed well Lane's familiarity with latter-day repurposing of old ideas. Over the years, Lane seemed to get better at what she was already good at: assessing the thing in front of her, enjoying itself for itself. She seemed to become more receptive to innovation in poetry, though I'm certain she'd claim that she was celebrating innovation qua innovation, not programmatic writing. In any case, Lane didn't grow into a critic who closed her mind as time passed. She kept it open, and, if anything, her taste broadened, although she remained convinced that poetry must be rooted in emotion to have value. To take a page from Lane's critical practice, I admit my own prejudice as editor of this volume: I agree wholeheartedly with her, and that is probably the greatest limitation this volume has, if one wants to think of it as a limitation.

Now that she is eighty-one years old (and still reviewing as often, and as well, as she ever was), I no longer imagine that woman intrepidly crossing the campus and looking for books. Now I imagine her infrequently driving to *The Fiddlehead* office. But just as I always have, I wonder: What will Travis pick up to review? What will she write? In my mind, she's become myth: writing criticism that eschews rhetoric in favour of description and analysis, her opinions like the night sky one can navigate by. She thinks in terms of the literature of millennia, not the past three years. Lucky is the poet who is reviewed by her, her criticism as close to an agenda-less opinion one is likely to get in Canada's politicized critical climate (barring the constitutive feminism which makes her a valuable critic in her era.)

To give the reader a representative sample, I tried as much as possible in my selection process to balance the quality of Lane's prose with the relative reputations of individual poets. Sorely treated are the poets who Lane wrote about more than once; in most of the cases in this book, you'll see only one piece on them when actually several exist outside these pages. Lane was the kind of critic who followed poets over a lifetime. Many of her reviews err on the side of over-quotation, which, although a thrill for the poet being reviewed, offers less to the reader of this volume who comes to the table to read Lane. Furthermore, Lane's omnibus reviews were thinner with respect to individual poets and, with such a wealth of prose to choose from, I always went in for the more substantial analyses. One of the problems of *Selected* volumes is what's left out, and I salute the pieces left out—may you be gathered together one day in a *Collected* (which would need to be quintuple the size of the book you have in your hand).

Unlike many other critics publishing in the present century, the grand majority of Lane's criticism is neither available on the internet, nor is much of it obtainable in humanities databases. It has been a labour of love to handle old issues of *The Fiddlehead* and to transcribe Lane's words for an audience who would otherwise have to travel to an academic library to get them.

Digging through shelves of issues turned up a number of surprises, but that's a different essay.

In this book, I give you a different Lane, a prose Lane—the equal-to-poet Lane, though I am sure Lane herself, and with justification, considers herself a poet first; but to many, her poet and prose selves are indivisible. What comes to my mind as I picture Lane reading this sentence is a vision of the great poet-critic shaking her head, scornful of the categories I have curated her work into, questioning my mythmaking, muttering something like the verdict she once gave a hapless anthologist, one who "thus blurs his own intentions by flattening the individualities of his authors and over-universalizing their themes." But onward!

Shane Neilson, Oakville 2016

ONE:

On Writing Criticism

On Reviewing

Most writers mourn the scarcity of thoughtful reviews. Perhaps the major reason so few reviews exist is that there is little academic or professional prestige, and only pin money, to be had from writing them. Someone with a full-time job has little time for such a profitless and time-consuming activity. It is hard enough to find time to write at all! (The reason that there are fewer female reviewers than male reviewers is that most women have a full-time job, but no full-time housewife.) In short, reviewing—especially reviewing poetry—is more of a hobby than a profession.

So why do it? Speaking for myself, I review because I love to discover good poetry, to share my pleasures with others, and because thinking about writing that I admire exercises my mind. I also review because I've never had a full-time job. Poetry and keeping house has been my life.

Although writers yearn for reviews, the market is very small. Too few prestigious places publish them (newspapers and paper journals) and there is too much turnover with the less prestigious places (blogs and online journals). Then there are the editorial expectations. Newspaper reviews are obliged to be short, "timely," and say something about plot, subject, or the "theme"; this makes it hard to go beyond generalizations and praise into a close examination of the material. Blogs vary, of course, but have a tremendous advantage: bloggers can indulge themselves in long speculations, comparisons, quotations, and because they allow themselves such freedom, they are often interesting. But how do we know what blog to look for? (And blogs tend to have short lives.) Online journals, although very much like paper journals, suffer from being on screen. How long, I wonder, do these thoughts remain retrievable?

Should every book produced be reviewed? No. There are too many books, as Orwell said a long time ago. If we are to have useful, thoughtful reviews, reviewers should be allowed to limit themselves to material that attracts their attention. When reviewers are assigned books that they would not otherwise have chosen to read, we can get very foolish or lazy reviews. In such circumstances, undeserved or ill-aimed praise is more common than surly dismissal. But what does the reader need? Readers need close, not hasty, reading. For example, *Crossover*, my latest book of poetry, was recently beautifully praised—and summarized as being primarily "about flowers." There were no poems about flowers in it. Mistakes like this ruin credibility.

Because I particularly like "discovering" writers off the beaten track, *The Fiddlehead* allows me to browse among the masses of books submitted to them until I find two or sometimes three that catch my interest. Since this is an introduction to a volume of my selected reviews and essays, you might want answers to the following questions: What am I looking for? What do I like? Dislike? And what do I ask of myself as a reviewer?

First comes sound. I sound out the sentences or phrases of the poems, and if the poet seems to have no ear for the cadences of our language, the poems will sound lifeless. Sound is inextricably linked with the emotion of the poem. All living creatures (including you, dear reader) exist in an emotional state—*acedia* is as much an emotion as fury, but it doesn't make for much of a poem. What I want from a poem is an opening, an enlargement of our sense of life, even if the "sense" of the poem is as untranslatable as music. Pater exaggerated when he wrote that "all art constantly aspires toward the condition of music"—which communicates without pictures or words. For me, the most important part of a poem is the part that can not be paraphrased. But what *can* be said in words is what music *can not* say.

Next, I consider a poem's imagery. I dislike images that are unimaginable, un-visualizable, and therefore irrelevant. However amusing such material may seem to the author and to his or her immediate audience, it resembles the pasting of a paper collar on a dog—futile, and somehow irreverent (to both dog and poem). The idea/narrative/argument of the poem should be integrally rooted in the expression/exposition of it.

One quality in poetry I am delighted to find, but do not find as often as I would wish, is a sense of theatre. I don't mean making odd noises or waving fists in the air, but rather development, discovery, or change in plot as part of the progression of the poem. I apply this wish even to the poem micro in scale, the haiku: too many of us write a version of "pretty thing pretty thing pretty thing" in the correct number of syllables. But the best haiku have a twist, a but, a tang of salt in their conclusion. The best sonnets, too, employ dramatic progression. At the macro level, a long poem absolutely must have changes of cadence, address, emotion because it will be on stage for pages and should not keep the same tonalities. No matter how seriously and intelligently observed its subject, without drama it will be soporific in production. Erin Mouré has observed that poems are "little theatres." She is right (and she is not boring).

Thought matters, too, but original thinking is rare and, because of the rarity, a casual reader may miss or misunderstand what is being communicated. Like Robert Frost in "A Considerable Speck," I, too, am glad to "find / On any sheet the least display of mind," but I try not to have any preconceptions about what is, or should be, written. Which is not to say that I am without the following dislikes:

I dislike extravagant generalities about race, gender, and religion. I especially dislike writers who believe that it has been "scientifically proven" that men are less emotional and less linguistically gifted than women. In spite of the prevailing cultural preference for girls to be pretty and boys to be clever, this yin-yang thinking is extraordinarily unobservant. I'd almost be inclined to think men are *more* emotional than women—and certainly talk a lot more than we do—though I wouldn't argue the point.

I am not charmed by language or ideas that seem to relish horror to the point of exaggeration and fantasy. Dracula leaves me cold.

I do not search for, nor do I try to avoid, topics such as gender, race, class. When building an anthology, an editor may find selecting a category of poetry useful. And indeed much material of historical or sociological worth can be discussed by sorting out poets into social categories. But categorization is crippling in a reviewer because it directs the readers' attentions to the subject and experience of the poet and away from the poem. Moreover, such categorization always hints at a second-rateness of the categorized, because in such sorting we do not tend to find a defined *and* discussed category of "white, anglophone, hetero, able, male"—instead this category is presented as the default definition of "poet." Because I am not a sociologist, but a reviewer of poetry, I will not emphasize the experience and social/historical/racial conditions of the poet in my reviews, even though these may be the poet's primary topic. Do we not all of us write out of our own experience? But it is not the subject of the poem, nor the history of the poet, that makes a good poem? A poem should not be treated as a symptom, nor should a poet be segregated.

●

What else directs my choices?

I prefer not to review a close friend or someone to whom I owe a great debt of kindness for fear that those knowing this debt might undervalue my praise. Although I prefer not to review someone I have reviewed before, I do so if I find I have something different to say. Whether I review several books together or only one at a time varies. Sometimes interesting comparisons can be made—but not always. I try to be neither boring nor unclear. And, although I have written a few hostile reviews when fired up against some idea or attitude in a poet whose work I may find otherwise admirable, I think it would be wrong to write a wholly unfavourable review.

In my opinion a good review should have ample quotations, not just to illustrate the reviewer's points, but also to allow the reader the opportunity to see whether they are likely to agree with the reviewer. A line one person finds admirable another may not. But this is not the only reason for ample quotations. Matthew Arnold has been much criticized for his term "touch-stone"—referring to those particular lines or phrases that seem so stirring, magically wonderful, so emotionally true, so beautiful, that reading them for the first time comes almost as a shock. But "touchstone" lines are rooted in their contexts, without which their power can not be fully felt; "I know why the caged bird sings." "Horseman, pass by!" "To her divine Majority— / Present no more!" "And miles to go before I sleep,"—it is only because we know their contexts that they move us so. A reviewer, wanting to praise some lines of a poem, should quote enough of it to give the reader some idea of the context.

I am reminded of the Navajo blessing "Walk in beauty!" To read a well-made poem is to walk in beauty regardless of the subject of the poem. A major part of a reviewer's duty is to bring good poems to the notice of others. But reviewing must go beyond praise and description. Reviewers are the servants of poetry, and we serve by educating the reader, by creating a more sensitive, more sophisticated audience for good writing. A good review must also be a response—a reading, a criticism, always partial, often imperfect—and no good poem should be met with silence. We represent the poet's best audience, and a well-written review is a chapter in the never-ending discussion among poets about poetry. Which is why reviews matter, and why I write them.

Contemporary Canadian Verse: The View from Here

Many of us are now aware that most people who write about Canadian poetry have tended to write about it in terms of its themes, or in terms of its geographical, political, or philosophical origins.[1] Critics following the leads of Northrop Frye, Margaret Atwood, and D.G. Jones discuss Canadian poetry in terms of its pervading themes and the national character such themes reveal, a method which fails to cope satisfactorily with atypical themes, foreign influences, "the spirit of the times" or international *weltgeist*, and disparities of poetic skill. Moreover, that the pervading themes are indeed garrison/survival/victim or butterfly-on-rockishness has been questioned. A case could be made that the pervading tenor of Canadian poetry is "loyalist"—loyal to the past or to an imagined past, its tone nostalgic for the wilderness few Canadians nowadays must cope with. This would account for the rhythmic mildness and elegiac tones of much Canadian verse, and for the comparative rarity in Canada of future-projecting, revolutionary, or visionary verse. Douglas LePan has noted that the Canadian mythos (as contrasted to that of the United States) is founded on mid-nineteenth-century sentiment, post-rationalist, post-romantic.[2] But this sort of writing is cultural history more than literary criticism.

Geographical distinctions are standard in historical resumés of Canadian poetry, distinctions once partially justified by the geographical distribution of influential figures with typifying interests (James Reaney/myth/Toronto). But time, the mobility of the Canadian poet, and our tendency to read and be influenced even by poets who do not live next door have blurred these distinctions. Regionalism, of course, exists; we write most about what confronts us, and the landscape, the weather, and the neighbours will always have their effect. But the necessity of earning a living—wherever—is even more influential. Nor are poets obliged to be regionalists. I was once asked if I could be considered a British Columbia poet (I had just brought out a long poem set partly in BC), but I have never been there. And I was once excluded from a list of New Brunswick poets on the grounds that I had not been brought up in NB. Actually, quite a number of Canada's poets have not been brought up in Canada—but they haven't all been brought up in the same non-Canadian places either. Geographic distinctions, whether in terms of "school" (the Black Mountain-Tish equation that fails to account for the similarly strong influence of American post-modernist poetry on non-western poets) or of "influence" (Irving Layton/Montreal, but not, somehow, Newfoundland or Alberta) or of regionalist landscape (Elizabeth Brewster/Maritimes) seem to me inadequate.

Political distinctions among poetries are a trifle old-fashioned, but continue to exist, most often as thematic distinctions between poems of social concern—Milton Acorn, Dorothy Livesay, Raymond Souster, Tom Wayman—and poems not socially concerned. And there is a kind of logical consistency in Robin Mathews's lonely criticism of the majority of contemporary Canadian poets as un-Canadian, that is, insufficiently combining the anti-imperialist message with the homespun, communal, un-hippie style. But there is also the distinction made a generation or so ago by poets rebelling against the pre-World War II high modernist poets, so many of whom were politically conservative, some of whom were fascist. These rebelling poets set up an ideal of poetic style: "naked"; less literary, less crafted (or "cooked"); less obviously rhythmic—and then identified their "post-modernist" style with mildly leftist politics and the high modernist style with implicit fascism. See, for example, a letter by Lloyd Abbey in *Canadian Literature* that takes the Coleridgean term "organic form" as indicating the favouring of American intervention in Vietnam.[3] Or Frank Davey's assertion in *From There to Here* that "modernism was essentially an elitist, formalistic, anti-democratic, and anti-terrestrial movement."[4] Throughout *From There to Here* Davey ignores the literal meanings of sensuous, life-affirming, social-value-and-community-affirming formal poetry (such as poems by Ralph Gustafson, Louis Dudek, P.K. Page, Phyllis Webb, Robert Finch) for the somehow nobler abstractions of inky post-modern experimentalists.[5] In fact, since poetry is not yet the common entertainment of the English-speaking, all contemporary Canadian poets are read only by an elite few.

There continues to be a great fashion of talking about poetry according to the theory of poetry possessed by the poet, or even according to the philosophy of life the poet professes. Thus Davey condemns an anthology of Maritime verse as being full of transcendentalism and objectivity,[6] a matter of taste rather than of artistic morality, and eulogizes bill bissett's "profundities."[7]

Both Eli Mandel and Davey have praised poetry that, in its dullness, disorder, and meaninglessness, reflects (or exaggerates) the dullness, disorder, and meaninglessness the poet sees as the Truth about Life.[8] Since the universe and humanity's difficulties with it have always been liable to being "meaninglessly broken off" (Robert Frost, "The Lesson for Today"), it is just possible that the construction of dull, disorderly, meaningless art is a retreat from the demands upon our courage and intellect that life has always made. I prefer Dennis Lee's conclusion to a poem on this subject, "Not Abstract Harmonies But": "the jangle is hard, but not to be quickened is death."

Many current discussions of poetic theory tend, to my mind, to combine truths too obvious to mention with a prose tediousness that makes Kant's prose, in contrast, sound like Jane Austen's. The magazine *Open Letter* contains stunning examples.[9] The favoured terms are "phenomenology" and "process." The gist, as I faintly gather it, is that the personal experience of writing a poem is either more interesting or perhaps more real than any object produced, and that the conscientious poet will include in the poem a description of the poet's mental processes while writing it.

However, once a poem is written it ceases to be a process and becomes a finished thing. Neither phenomenology, if that is what it is, nor post-modernism prevents its advocates from writing good poems, but both provide no principles of excision or pruning, and very little principle of entertainment. The result can be the earnestly sensitive, if awkward and over-prolonged, "journals" of Daphne Marlatt, or the numbing intricacies of bpNichol's *Martyrology*—material with the sensuous charm of knitting instructions. If there is an argument against this kind of phenomenological poetics, it is not logical but emotional: any poem by Yeats. "Time drops in decay / And the candle blows out"—but the poem lasts.

As for the old-fashioned but still vital Jungian poetics, to my mind a more fecund philosophy, the muse as anima or animus does not work for all poets. Mythological archetypes that have life for one poet are inanimate for another. Towards most of these implausible spectres I find myself in the position of the speaker of Blake's "To Tirzah": "Then what have I to do with thee?"

Just as a well-written theory of parenting does not guarantee a good child, nor a lively cookbook an adequate meal, an interesting poetics is no guarantee of poetic quality. Even whether a poet needs a poetics seems to me debatable.

Some centipedes may not fall "distracted in a ditch / considering how to run" but aesthetic self-consciousness can be crippling. Many poets, myself included, prefer to trust the forming principles that emerge in a particular poem rather than any more abstract programme, though consistencies of creative process may be obvious to an objective or critical eye.

For me a poem is still a thing: a verbal construct in which meaning of word and grammatical phrase is not irrelevant to artistic intention, and where word, phrase, and sentence sounds, sequence of image, and structure of argument are more important to the artistic effect than in prose. That the reader's presence is always part of the reader/poem reality must be taken for granted, as well as the fact that the author once existed and once wrote. But any further philosophical excursion tempts me towards Dr. Johnson's illogical but irrefutable rejection of Berkeley. A poem is like a stone, concrete. By concrete I do not mean typed cunningly in the shape of the typist's bottom, but something artefacted, made, and finished, like a statue or a painting. Between poem as process and as thing two other analogies can be supposed: poem as opera, and as conversation. But I find neither of these analogies implicit in recent theoretical discussion of Canadian verse nor in the verse itself (although they may be applicable to verse drama). Poem as opera implies interpretation by performers not the poet; poem as conversation implies an especially active and creative response by the reader/audience.

Regarding recent Canadian poems, therefore, as things, and excluding typographic frivolities, I find it possible and useful to sort Canadian verse into roughly four formal categories (with hybrid or subcategories on occasion): the long, dramatic narrative; the meditative essay; and two different kinds of lyric, one of which I shall call "proletarian" and the other "self-displaying." The short anecdotal poem too short to be termed narrative usually makes a social protest or displays the poet's sensitivity, often both. Admittedly this way of looking at Canadian poetry has the disadvantage of blurring individual distinctions between poets, since poets do not necessarily limit themselves to writing only one kind of poetry. But it has the advantage of highlighting similarities between poems by different authors. Moreover, this way of looking at poetry allows one to distinguish between poems that surmount and poems that sink under the problems common to each category of verse: tediousness in the narrative and the meditative essay, sentimentalism in the narrative and the proletarian lyric, unoriginality in the meditative essay, and shallowness and vanity in the lyric of self-display. The characteristic virtues of each category, set against these characteristic weaknesses, will illustrate some of the strengths and virtues of contemporary Canadian poetry, and may also illustrate some truths about art in general.

The dramatic narrative is a form which includes near-epic recreations of historic events, patriotic celebrations of specific localities, and lyric sequences with psychological plots expanded to narrative length. After E.J. Pratt's heroic narratives in the grand, nineteenth-century manner, the Canadian dramatic narrative has tended to become subjective, substituting "we" for "they," "I" for "he," or, where the third person is used (rarely), keeping the point of view tied to the subconscious or instinctual level. Contemporary Canadian dramatic narratives basically come in two sorts: the plurally voiced, of which Don Gutteridge's several "poems for voices" are perhaps the best known; and the narrative monologues, much influenced by Earle Birney's "David" and, more recently, by Margaret Atwood's *Journals of Susanna Moodie*, which demonstrate the narrative potentialities of lyric sequence. (Verse plays, such as the masques or dramas of James Reaney or Phyllis Gotlieb, being presented rather than narrated, are not included in this discussion. Though the distinction between prose and poetry is perpetually blurred, that between drama and poetry is not.)

The seriousness of intention and importance of subject in this group of poems are a very great strength. Moreover, our writers of dramatic narrative have, as a whole, an excellent sense of structural unity, as if a clear understanding of theme naturally ordered perceptions and statements. (The narratives of Michael Ondaatje are generally acclaimed for these qualities, but similar praise could be given to those of Gary Geddes, D.G. Jones, Don Gutteridge, Stephen Scobie—and many others.) This poetry means to be major, and sometimes is. But the dramatic voice in present-day Canadian poetry also has its typifying weaknesses. The importance the poet attaches to his or her subject and the intensity of his or her gaze lead to the attachment of too much importance to every detail or quotation the poet can include. Thus these poems are liable to tediousness and to a kind of sentimentality, particularly noticeable in Gutteridge, towards historic or geographic detail. Narratives that focus on the development of an individual psyche, such as D.G. Jones's "The Lampman Poems," are less liable to these vices. But even Jones and particularly Scobie, in *McAlmon's Chinese Opera*, rely overmuch on the readers' sharing their own emotional reverence for historic fact. Ondaatje's ruthless shedding or rewriting of history has been, in his work, a source of strength.

A further weakness common to much recent Canadian dramatic narrative is its tendency towards subaqueous or somnambulistic characterization. The heroes and occasional heroines of this poetry tend to be passive, at their most vigorous merely the instruments of an obsessive dream. They do not intellectualize their behaviour; rather they dream and endure, moving instinctively through omen or nostalgia, as if they were never quite sober, never thoroughly awake. It is as if the writers could not imagine a conscious, alert mind doing the things these characters do, or as if only the instinctual self can be brutal. So pervading is this dreamlike tone in Ondaatje's verse, for example, one is sometimes tempted to think that the whole of his envisioned world would crumble instantly upon the application of a good breakfast.

Directly related to the somnambulistic aura of these poems are the poets' choices of "memorable" events—fornication and murder, and dreams about either, being apparently more essential to their characters than getting or not getting the daily bread. It is as if housework, farming, doctoring, governing, educating, managing money, or reasoning were too prosaic, too alert, too undreamlike for poetry. The language used by the dreamy characters of many of these narratives tends also to be dreamlike: the slow brooding of twentieth-century college graduates reading modern decadence into the imperceptive brutalities and alien philosophies of an earlier age. The imagined "natives" tend to speak ominously, humourlessly, Jungianly, as if they were not quite human. (Primitive voices in shorter Canadian poems, such as those by Marilyn Bowering or Kristjanna Gunnars, are often similarly unreal.) And the tepid rhythms and dreamy syntax in which our ancestors are supposedly brooding are sometimes gratingly set off by actual quotations from ancestral prose—incredibly lively, vigorous—a reality unaccounted for in the verse (see Gutteridge's *Borderlands*, for example). The problem may come from our poets' desire to create myth, from their relating myth to dream, from their taking from dream the sleepiest rhythms of the flesh. Where the poets stop trying to mythologize history and instead record anecdotes and living voices, as in Rona Murray's *Ootischenie*, or in many of the short narrative poems by Andrew Suknaski or Sid Marty, reality and the waking world return. Nevertheless the narrative voice in most recent Canadian poetry in English has tended to be the voice of dream—movingly numinous, and yet alien to waking life.

The meditative essay is the only kind of contemporary Canadian verse in English that assumes an educated audience which reads poetry habitually. Where the narrative and the lyric are mainly addressed to listener rather than to reader, the meditative essay is addressed not only to the audience's sensibilities but to its intellect. Meditative essays have been written by all Canada's Grand Old Masters—A.M. Klein, Margaret Avison, A.G. Bailey, Ralph Gustafson—but are less common now. To some extent this change in fashion reflects a swinging away of aesthetic interest from the objective to the subjective approach and parallels the similar change in the dramatic narrative noted above. And the militant post-modernist critics' identification of the well-formed thought with fascism may also have led poets to use this form less. The long meditative essays by Dennis Lee, the *Civil Elegies* and "The Death of Harold Ladoo," although eloquent and deeply moving, are, to my mind, weakened by what may be a reluctance to appear old-fashionedly rational. Lee's poem-essays deliberately wander and meander, confusing their syntax and their logical progression in order to display the confused emotions of their speaker. They are, in short, not quite as well written as prose—although some of their shorter, lyric sections are exquisitely well formed. Other circumstances have also lessened interest in the meditative poem. Recently I was astonished to hear an excellent younger poet condemn as "cold" and "intellectual"—apparently an inseparable combination—the poetry of our older generation: Ralph Gustafson, Phyllis Gotlieb, A.G. Bailey, Margaret Avison. She could not respond to a world of events, artefacts, ideas, and literature that had been real to them and is still real to me. The young have lost much of the past. References to history and to literature that characteristically recur in this kind of verse are meaningless to many readers. Long words or foreign words (French, Latin) offend. And a less educated audience is less perceptive, less understanding. So are its less educated poets.

No doubt the cult of reading poems publicly also discourages poets from working with ideas. The meditative essay is meant to be thought about in the privacies of our reading. Perhaps most of the audience for poetry today no longer reads it. The meditative essay tends to be the least naive of Canadian verse forms; it draws from the largest range of materials; it permits itself any reach of the intelligence or emotion. And this is the only voice in recent Canadian poetry that has a sense of sin. Where the dramatic narrative voice has a sense of Natural Evil, the proletarian voice a sense of Social Evil, and the self-concerned lyric a sense of Glamorous, Sado-Masochist Evil, à la *The Rocky Horror Picture Show*; the highly educated, highly thoughtful, and generally more experienced authors of the meditative essay tend to take a more complex view of the human condition. There is a tendency for critics to think of this verse as conservative even when it urges political reform, because of its lack of confidence in the nobility of common man, in combination with its reverence for the efforts, however partial and corrupted, of mankind in ages past. And though this poetry can care, strongly care, for the general welfare, its cultural references mark it as of the party of the elite. Its relationship to nature, too, is suspect to its opponents, for its writers see nature as mediated through experience, not "raw." In this poetry even dream is mediated through literature. Nothing comes to it spanking new.

Although the meditative essay is the least adolescent of Canadian verse forms, it tends to be the most sensuous. Consider, for example, the abundant use of tactile, olfactory, and auditory imagery in the meditative verse of D.G. Jones, Phyllis Webb, Robert Gibbs, or Ralph Gustafson. The tendency to analyze rather than to generalize, and the devotion to specificity and complexity rather than to myth or politics, make this verse the experientially richest of Canadian verse forms. Even Daphne Marlatt's long poems, which overtly spurn consciously formed ideas, derive their primary strengths from the fact that they are deeply considered meditative essays, however subverted by a post-modernist aesthetic and a self-displaying imperative.

Yet the meditative essay also has its liabilities. First, the well-educated writer always has other people's noises in his or her ears and can be overcome by metrical self-consciousness, becoming awkward or constricted as a way of trying to avoid imitation, as sometimes in Gustafson, or becoming a little too flaccid, as in Lee. These writers often lack the metrical assurance of the proletarian voice, or the self-assurance of the lyricist. The curse of academe dislivens this verse, as Louis Dudek vigorously noted at its prime.[10] Second, although the habitual study of art and history is essential to the development of any poet ambitious of greatness, the love that leads to such study has its dangers. Too many of our meditative poems, in a kind of Pavlovian response, depend for their effect on our emotional reaction to the work of art or the historical event to which they refer. They offer us someone else's *madeleine*.

The "proletarian" lyric expresses social concern—typically, with reference to the lives of ordinary, working man. (Despite Tom Wayman's efforts on her behalf, the common working woman, as subject, is not common.) These lyrics often include brief anecdotes but are primarily expressive rather than narrative. Some of these writers, Alden Nowlan, for instance, tend to share the socially concerned but moderately conservative views of the average worker. Most of these writers, however, are socialist and even, as Mathews deplores, internationalist in outlook. References to contemporary Latin American and European verse occur more typically in socialist lyrics than in nationalist lyrics or meditative essays. These authors (see, for example, Peter Trower, Kevin Roberts, or Tom Wayman) speak as knowledgeably from literature as from experience in the ordinary working world, although their imagined audience appears to be the common man who is their concern. An identification with the ordinary worker is the hallmark of this poetic voice; Dorothy Livesay, Anne Marriott, Miriam Waddington, Al Purdy speak not only *to* but *for* the common people. The meditative essay, in contrast, may speak *about* the common people, while the dramatic narrative imagines and represents them.

Distinguishingly, the proletarian lyric tends to be musical, perhaps because its intention, to celebrate the common man, leads it to adopt instinctively what the common man identifies as poetry: a poetic voice that falls naturally into identifiable metric. Often these poets begin a poem in matter-of-fact tones and seem to get carried by their argument towards more regular rhythms—the effect is quite common in Purdy. Others (Phyllis Gotlieb, Peter Trower) use the rhythms of popular or traditional song as part of their working material. And of course much physical labour, well done, tends to be rhythmical, a fact eloquently exploited by Sid Marty. So a regular, pulsing metre is natural to the world these poets celebrate and address. Secure in their relation to common man and to common man's reality, secure in the moral principles that touch their emotions, these poets do not fear their poetic moods, they do not fear rhapsody. Indeed, much of the best work of Tom Wayman, Milton Acorn, and Al Purdy is unembarrassedly rhapsodic. The problems of modern form that concern the intellectuals and the modernists can not concern writers who do not address their verse to intellectuals and modernists; thus these writers are never tempted to distort the flow of their line for a formal theory. Also, since the writers of proletarian verse are willing to think in verse informally and colloquially, without an intellectual's qualifications and hesitations, their verse is livelier than most dramatic narratives, most cultured meditations, and even most lyrics. Their rhythms lie nearer, one feels, to the pulses of reality.

Moreover, this poetry has the great strength of its ideals. It treats the common man and his common problems seriously, and thus it can not be egocentric or trivially aesthetic. The common man expects poetry to be something to which he can emotionally respond, and this common man's poetry appeals to the emotions—to the heart and the ears in conjunction. (Thus the affection for writers as diverse as Fred Cogswell, Alden Nowlan, and Miriam Waddington among the unsophisticated—which is not to imply that the sophisticated can not respond.)

The potential weakness of the proletarian voice lies squarely in its noblest principle: the ideal of the common man. God knows, the dearest and most valuable human beings on earth may have and often do have the intellectual and aesthetic responses of Shetland collies. We do not want to make a class distinction in our love. The poetry I have been calling proletarian lyric tends to have a warmly socialist distrust of anything suggesting an intellectual or cultural elite. In the great common eucharist of the pub, which Purdy so feelingly touches on in his introduction to Peter Trower's *Bush Poems*, no ideas are clearly articulated, qualified, or examined; nothing in the world of ideas is complex. Anything wrong other than death or the weather can be cured, somehow or eventually, by brotherly love, courage—by something simply defined, noble. Of course many if not most of these proletarian poets are themselves intellectuals, but where they can not conceal their education, they do not boast of it. The heroes in their poems are by and large blue collar, ordinary. Often listed on the back or front page of a volume of proletarian verse are the author's blue collar and macho credentials. (They do not ever seem to boast about having been clerks, accountants, nurses, waitresses, grade-school teachers, grocers, librarians, or barbers.)

This beautiful, serious body of verse can cripple itself by its frequent unwillingness to go beyond the sentiments of the average person. The average person does not much read this poetry written for him, a poignant truth. Perhaps here the schools could help. But the mind, like the hands, is an honourable tool. The average person resists hard thinking, and the poetry that only hymns him as he thinks of himself is less than the poetry that thinks beyond him.

The term "lyric" used to mean "song." In practice, however, it has come to mean relatively short poems that need not have any relationship to song or metre but in which the poet/speaker appears to be expressing his or her own feelings. The lyric, whether proletarian or self-displaying, lacks the structural development or breadth of subject of the dramatic narrative, although a narrative poem can and often does include lyric or lyric sequences. The proletarian lyric and the meditative essay are typically more interested in what they have to say than in expressing or displaying the self that says. The essay is more objective and analytic than the lyric. But clearly a poem by Phyllis Webb, for example, may be both lyric and meditation, both analytic and self-expressive.

However, an emphasis on displaying the persona-self of the poet in the lyric form has increased over the years, and has become particularly marked recently in a time when it is fashionable to say, as most modern critics of all nations seem to be saying, that mankind has lost its sense of community, its sense of shared values, its sense of wholeness. Eli Mandel seems to have persuaded himself in *Another Time* that nothing but the inchoate experiences of a fragmented personal experience exists as the possible subject for verse.[11] A display of sensibility becomes the pervading theme of verse that rejects the world of an objectively describable nature, or of generally communicable ideas. That our poets do not consistently immerse themselves in solipsism is to their credit. But an exaggerated sense of the importance of displaying the sensibility has promoted exaggerations in expressing it. For example, Margaret Atwood's poetry and Patrick Lane's both, in different ways, have already expressed such violent emotions about their poet/persona selves in personal relationships that, given their education, sanity, and middle class comfort need not be in reality so Maileresque—that their sincerest feelings about, for example, the circumstances with which Amnesty International deals can not summon a more ferocious eloquence. (A much wider range of communicable emotion is that of Sid Marty, who may well be our finest lyric poet.)

Most lyrics of self-display explore the poet/persona/self in its relation to something outside the self—in relation to family and local history (Robert Gibbs, Leona Gom), in relation to nature (Stuart MacKinnon, Sid Marty, early

Michael Yates), in relation to mythic archetypes (Marilyn Bowering, Susan Musgrave) or to literary precedent (James Reaney, Phyllis Gotlieb), and in terms of sexual identity (Irving Layton, Dorothy Livesay, Paulette Jiles). Certainly the most original thinking about the self has been that of Jiles, whose work, because of its very originality, does not fit in with the conventional dispositions of most critics, and has thus received less attention than is its due.

There is also a body of Canadian verse which displays the poet's self as Clever and Deep without reaching after an enlarged understanding of the self, a verse whose goal is entertainment and prestige. Essentially light verse (Joe Rosenblatt, bill bissett), it is praised earnestly by some critics for theoretical reasons—making of post-modernist criticism the touch of King Midas. Such light verse aside, the majority of our lyrics of self-display show the strengths of emotional sensitivity and the sort of truth that one self, speaking of itself, can speak of us all.

But the self-displaying lyric, as we commonly have it in Canada today, is liable to two closely related weaknesses: first, the over-valuing of spontaneity, because of a widely held belief that spontaneity reveals the true self as premeditation and reconsideration can not; and second, the valuing of poetic feeling over poetic production. But what we say spontaneously, thoughtlessly, "off the top of our heads," is apt to be conventional, habitual, clichéd. The equation of spontaneity with truth prevents the analysis of idea, inhibits the analysis of self, and discourages artistic control. Hokusai, after eighty years' fine drawing, could draw a masterpiece spontaneously but, as he assured the emperor, it was not in truth spontaneous—it had taken eighty years.

Related to this valuing of spontaneous expression over premeditated speech is the valuing of poetic feeling over poetic production: the assumption that whatever is spoken or written by someone who feels deeply moved at the time of speaking or writing must be, as speech or writing, a poem. This weakness is most prevalent in poems admired by teachers of Canadian literature, perhaps because of the ease with which such poems can be taught, and has become a prevailing weakness in Margaret Atwood, Irving Layton, and Earle Birney. A variant of this weakness, not infrequent in Susan Musgrave or Gwendolyn MacEwen, is the lazy use of a good metaphor—like a soup made with a bone and one onion, no herbs, no simmering. It is as if, instead of working with the *donnée*, these poets proceed briskly to a point or, as in Atwood, to an

O. Henry-like twist at the tail of the poem,[12] a trick to give an agreeable *frisson* to the audience. But not an explored perception.

For the romantic emphasis on spontaneity scants the potential difficulties of poetic composition. A writer, valuing his or her own emotions, pleases himself by expressing them and, reading his lines emotionally to a group of *semblables*, pleases them. But, like Browning's last duchess, they are "too soon made glad." It is a humane charm in the young that they should regard whatever occurs to them as luminously important—what year they are born in, their first romance, their first family funeral, last night's dream. However, when this universal vanity is naively combined with a belief in the elite importance of any human being who writes poetry, the result is not admirable. It should be said here, in Margaret Atwood's defence, that she does not convey that sort of vanity, however prevalent it may be among her peers. Yet where vanity leads one poet to shallowness, good intentions can lead another to dullness.

Nowadays the idea of being a poet is too often associated with the idea of being somehow more sensitive and more valuable than anybody else. Some poets wallow in the glamour of unearned pain. That they write becomes more important to them than what they write. They do not study their art. But even the less self-centred poets nowadays are too often unwilling to think over their original poetic impulses. Dennis Lee's ability to step back and rethink or qualify his spontaneous expressions, best displayed in the involuted, self-re-examining structure of "The Death of Harold Ladoo," is a strength too rarely found in our poetry. The majority of our poets publish too often, too soon. The round of poetry readings must not only drain poetic energies but tempt poets to vary their routines with new material. Certainly only a few poets, our very best, re-examine their ideas. More commonly, even though the verse itself be revised, the initial impulse is left unrevised, the core remains spontaneous. Unmeditated spirit is grape juice, not wine. Some poets are instinctively wise; some instinctively lucky—like the girl in the fairy tale whose lips dropped pearls. The rest of us should, as Robert Frost advises in "Build Soil," turn our ideas over and over again, instead of running them still immature to market.

For poetry is not only expression, it is a making. It is, as Phyllis Webb says in "Making," an "exegesis of the will," "making the intolerable, accidental sky / patch up its fugitive ecstasies," making from our fragmented experience a

35

grace, a usefulness, a patchwork quilt "madeness out of self-madness" that warms the "mild unblessedness of day," a thing of real, if partial, value, whatever our themes, whatever our theories.

from *University of Toronto Quarterly* (Winter 82/3)

NOTES

[1] See Eli Mandel's eloquent demonstration in *Another Time*, vol. III in the series *Three Solitudes* (Erin: Press Porcépic, 1977).

[2] Douglas LePan, "The Canadian Dialectic," *Notes of a Native Land*, ed. Andy Wainwright (Ottawa: Oberon, 1969), 59.

[3] Lloyd Abbey, letter to editor, *Canadian Literature*, 46 (1970), 103-4.

[4] Frank Davey, From *There to Here*, vol. II of *Our Nature—Our Voices* (Erin: Press Porcépic 1974), 19-20.

[5] See Davey's From *There to Here*, 41-43, 49-53, 57-61, 78-81, 95, 103, 132-7, 209-15, 231-5, 261-5. The characterization of Dudek as "anti-humanist" (95) is typical. But see also Robin Mathews's refutation of Davey's politics of form in Mathews's *Canadian Literature: Surrender or Revolution* (Toronto: Steel Rail Educational Publishing, 1978) 157.

[6] Frank Davey, review of *Ninety Seasons: Modern Poems from the Maritimes* (Fredericton: Fiddlehead Press, 1974), in the *Toronto Star*, 6 July 1975.

[7] Davey, From *There to Here*, 49-53.

[8] See Davey's From *There to Here* on bpNichol, esp. 214. And see Mandel's *Another Time* on bissett, Rosenblatt, and Nichol, 108-13, and on Cohen, 124-35.

[9] A similar example of critical prose is Dennis Lee's *Savage Fields: An Essay in Literature and Cosmology* (Toronto: Anansi, 1977), whose impressive metaphors imply the presence of more originality and meaning at the literal level of his discussion than the literal level can sustain.

[10] Louis Dudek, "Academic Literature," *First Statement*, 2:8 (August 1944), and "Patterns of Recent Canadian Poetry," *Culture*, 19:4 (December 1958), both reproduced in Louis Dudek and Michael Gnarowski, eds., *The Making of Modern Poetry in Canada* (Toronto: Ryerson, 1967) and in Dudek's *Essays and Selected Criticism* (Ottawa: Tecumseh, 1978).

[11] See in particular Mandel's essays in Another Time: "Cohen's Life as a Slave" and "The Language of Silence." But see also his remarks on Nichol and bissett, 108-13.

[12] But George Woodcock praises this effect as a "poetic booby trap" in his *The World of Caruldian Writing* (Vancouver: Douglas and McIntyre, 1980), 150.

How Has Canadian Poetry Changed since 1960?

I had read no Canadian poetry until I came to Canada in 1960. Most departments of English literature in the States limited their attention to Britain and the US. And they still do. Following after the American fashion, courses in Canadian poetry at our universities sometimes have a hard time getting enough students to persuade the administrations that such a course would be cost-effective.

When my husband accepted a job to teach at the University of New Brunswick I started to look out for Canadian poetry, making up for my earlier ignorance. I haunted the UNB library, reading as much as I could. There was so much of it—and so much of it was so very good! I began by thinking I could read all that I found in the library, but that was too much, so then I thought I would read all the poems by women—and that, too, became too much. I couldn't, and can't, keep up!

Not that many years before our arrival, Canadian poetry had begun its modernist flowering, helped a good deal by UNB's Alfred G. Bailey and his *Fiddlehead* poets. Bailey told me that he was first introduced to the poetry of T. S. Eliot in the 1950s, and felt himself influential in introducing the modernist poets of the US and Britain to his fellow Canadians. It's not news to admit that Canada came late to modernism. The high modernist style espoused by Bailey, Avison, Gustafson, etc., was felt by many to be "difficult." Even today, some Canadian readers of poetry find modernist poetry difficult. Fashions being what they are, not long after the Canadian modernists had made their impression a younger generation of poets began to find them old fashioned. And difficult.

When I arrived, UNB was a great place for poetry. *The Fiddlehead* was still young. Fred Cogswell was its editor and was producing masses of chapbooks. He once said to me that he never wished to tell "a bird not to sing," but I hasten to mention that despite his reputation as a man who would print anything, a whole generation of our best poets started out in chapbooks from Fred's Fiddlehead Press. I met several good poets on campus: Bailey, Gibbs, Nowlan, Bauer—and many talented amateurs. Nancy Bauer was starting up her chapbook line, the New Brunswick Chapbook Series.

In the larger Canadian context, the League of Canadian Poets was just starting out, and I remember vigorous quarrels about whether or not performance poetry should be considered poetry. Feminist criticism was sneaking into attention. So much was happening, so many things discussed! Perhaps not everything happened at once, but from here, 2016, it seems so. It would be easier for me not to speak chronologically, but instead to consider the question of changes in Canadian poetry as divisible into several topics, even though the topics necessarily overlap: colonialism, social justice issues, poetic style, and professionalization.

COLONIALISM

At about the same time as I was introducing myself to Canadian literature, I was also introduced to "world literature written in English"—discovering the written-in-English poetry of Africa, the West Indies, Australia, etc. I thereby introduced myself to the tremendous thrust of anti-colonialism that goes by the name post-colonialism. There were two aspects of post-colonial criticism: first, it led us to perceive that perhaps the best poets and writers today were not necessarily British or American—which is still true; second, it led us to emphasize the importance of defining ourselves as Canadian rather than as unsophisticated imitators of American verse, and, by defining ourselves, to write a richer and less derivative poetry. But although the Canada first-ism of the post-colonialists may seem extreme to the subsequent generation (after all there is important poetry that *isn't* Canadian, and some ultra-Canadian poetry that isn't all that good), I continue to believe that the post-colonialists have not yet succeeded in weaning Canadian writers from a generally held belief that the best poets, and the most important poetry magazines, are American, and written in English. "World literature written in English"—that is, in less powerful countries—remains largely ignored. As for Canadian poetry written in French, what to say! Most Canadian poets who write in English don't bother to read the very different poetries of their compatriots. And, since the death of Fred Cogswell, no anglophone Canadian poets have spent much effort translating the work of their brethren.

The first social justice issue I noticed in Canadian poetry was the "class" issue—a reaction against highbrow, "inaccessible," upper-class university-style poetry, in favor of a "people's poetry" in plain language on easily recognizable subjects of general concern. This division has been pretty much absorbed into the difference between Spoken Word poetry (i.e., Performance poetry) and Bookish Stuff. Spoken Word poetry relates to print poetry as Theatre does to the Novel—it is an art form that insists upon performance. Inaccessible theatre does not flourish. The Spoken Word poets address their audience intimately, clearly, and often on strongly-felt social issues. Social justice issues like race, culture, and gender demand attention; Spoken Word poetry gets attention. At present, some Spoken Word poets are accepted as, somehow, "one of us," even if their recordings are more interesting than their scripts, but most descriptions of contemporary Canadian poetry ignore Spoken Word poetry, as if it were somehow not "art," as if it were insufficiently highbrow—(or insufficiently WASP). This stupidity may not last much longer; increasingly poetry festivals have included sessions of Spoken Word, and the internet allows us many opportunities to appreciate and evaluate Spoken Word performances.

Social justice issues were being addressed before 1960, but writers concerned with racism and cultural prejudice were not then prominent. I think that the emphasis post-modernism placed on our examining the assumptions behind the language we use has helped to move from being quietly "kind" to becoming respectful, even awed, of "non-WASP" writing. The growth in perceiving, understanding, and accepting gender issues other than "rights for women" came much later, in part because the magazine publishers gradually became more willing to print material that, in my college days at Vassar, would have been "under the counter." Our sense of what is human, and, therefore, our humanity, has been enlarged.

Feminism is the social justice issue I can speak most about. Between my graduation from Vassar in 1956 and my departure, with an MA, from Cornell in 1960, I learned to not speak of "the poet" as "he." Book after book and article after article opened my eyes to what was immediately around me. But in New Brunswick, and in Canada, feminism had not come so far in the arts. The UNB poets (Bailey, Gibbs, Cogswell, Bauer) were all supportive of women's writing but there remained at UNB serious issues. Two examples: quite some time after my husband and I arrived, he discovered that the one female professor in the English department, Marjorie Chapman, was being paid less than the male professors whose PhDs were no better, and sometimes not quite as good, as hers; another eye-opener was Barry Davies's reading list for his class in contemporary Maritime poetry. About thirty or so names appeared on that list, and all of them were male except for one: Elizabeth Brewster. The names included several members of UNB's English department who had, like most English professors, written, possibly even published, one or two poems or even produced a tiny chapbook. Incensed, I instantly typed out a much longer list of Maritime women poets who had actually published books (including me) and taped the list on all the doors of the English department offices. If my husband had not brought home the list to show it to me I would never have seen it, and I don't think any of the professors, including Larry, would have thought to raise a formal objection to the list! Bad manners, perhaps, to criticize another's teaching!

With the creation of the Feminist Caucus within the League of Canadian Poets, there came a demand for greater attention to feminist issues. The idea of a Pat Lowther Memorial Award for women poets only was decried on the grounds that women and men should be competing equally—we were told we did not need extra encouragement. When I won the first Lowther, the prize was the copies of the books sent to the judges, plus a calligraphy scroll presented to me by a man who "gallantly" knelt to hand it to me. It was about this time that Sharon Nelson started the statistical study, recently repeated by CWILA (Canadian Women in Literary Arts), of the gap between the numbers of women writing and the numbers of women writers reviewed. (CWILA has since widened its interest to include the effects of other social prejudices but, although the young are believed, statistically, to share their concerns, the battle is by no means won).

POETIC STYLE

The prevailing style of Canadian poetry has considerably changed since 1960. Then, in spite of the modernists, most Canadian poetry was written in a plain

40

undecorated style, largely anecdotal, somewhat prosy and with little formal experimentation. There was a tendency towards nostalgia, and sometimes it seemed to me that most Canadian poets had been brought up on a farm and dried their mittens on a wood stove. An old cliché, I know. But clichés hit too close to home. Rhyme was just going out of fashion. (Cogswell's sestinas, with all the rhymes pencilled in before the rest of the poem was composed, were at the time a source of embarrassment to many of his friends.) Some poetry magazines announced that they did not wish rhymed poetry submitted to them. Instead, we were to be inventive, and experimental…and some of us, but not most of us, were.

The attitude towards rhyme has changed once again, and it is back in fashion, much admired. And with the return to admiring rhyme has come admiration for traditional forms. Indeed, it now often seems that form, whether experimental or "classical," is more valued than content, an emphasis I think paralleling the increase of creative writing courses in which infant poetasters are urged to write sestinas during the hour or so of the class. (I once witnessed such a class with Thomas's sestina on his father's dying as an example of the sestina to be imitated, and hope someday to be able to forgive the instructor.) Along with the swing towards form came an interest in adopting or adapting forms with foreign titles or derivations, generally in imitation of senior poets. P. K. Page is one whose excellent glosas have inspired hundreds of poems in which all the best lines are not written by the poet "author," but borrowed.

Yet, even with all our rage for invention and imitation, Canadian poetic language remained for many years fairly bland, somewhat colourless, and often unmusical. I recall vividly how excited I was to find rich imagery and musical eloquence in the poetry of George Elliot Clarke. Since then, Canadian poets have increased the colourfulness of their imagery, perhaps imitating Clarke's word hoard. Fewer, however, imitate his dramatic eloquence. This may be because we have become a nation of eye-readers and have lost the ability to "hear" as we read a printed page the cadences of our language. Canadians with a background of aural culture, Newfoundlanders for example, still seem to be able to write with an ear for cadence. Clarke's background is richly aural. But a great deal of contemporary Canadian poetry, for all its colourful—and sometimes wildly heterogeneous—imagery still sounds drab.

Royalty, parliaments, universities have long believed it prestigious to support "the arts" by appointing one representative: the Court Poet, the Poet Laureate, the Poet-in-Residence. As for the rest of the poets? Poetry does not pay. But teaching creative writing pays and has become a profession. Increasingly, young poets plan to make their living teaching creative writing and wish to make their profession as respected and as well paid as the teaching of literature.

Creative writing courses are a growth industry as teaching literature is not. We seem to value creativity more than the thing created. Writing workshops flourish while bookstores fade. To some extent this reflects our interest in "self-ies" and our delight in posting trivialities online, but it also reflects our genial interest in the trivialities of others. The teacher who can increase our pleasures increases our sense of our own creativity. An example of what a perceptive creative writing teacher can do: Barry Dempster was once presented with a group of children recently transplanted from the urban densities of China. He took them into the Ontario woods and induced them to actually touch (though with fear and trembling) moss, bark, and fungi! Our understanding and response to poetry, which enlarges and enriches our experience through words, is rooted in pre-verbal experience. Those of us whose experience has been excessively closeted can not respond to anything that is to them wholly alien. Dempster, addressing their lives, their "souls," was giving them the gift of a life open to new experience, to nature, to poetry.

Although good writing must begin with our contacts with the world around us, most creative writing teachers stay in the classroom, and many only occasionally draw their students' attentions away from themselves towards nature, history, or literature. Instead they teach how to write like their contemporaries, how to apply for grants, and how to get a graduate degree in creative writing.

Getting a graduate degree in creative writing is a lot easier than getting one in literary studies. Anyone who reads poetry at all, and who has majored in English literature, can write at least one sensitive, intelligent poem. Writing an essay on a writer not oneself that will be publishable in a serious academic journal is difficult. And any professor who has been refused, on the grounds of cost-effectiveness, permission to teach a graduate course in contemporary Canadian poetry or African fiction to five or six students may be inclined to cast a dubious eye on a graduate creative writing course with twenty students.

What was not done in my youth, when creative writing was not an academic subject, but what is currently done, is to insist that each student write a prose statement of their "poetics." This respect for "poetics" or literary theory is the result of the intellectual respectability of post-modernist criticism. (I am reminded of Eli Mandel who, at a conference on The Long Poem, replied to a student who had asked him something post-modernistically: "I am not quite sure what you have just said, but it *sounds* right.") If a student knows how to write learnedly *about* his or her poetry, surely that is enough for an MA? At present a PhD in Creative Writing is contemplated. Will a PhD dissertation on the poetics of a collection of Spoken Word poems be read—or performed? I do not believe a dissertation on "poetics" should be required—unless we become silly enough to insist that the philosophers and scholars append to their theses poems and short stories. "Poetics" is philosophy, not art. To demand from creative writers a "poetics" seems to me to reveal a dislike or distrust or disvaluation of art (and certainly most academics do not attend poetry readings). It seems to me reasonable for the university to award creative writers for their perceived excellence as writers—and if the universities want to do so by the titles MA or PhD, I see no great harm. But the title should be awarded for art—for poetry, not for philosophic prose. It is not for his "poetics" that we value Homer. Aristotle, who did concern himself with poetics, is a dull read.

TWO:

Maritime Gallery

Roads Round about Here: The Poetry of Robert Gibbs

The country of Robert Gibbs in *Five New Brunswick Poets*, *The Road From Here*, *Earth Charms Heard So Early*, and *A Dog in a Dream* is a real country—just off Saint John, perhaps, shimmering in mill-stink and beach swabbings. But it is also a country of the mind, a patria of the imagination.

A traveller in the poems of New Brunswick finds often enough the minimal, a nostalgic plainness, like dulse scraped up and handed to you—it's the chewing makes the flavor. Such simplicity can reduce itself merely to mentioning the dulse and relying on pre-trained taste buds to imagine the taste. The unfamiliar stay hungry. But in Gibbs's best poems there is no minimum served minimally, but, instead, a maximum approach to the minimum, "skipping round the biosphere" (as he entitles one of his better poems). Gibbs is a gourmet of the minimal. In some of Gibbs's shortest poems we are reminded of the ancient Chinese philosopher who pulled himself out of megrims by conquering the perfection of ox riding, finding in the achievement of a minor art the mental tonic. Consider, for example, two Gibbs poems on almost nothing at all, the Zen riddle. First:

> the attainment of nothing
> is for sure beyond me
>> pussyfooting in here to nose
>> my way through dark rooms

says Gibbs in "Bait for Hamlet's Mousetrap"—and the light in his darkness? The moon, "that fat broody golden hen / called the lord Buddha" that is

> cheese only cheese
> for many a mouse to nibble on
> but nothing like nothing for this poor dog.

Or, summing up Zen in "Transmigrations in the Five Worlds":

Reading these koan of the masters
I think I hear a little
                    as much through nose as anywhere
            the solid music of their unhollowed
                    hallowed iron flute
                    the kind of carol
            Alice might have heard
                    where time is never beat
            and standing still keeps you
                    running fast
            on both feet.

With the minimum of sensory data and a maximum of intelligence; and we too have transmigrated in our five-sensed world—to "nowhere"—in this case.

This connoisseurship of precise circumstances is even more the distinctive note of Gibbs's best, thickest poetry, a note—along with the witty, modest grace of his handling—that makes his richer meditative lyrics a brew as pleasing as the skunky, positive St. John river beers: not immediately inebriating, but moderately liberating.

Gibbs details best the ocean's sides (and the way they affect us, living by them):

Anything so restless and formless as an
ocean rubbing under your scalp troubles
your dear but hardly secret illusion of being
able to measure such expanses of time and wind
out in drops
to suit yourself, and water taken in large doses
often brings on muscle cramps of swell rhetoric.

Living by it, I acquired some indifference,
a shell to keep it out much of the time,
and walking by it, squilching
through bladdered focus after periwinkles
feeling its grit and mucous in the cracks
between my toes, I got to know how
little of its debris is picturesque. It's
like the local paper, a daily blotter
absorbing and emptying you of impressions

King Jumbo Potato and the bicycle race
J. Glen astronaut.

"Trying a Peter Walk"

In Gibbs's best poems we feel ourselves to be taking our own good time about matters. There is a sense of sane, even obdurate, mental balance, of laconic relaxedness, of measuredly recollected and rigorously articulated detail:

For the city boy it's
waterfronts, a rubbie's delicate
wipe of white lips after
lemon extract behind a stack of lobstercrates
a half blind negro baiting up with bloody
chunks of gaspereaux, smelt fishing
from the top step at the end of the pier
sulfur stink at low tide and the ship lights
at dusk, accordion distensions in the slack.

And for the poet? Seas are "cesspools shaking under fairy green" the poem continues. Thus the necessity and the difficulty of making a "Peter Walk," Gibbs's metaphor for the poem itself—walking on water by artifice, fishing for the "strange fish," the imagination's hinted visions.

Gibbs manages particularly fine rhythmic effects where he allows his soberer rhythmic to be counterpointed with remembered song. In "Earth Charms Heard So Early" this counterpointing parallels distinct levels of consciousness; what is possessed by the adult intellect exists alongside what is possessed by the earliest memories of childhood and by the secretest of infantile dreams. Thus "Earth Charms Heard So Early" presents a more faithful reality than those poems by "naive" writers that refer only to the material of the "subliminal imagination" or the "objective circumstance."

II

"Earth Charms Heard So Early" integrates the child's riddles: his fears of the relatedness of death, unrepressed sexual ambition, growing up—"cutting loose"—and "subcutaneous itches" of the sensual self integrate these with four other levels (at least) of image suggestion. At another level we have the

49

simplicities of the renewedly self-conscious, subcutaneously-itchy earth charms, the aware physical present of the poetic speaker:

> The empty chair beside me creaks
> The drapes knock at the screen
> The air shifts its heaviness a little off

Third, we have the recollected experience that serves as trigger for the poetic statement:

> me and you too big with child almost
> to get into the elevator together
> meeting there at once
> went up together
> me singing inside for your child
> the leap I didn't take
> the dazzling rainbow

Fourth (so truthful is Gibbs, for we do not come unlettered to our adult rainbows) the speaker remembers a poem he has read, a poem by Chardin, who, under similar circumstances, felt similarly:

> "proche l'un a l'autre
> une fois de plus" ...

> "as if some great force
> had routed me out of myself ..."

But the poetic speaker still remembers as part of the "great force" those sensations from childhood that appeared to be linked to "the leap I didn't take," the child's scary riddles of death and sex:

> the hummock the bummock
> the two durry dummock
> knock off the fuzz
> and send the dash home
> (a white bedstead gate on a country graveyard

creaks where my grandmother's mouth went dry)
riddle-oh-riddle-me riley-o
this child went to Shilaoh
the wind blew   the skitters flew
and cut this child right fair in two

The garden of "Shilaoh" is somehow dangerous. The authenticity of this semi-nonsense lies in the fact that this is what is really sung to real children (not a coy invention of childish speech as in, for magnificent example, Roethke, whose child's voice rarely says exactly what a child might say or have said to it): "The wind blew   the skitters flew / and cut this child right fair in two." This sort of thing was recited to me—in a skipping rhyme, perhaps? Like the bedstead gate on a graveyard, "Shilaoh" is a real spook.

"Silk was the saddle," and "brass was the bow." The answer is All—but All in terms of sex:

down in a dungeon
I saw a bright light
all fit for a fight.
Silk was the saddle
brass was the bow;
I've told you three times,
and yet you don't know.

Had we understood this riddle before Gibbs's poem? And the riddle is his fifth level. But he finishes even better—he finishes with a reappraisal of the poetic speaker's self and situation:

and yet you don't know
    What did you expect?
    A squaring off?
    Nothing closes
    that stops this close.

Nothing closes. The open ending of this brisk, contrapuntal poem is like the bright light in the dungeon—all ready to go, whole, an All.

> The answer is All
> all that goes up
> sparks in the air
> fish in the river
> me and you too big with child almost

The answer is the vigorous and unrelenting earth charms themselves.

The visual patternedness of "Earth Charms Heard So Early" correlates with its themes. First, the images and meanings of square things are repeated: the dungeon, the window, the bed/ gate, the elevator, the finger that, keeping "a tight line on my direction" makes a "square" around the "point," the itches that suddenly "square with nothing now" and the conclusion: "A squaring off?" as if "fit for a fight." Against these squares Gibbs poses images of linear movement: the lines sparking off like "sparks in the air," the controlling fingers described as if playing a fish line with the self's tugging, and, in addition, all the streaming, swimming, running motions of sweat, car wheels, rhymes that "sing you down" and "swim across" the page, the sexual "knock" and "dash," the wind blowing, and the leap not taken. The alternate movements of leap versus square almost, in themselves, explain the poem. And parallel to this delightful ambivalence, the interspersing of the riddle poem's lines one at a time among chunks of the meditative poem, as if the two motions were going on at one time, gives the impression that the riddle is nudging the leap (as the lines taken out to the edge of the page and underlined reiterate the linear, sparking movement of the leap); while the meditative sections, indented, their several lines thus making the shapes of squares, give the holding back from the leap, so that the poem itself, pictorially, line against square, is a perfect, balanced, ambivalence.

III

Gibbs's rhythms, whether musical or conversational, reflect the tact and decencies of Maritime habit. He tends to avoid the unnatural confidences of the fashionable confessional, and relies on an easy reader-author relationship that can sustain considerable confidence. Rather than looking within himself, Gibbs observes the relationship of the human to the world around him—he looks out the window—for:

> The roads and we that take the roads
>> (with us as we must)
>> become ourselves in going out.

"The Road From Here"

The roads are our experience. A window out, feelingly observed, can be a window in. And Gibbs's roads are not paradisal.

"The Road From Here" is a Bunyanesque trek from "here" to "Saint's Rest" which must take us past the "asylum farm" "for the mindless bones of old ones" and the "hospital school" for the "slow beginners"—through a kind of limbo for the mindless and the innocent, a modern analogy for the unborn and unbaptized infants' limbo in older hell-routes. We travel through a thickly graveyarded countryside, and there is even a customs house, a secular hell-gate

> razed now and replaced
> by a more customary and unbedevilled
> concrete box

(note the two puns) on the road to Saint's Rest, this Acheron crossing, whose best and "easiest path" is actually a "hellmouth inaccessible except by water." The accessible way is longer and more difficult (as the path of virtue always is), but it is also streaked, as virtue's path is, with thorny temptations, with creatively vigorous signs of "infernal fire." This true path is shaken with lightning and fears and is as dangerous to tread as the Whinnymuir of the old song "This Ae Nicht"—for this is the archetypal path to Saint's Rest, where fear, terror, and desolation so often turn us back:

> the groaner often turns me back
> sucking its breath
> from some inward spasm of the bay's sickness
> off Partridge Island.

but the Pilgrim must go on. And like Pilgrim, indeed even more like Browning's Childe Roland, the travellers of this poem go on through a landscape of the dead, wounded beasts, mad men, grave upon grave:

A paved road through woods
spreads a banquet table
red fox, skunk and crushed porcupine
for unsettling crows' craws …

Signs, signs everywhere advertise
    graveyards for every conceivable death
    and parish houses for every
        conceivable madness.

"Conceivable" is a finely chosen adjective for every kind of death, every kind of madness, in this passage through life.

Yet this road "from here" is travelled in a faith—not a religious faith—but a faith in the nature of stones and sea and the landscape around it—in a faith in the basic health of this "compoted mud and granite," these "sweetmeats for vultures"—in a faith in death, in the ultimate cleanliness, beauty, and "light" of natural process:

I know how the stones will be
    when I get there
    (taking the Chichestrian way)
    salt-white in the sun
    and milled smooth as marbles
    ungarbled in the mouth
    of the lapidary ocean
    yet not done
    as nothing stone is done
    until it is sand
    and nothing sand is done
    until it is dust
    and nothing dust
    till so dispensed in light
    as to become light.

This road from hell to the pure light of natural process does not demand from us any philosophy that science and healthy-mindedness can not simply assign us; the confidence of Gibbs's mapping supplies the rest. This is the road from here, the road we know, the countryside we daily travel, both the horrors and

that into which the horrors are milled by lapidary time, the ultimate "light,"
"Saint's Rest."

IV

Perhaps because Robert Gibbs dislikes asking us to accept more than we rea-
sonably can, he usually devotes himself to asserting the value of the ordinary:

> Whatever the lighthouse means flaring round
> offbeat with the foghorn
> making its connections and disconnections
> in this watery envelope ...
>
> and the herring weir makes thin lines and crosses
> a Japanese virtue
> or virtuosity of restraint ...
>
> Whatever this whole watery egg means
> that holds a half-hatched world ...
> is not of my making nor is it as you might think
> making a lot of a little
> looking agreed for more than what's there
> but more like putting down
> most of what I see or want to see
> and what I don't
> (caught by fog with my ballpoint skipping)
> in invisible ink

"Skipping Round the Biosphere"

Value, not clear meaning—invisible meaning, perhaps, human desires. But
in speaking about value, or about one's impressions of it, a "virtuosity of
restraint" is what the poet must employ. Unlike Dickens's fat boy, Gibbs
does not want to chill our blood but to win our assent to his statements: so
that the viewpoint and the stated beliefs of Gibbs's poetic speakers are almost
always located in the mundane, ordinary "biosphere" of common experience.
When this viewpoint is not developed with Gibbs's intensest wit, the poetry

can sometimes get thin. For the poetry of the ordinary must gather overtones, complexities, distance from its initial impulse; it must not be brought too soon out of the barrel.

A constant temptation to all poets is the desire for an immediate response from a listening audience. Nostalgia, simple description, and quaint anecdote are always popular, and Gibbs, like the rest of us, is not without sin in this area. His "Six-Stage Crossing," for example, is better heard than read for this reason, for it is a one-dimensional poem. But Gibbs's best poems provide us a richer experience:

> From here it is no easy walk away
> > without foot benefits
> > of seabird-feathered sea-ribbed sand ...
>
> Walking here's a boulder hopping
> > or a crabwise scrabbling back
> > out of sole-breaking slippery clefts
> > where tide-ends slicker over slime.
> Sometimes on top
> > room enough for one foot
> > to drop the other
> > and tread air.

"The Road From Here"

For, as Gibbs entitles, explainingly, the last poem of *Earth Charms Heard So Early*, "To imitate nature involves the verb"—the active verb:

> What a sharp selfhood
> he must have brought
> to his cutting edge
> to uncover them both here
> his own and the wood's
> You'd have to handle this
> unsmiling head yourself
> to know how man and tree
> secure each other

We do have to handle this poetry ourselves; it is not poetry for passive audiences. We take the roads "with us as we must," and they become part of our selves, as they must. We take these poems. And it is our selves that are sharpened, our identities that are formed—by this unique, idiosyncratic, and inimitable verse.

---

from *The Humanities Association Bulletin* (Fall 1972)

The Muskrat in His Brook: The Poetry of A. G. Bailey

Any substantial collection of a poet's verse over a long period of time is likely to have weak moments, but A. G. Bailey's collection *Thanks for a Drowned Island* contains as well some remarkably fine poems to some of which I would like to draw attention.

A fusion of intelligence, craftsmanship, and, markedly, creative joy distinguishes Bailey's best verse. Both the felicitous juggling of the elaborately rhymed and metered pieces and the witty dignity of the prosier meditations please as much by their grace as by their sentiment. Bailey's poems underline the importance of technique, for they never rely chiefly on subject or symbol to make their effect; rather, they succeed or fail mainly by technique—by word order, stanza pattern, sound. Yet Bailey does not have a single technique, a "manner" that he has studied and perfected. He has never settled into a mould, but tries nearly all the kinds of poetry our century has produced, all the various degrees of free verse, of controlled pattern, partial or thorough, variation of stress or of breathed phrase. Such constant experimentation keeps his technical abilities green and flexible even as it risks occasional weaknesses.

But with all this technical variety, Bailey retains consistent and distinctive characteristics: a love of nubbly, hard-to-mouth word patterns and material nouns, and, even more characteristically, an embracing sensitivity towards the "feel" of history. His poems come, roughly, in three varieties: first, poems that celebrate the sense of history, place, biographic; second, poems that indulge a "mood"—as a piece of music does, or a traditional symbol for a set of emotions; and third, poems that are primarily exercises in wit or idea/metaphor. Bailey, himself, of course, a distinguished historian, is probably best known for his historical poems, since they can contribute so much to the sense of being Canadian, and *Thanks for a Drowned Island* contains many excellent examples.

That a historian should recreate the sense of history poetically is fitting; that he should convey so well the sentiment of history, which lures us all to be historians and rememberers, is our good luck. For the sentiment of history is something that can not be articulated in words, but in gestures. "Confederation Debate," for example, which rehearses fairly conventional speech-maker's themes, gives to its subject a tremendous dignity of emotional depth through technique alone. For example, towards the end of the poem, the longer lines are given the primary meanings and these longer lines, weightier in subject as well as in length, are succeeded by lesser, and shorter, lines like the left-hand part on a piano, chording below the tune, or like the phrasing repetitions in psalms. And the language of this poem, while never strange or exotic, delicately avoids the absolute clichés of the patriotic speech it represents, and moderates itself, and widens its appeal, by the sense of historical perspective, which, as remembered and uttered at the end of the poem, is spoken with slowness to represent the slowness of the nation to come to the poem's vision. The sense of the nation remains evoked, not defined, as something palpable, emotional, indefinite, developing—and slowly come to, grown into, under the weight of time:

> Perhaps it was something that could not be
> > put into words
> like a railway advertisement
> of a sequence of magnificent vistas
> but a way for men to live in peace and freedom
> with mutual forbearance
> speaking in half the languages of Europe and Asia
> with rights grounded in law.
> Whatever else it was it could have been all of
> > these things,
> but there were not very many who could see this
> in the session of eighteen sixty-six,
> and not many the year after.

Another such patriotic poem is "La Route Jackman," in which we travel in our present while remembering our past. The poem parallels the rough natural contours of the Boundary Range and the thickly forested border with the remembered harsh pangs endured by Arnold's invaders while crossing them. Although the poetic speaker's automobile ascends the smooth modern roads with ease, the memory climbs the hills with a metre that reflects the laborious climbing of old times:

> day of sleep and rain,
> his men haggard and sore, the smallpox

growing in their faces,
starved and white with
grit, and lame hands
torn and bleeding from rope burns:

This clenched rhythm is relaxed in later lines as the modern car begins to coast down and the lines lengthen and coast themselves, reflecting its movement:

not needing ropes, without need to haul barges
through dead birch thickets and over the scarred tops,
                              breaking open hands

until the car comes home to level lands, the comforts of the modern world, and a sense of historical relief:

Penobscot water running back
ourselves forward towards
the level fields of Beauce,
the populated pasture land,
having all at once the feeling
of having come home.

History in Bailey's poetry is most often felt as a genetic working out in the present of the patterns of the past as part of a still living web: the link is biological, vital, present. So Bailey does not research the past so much as he recognizes it in the present. This sense of continued historical pattern contours many of his poems, one of the best of which is "Hochelaga." The name of the Indigenous village upon which Montreal stands now is used to remind us, throughout the poem, of the continuity of bloodshed, a continuity which reflects itself in the hard and blood-coloured ground of Montreal. As the poem opens hard clay is being cultivated by urban machinery; in stanza two it is cultivated by the Indigenous of the agricultural past. In both stanzas the hard ground of Hochelaga is sprinkled with the blood of murder. The poem uses the short lined brusque metre of the driest of modern verse; the metre appears to reflect the harsh brittleness of daily living, mundane, careless, callous—like the hard ground. Indeed the earth of modern Montreal seems harder than the ancient

Indigenous farm, which, as Bailey puns, is in the process of becoming "hard to beat" as the Indigenous people fertilize it with the surefire combination of fish and scattered brains. The hard ground stands for the heart's hardness. Murder is normal; the past remains in the present.

Bailey nicely uses irregularly spaced rhymes in "Hochelaga" for two purposes. With the unmusicality of this irregular and harshly metered rhyme he points up a sense of artificiality somewhat akin to the "Easter hats" of the third stanza—irrelevant to the murder-fertility festival of Easter, unsensuously decorative. In addition, however, Bailey echoes through these rhymes the similarity of new times to old times. The lines of the last stanza, about the present time, do not rhyme with each other, but with the rhyme lines of the earlier stanzas: the present is echoing the past.

A fourth "historical" poem I much admire is not, in my opinion, really historical, but a "mood" poem. The metaphor that compares the battle of the Seneca against the Montagnais with a present rainstorm over a field of corn does not evoke any picture of human battle; it is not even the lament of ghosts, as it purports to be, but the lament of earth spirits, a memory that has been rinsed of the human until only the weather grieves:

> Yet when the wind in the night moves
> we move in our sleep
> seeing the band's flight
> over the blueberry swamps
> and down to the eel-stations
> in the wild light of Spring.

Another "mood" poem of wind and weather is "Noroua," ostensibly the history of a shipwreck. "Noroua" is built from newspaper-like material, which could have been made, as found poetry, into something quaint and wry. Bailey, more creative, allows the weirdness of the natural incidents to possess the reader's imagination, cajoling us by his wickedly deft technique into enjoying disaster as in a theatre of the absurd. The poem is funny: windy, dream-like, full of the heartless grotesqueries of natural incident, where what is destroyed is destroyed with indiscriminate gusto, and where the signatures of danger are as marvellous as fairy tales:

> A thin fog formed. The lighthouses were seals,
>   standing on their tails.
> At unheard signal they dove, leaving the
> capes untenanted and bare, like a
> room without furniture.

As a result of the fog the *S.S. Old Carolina* wrecks on an off-shore rock with high winds and deep waters between it and the safe shore.

> Huge waves race like galloping horses
> past my friend Lieutenant Herbert
> Arlington-Jones doing the crawl.
> Arm over arm he speeds towards Dead Man's Current.
> "He'll never get through," shriek the girls on the point,
> waving handkerchiefs, but he does.
> A shoal of porpoise following get through too.

Notice how line divisions as well as un-sombre detail add to the sense of strange comedy, which continues as

> cork life-belts, egg-crates, passengers,
> laundry baskets, deck chairs, and grape-fruit skins

are wrenched out from the wreck, and all, except Lieutenant Herbert Arlington-Jones, drown. Indeed, in the glorious coda, the fish of the sea are lifted out of the water and drowned in air. The "fish" of course are beluga, for the consonance with balloon, and the comedy of the noun:

> Fleets of beluga rise from the churning sea,
> like balloons, and are carried away by the wind.

This poem is a bracing hymn to the destructive vigour of reality; the Noroua, the wind of the Saguenay, as the footnote tells us, is a manic, comic demon.

Another "mood" poem with the gusty vigour I like so much in Bailey is "Water, Air, Fire, Earth," a paean to spring, sex, fertility, and natural glamour—mainly from the point-of-view of a frog, but, lastly, also from a mole's. Frog-rhythm, frog-sized scenery—the size scale is changed and we are frogs, complete with a "fearful lay / of lilies" and "logs / gone monstrous in the dark" and a storm of lightning bugs.

Equally attractive, but in an entirely different style, the title poem "Thanks for a Drowned Island" uses rhythms of song, not four square ballad, but song-lyric, as in Tennyson or Thomas:

Into the flooding tide
to seek the consolation of the waters,
to find the depths a life of blessed peace
after the sable ride:

I would lie in the sea
and light not cease
nor water gather stagnant in the grave

and so on. The music does not break till the poem's end. The blessed island of the imagination, the re-creative retreat, like Yeats's Innisfree or the "octopus's garden 'neath the waves" of popular song, is an ancient symbol that has never lost its appeal for us.

Another traditional symbol nicely re-worked by Bailey is that of the ship struggling at sea as image of the mind, "how in the dark our index page to find" is wonderfully witty. Its tone, comic, "ammonia-sharp," prepares us for thought. The punning parallels "dock" with "dark," and the freshening of convention with slang (as in "blooming goal") lightens the philosophic level of the poem with Joycean humour.

dock take ship
    trundling

bundled in funnel's
smoke; devil take
sea chop and oil slick

So, stoutly, good-humouredly, swearingly, the poem starts. But the ship must commit itself to dark in order to be docked in its "blooming goal," its paradise: the smoke that bundles the ship is specifically compared to the Holy Ghost (and "trundling," used with "bundling," suggests the ship as baby). Here the efforts of "good-hulled ships" and "vertical virtues" are seen as hard work—and as fun. The danger, the sea chop and oil slick, are fun. (The possibilities of "goal" and "dock" only point up the difficulties of the venture.)

A joyfulness rooted in the efforts of experience is a pervading aspect of Bailey's collection, and is perhaps his chief poetic gift, a contagious eupepsia. The witty poem "The Muskrat and the Whale" I think can be taken at least in part as a humorous apologia for the author's poetry. The muskrat's peculiar gift is seen as lying in his play. For the muskrat, "not a contemptible fellow," though small, playing in his natural medium and liberated by reason, is a fine metaphor for the kind of poetry we find in *Thanks for a Drowned Island*, joyful, deft, unpretentious—and reasoned, liberating. Bailey's muskrat is contrasted to the whale, that Pratt-Melville creature: the two animals are clearly unlike. The tiny muskrat is unportentous and not uncommon; he is confined to a smaller habitat. Whales are huge, rare, frightening—and, the image implies, profounder of element—perhaps thus, indirectly, of subject. They surely write larger—and longer poems, and less playful ones. The Whale is the Great Poet and the muskrat isn't. But, the poem truthfully asserts, the muskrat has his own dignity, and, even, the poem hints, a plus of liberty.

> Let whales wake and sleep in their own water,
> the muskrat in his.
> His bliss, like an emulsion, injects
> his veins and arteries; a whale's
> capillaries accommodate a liquor
> immense and sedate.
> Dignity and industry lend size to the muskrat.
>
> His size is his own, and mete.
> The whale may think his dignity is greater.
> The muskrat would be able, if the
>   thought struck him,
> to prove his own title to this quality,
>   sooner or later.

Although "The Muskrat and the Whale" is primarily about the unselfconscious dignity and animal joy of intelligent animals—and any wild animal observer does recognise the literal truth of Bailey's description of such industriously playful beasts (I have seen just such muskrats) the poem remains, still, wonderfully illustrative of its author, whose reason

> liberates his nights and days
> in the medium this reason both foreshadows
> > and reflects.
> He is satisfied and we are satisfied
> > to see him so.

Not just satisfied. Delighted.

---

from *The Fiddlehead* (Winter 1974)

NOTES
Thanks for a Drowned Island by A. G. Bailey, McClelland and Stewart Ltd., 1973.

A Sense of the Medium: The Poetry of A.G. Bailey

It is time we took another look at the poetry of Alfred G. Bailey, who has for many years excelled in the practice of a poetics that has increasingly interested contemporary critics: an emphasis on the imprecision, textuality, and potential duplicity of the "word," whether as "writing" or as habit of thought, and on the uncertainty, fluidity, and verbality of "fact." Bailey, in his poetry, has always emphasized the fluidity and mutability of the contextual situation and/ or medium, and the relativity, dubiety, and metamorphic nature of "guiding words" or sought-for principles. He has presented history as memory, legend, emotion, conflict and interaction, and as presence—not as a stable description, but as a living and mutable web. Further, as Bailey's frequently Joyce-like word-play robustly reminds us, he has always been aware of the context, intertext, and textuality of the text—of the function of poetry as a liberating play in the medium (verbal, emotional, prejudicial, skeptical) of our intellect. Above all, Bailey's poetry reaffirms for us his strong sense that life is lived most intensely in the emotional intellect rather than in unexamined sentiment.

It seems to me that the contemporaneity of Bailey's poetry may be ulti-mately more ascribable to his training as ethnohistorian than to the "New Poetry" that belatedly caught his attention upon his return to graduate school in 1930. Yet for Bailey himself, the introduction to the poetry of T.S. Eliot was a significant revelation. Although from earliest youth Bailey has been interested in reading and writing poetry, he has never been primarily a poet. After the publication in 1930 of his second small chapbook, *Tao*, and upon his return to academia after a post-undergraduate period as journalist, Bailey became aware that he was out of touch with contemporary writing: "I had never even heard of Edna St. Vincent Millay, Elinor Wylie—hardly any of the contemporary poets except Edgar Lee Masters!" Then, while a graduate student at the University of Toronto (in history, anthropology, and econom-ics) Bailey became a member of the "Nameless Society," a group interested in the study of Canadian literature, presided over by E.K. Brown, and, as well, made friends with Malcolm Ross, Roy Daniells, Robert Finch, and Earle Birney. When Roy Daniells returned from a year abroad and introduced

Bailey and some others to The Waste Land and "Prufrock": "we had never heard of Eliot before." Eliot seemed to offer new ways of writing about what most concerned Bailey's contemporaries: "The subject of the urban wilderness was so concerning us then—and Eliot's rhythms caught in one's mind. There was a lot of imitativeness for a while. Smith, Scott, all the people who were writing at that time were very influenced by Eliot. I had a few of my poems in my new manner published by *The Canadian Forum* in 1932, 1933, and 1934." ("Best Seller" is one of the earliest of these.) Bailey felt that "Eliot had pronounced an epitaph on the past. It was necessary to pass through that phase, incorporate its effects, and transcend it."

While going through "that phase," Bailey and his friend Daniells, and later Finch, met weekly and "did exercises in poetry, on T.S. Eliot's advice that one should keep ready like a well-oiled fire engine."[1] They wrote on subjects chosen at random—the result of one such exercise with Robert Finch is "Pieces of Silver." A similarly Finch-assisted effort was a translation, "The Troubled Fawn" (from a French poem neither can now locate). The effect of such exercises seems to have been far more lasting upon Finch, with his early developed and long retained facility for writing gracefully even occasional and light verse. Bailey's own lighter poems are rarely graceful, and the poems in his "new manner" show the complexity of thought and the historical and sociological ponderings that typify his mature writing. It is probable that Eliot's historical and anthropological casts of mind were more available, because more sympathetic, to Bailey than to Finch. Certainly "Hochelaga," a poem of that period which Bailey characterizes as being a little too much Eliot-like, not merely in its rhythms, but in its combination of the image of the modern citizen drinking tea superimposed upon a doubled image of the bloody and wicked present and the bloody and wicked past, is most un-Finchian.

Bailey did not work closely with Birney, the strongest poet of the group, and while there are affinities, especially in intellectual and historical interests, between Bailey and Birney, Birney has been much less interested in self-conscious intellectualizing than Bailey, and much more interested in nature. Bailey's interest in the speech rhythms of Maritime and professorial Canada show an affinity to Frost (to whose poetry Bailey's "His Age was On" may be read as an indirect reference), although Eliot, too, made colloquial speech rhythms poetically available to his readers. Of the group, Daniells's work now seems the least influenced by the "New Poetry."

Thus, although the effect of the "New Poetry" upon Bailey's generation was shocking, in Bailey's words, "putting into the discard"[2] the reputations of earlier Canadian poets, what each poet learned from the "New Poetry" differed according to each poet's interests and needs.

Bailey did not go on to become a major Canadian poet of the 'thirties. He was too busy as historian, archivist, librarian, administrator—working to rescue and reawaken New Brunswick's cultural heritage. His first collection of mature work, *Border River*, did not appear until 1952—by then he had not only read and assimilated Eliot, he had also read and assimilated Frost, Auden, C. Day Lewis, and Dylan Thomas. Bailey's poetic style has not significantly altered since *Border River*, although the majority of his latest poems, as collected in *Thanks for a Drowned Island* (1973) and *Miramichi Lightning: The Collected Poems of Alfred G. Bailey* (1981), are more often specifically "historical"—either as speculation or as re-creation. But it was, indeed Eliot, who first showed Bailey how to use his historical and sociological training, his cultural insights, and his native wit in the poetry that replaced the Carmanesque poetry of Bailey's youthful writing.

Eliot had shown the way to writing about something other than nature or love. He brought back vividly to the imagination the possibility of writing about the things that, to Bailey, seemed most intriguing, that demanded new thought. Bailey's own interest in the "urban wilderness" is strengthened by his historian's belief that there "is a dynamism in the life of people stimulated by different varieties of cultural strains ... Contemplating the beauty of nature is all very well, but it doesn't accelerate mental interaction. I prefer the city."[3] The place where ideas interact, where cultures conflict and mutually stimulate each other, the city of the mind, is where the poet should be, and the historian. So believes Alfred G. Bailey.

Poems such as Eliot's *The Waste Land* and "The Love Song of J. Alfred Prufrock" were using the ideas of the modern world—and the experience of the mundane, urban, and unlovely—as both the matter and the medium of poetry, as much the medium of poetry as myth and natural images. Eliot had broken the constrictive, thematic definition of the "poetic subject" and had returned wit, intellectualization, and even the grotesque to the uses of poetry. Without rejecting the beauties of nature, or of poetic melody (as so very present in Bailey's beloved predecessor Bliss Carman), Eliot introduced the effective use of the unbeautiful, and, in particular, the construction of an image for an emotion or an idea rather than simply as a way of describing one *thing* in terms of another *thing*. Eliot showed us how to use the anti-poetic and the irreverent—he showed us, above all, the wordiness of words.

With the "New Poetry" came a much greater freedom to regard words as artificial constructs, a much greater feeling for words as things, as objects, subject to context and mortality—there came along even a degree of Humpty-Dumptyism ("When *I* use a word it means just what I choose it to mean—neither more nor less"). Pleasure taken in the buried words within words, the semantic possibilities of the pun, the decorative and sometimes almost irrelevant surface detail of the text, and the literary suggestiveness of context—all added up to a kind of verbal dandyism that remains one of the characteristic traits of Bailey's writing (and also continues to exist, but to a lesser extent, in the writing of Gustafson and Finch).

Much of the verbal dandyism in Bailey's work occurs in the playful poetry (the majority of his work), but it occurs also in some of his serious poems, where it can assist the effects of intellectual and emotional tension. Like anchovy paste, it can be spread too thick, as in "time down end."[4] More commonly, however, Bailey's verbal dandyism is mild. Rarely obscuring his meanings, it exists primarily for the effects of metrical compression and textural liveliness. Typical examples can be examined in the dedicatory poem to the collection *Miramichi Lightning*, "The Winter Mill." The line "And there's no stoic tethers soul to eye" is an example of Bailey's frequent omitting of metrically dull parts of speech. He also allows himself to use the shorter forms of words, even where not grammatically correct, as in "like tooth once bitten and forever ache." And Bailey likes to use phrases that can be read in more than one way. We are in the just-quoted phrase reminded of "once bitten twice shy"; we are reminded that a tooth bites; but the subtext reminds us of a toothache. Winter's bite is like having a toothache. And Bailey likes to use puns and secondary meanings. "The winter mill will not return" includes come back, bring back, and revolve. The last line of the poem, "with batting of this scene," adds the meaning fending off to the cotton-batting appearance of snow. And the term "winter ambit" means boundaries, but suggests ambition, bite (and bit, auger, ache? Agenbite?) The oddness of Bailey's diction provokes such semantic ponderings. "The Winter Mill" is stuffed with literary allusions. Falstaff, discovered dead, lurks in its complexly textured, half-grotesque, half-romantic lines—so, too, does Carman's yearned-for April. "The Winter Mill" spoofs itself yet is, at heart, still serious: "with book and pen record these / cries" the poet urges himself, introducing the gritty tonalities—playfulness and seriousness together—that inform his collection.

Frequently Bailey's verbal dandyism consists of a witty use of and reference to formal academic language; he enjoys deflating pomposities and the grandiose by relishing their manner, as in, for example, the poem "The Habitat of Unexorcised Notoriety," which remarks: "If indeed it can be said that 'try' is the right word for the sightless and clearly undocumented instigations that resemble the antics of a trybal global village of the purposeless and unrequited." (The "trybal" is a whole commentary in itself on the familiar McLuhan term "global village.")

Bailey also likes to play with images for academic or philosophic ideas—"Waasis," a surprising illustration for Lamarck's theories, or "Gluskap's Daughter," which plays with a Kantian/Berkleyan theme. "Jones" presents the "hopeful" human creature from "australopithecan root" to "cherubim bar-dextrous." In "The Sun the Wind the Summer Field," an image of pathos from Spengler's *Decline of the West*, Volume One,[5] becomes celebratory.

Many of Bailey's poems celebrate the fertility and vitality of nature, usually in terms of its oceanic or fluvial condition. Poems such as "Water, Air, Fire, Earth" celebrate sexuality and creation. Poems such as "Plague Burial" and "Noroua" celebrate destruction. "Noroua" is "full of the heartless grotesqueries of natural incident, where what is destroyed is destroyed with indiscriminate gusto, and where the signatures of danger are as marvellous as fairy tales." The poem concludes with "all, except Lieutenant Herbert Arlington-Jones" drowned. Indeed, "the fish of the sea are lifted out of the water and drowned in air." That the fish are beluga and drown like balloons is, like the Lieutenant's name, a further example of Bailey's dandyism. "The poem is a bracing hymn to the destructive vigour of reality: the Noroua, the wind of the Saguenay ... is a manic, comic demon."[6]

Obviously Bailey finds Eliot's comic streak sympathetic. It is instructive to read Bailey's tribute to Eliot's "Prufrock," "Variations on a Theme." Rather than presenting an image of immortal, mythic sexuality, Bailey gives us a Marvellesque Charon as Father Time (the historian's Fisher King) and, instead of mermaids, Queen Dido—mortal, individual sex. (Note, too, the lawyers with their "sandy briefs" who suggest the *sands of time* and *out, out brief candle* and add just the dry, legalese note that so often distinguishes Bailey's dandyisms.)

However the main effect of Eliot's art and criticism upon Bailey's thinking, his sense of the medium, must have been to reinforce attitudes, motives, and images that had been coming to Bailey already through his studies in history, anthropology, ethnology, economics, and Oriental and Western philosophies. *The Tao, The Golden Bough, The Decline of the West,* and Toynbee's *A Study of History*—were part of Bailey's world independently of Eliot. And, again independently of Eliot, Bailey had from his earliest childhood a strong sense of history as multi-cultured, multi-layered. The geological strata and the natural violence of the Saguenay; the historical strata, conflict, and tumult of Quebec and of Maritime history; letters and visits from travellers abroad, from China, from Europe—all reinforced Bailey's sense of human history as a fluid and altering web of interactions rather than of stable patterns.

The combination of patriotism, loyalism, and romantic love of nature—which was Bailey's inheritance—with his ethnographer's sense of change and relativism has produced two sorts of history poems. The first is a representation of the past, most often from the wider perspective of present memory and attitude, but occasionally as a "period piece" (like "Edwardian Outing") or as a kind of dream of the past in which the past speaks to the present (as in "Lament of the Montagnais"). In poems such as "Hochelaga," present and past are seen together, like geological strata intermingled by recent diggings and upheavals. The past is a very vivid ghost in such poems—"Grandfather's Gray Top Hat" is still redolent and quickened with anecdote; "The Shadow of Mr. McGee" is still eloquent in Parliament Square.

A second variety of "history" poem is the Bailey quest poem, in which the directing impulses of a society are imaged by an individual or a group (often shown as travelling in a fluid medium) consciously seeking a vaguely sensed destiny, definition, or enlightenment. These quest poems can arise from historical incident, as does "The Angel Gabriel," but more often they are abstractions, modifications of the Toynbean myth qualified by Bailey's sense of the ambivalences and uncertainties of the social, human situation. These poems repeatedly emphasize that the quest is not defined by a clear notion of what is being sought. It is the impulse Bailey describes, not a destination. Thinking is necessary and profitable, but it is a process, a motion in flux, not a seizing of precise patterns, as "Searched for, finding" reminds us. In "The Unreturning," Bailey turns Peter the founding rock into the insubstantial medium of the sky, and the travellers are guided by the "lost bearings of an unfound star" towards no "haven," and "no certain bound." The travellers of "Night Country" can only guess their destination, ask if "time's hand upon them" was "their own contrivance" (a Kantian question), and conclude with a decision, not uncommon in Bailey's quest poems, that

> unless they could make utterance
> of the holy names
> there would be no way out,
> and no end of the night country.

There is no end of "night country," Bailey would affirm, but so people feel—about "utterance, holy names," the guiding word. "North West Passage" and "Go, the Word, Go" reiterate the theme.

"The Isosceles Lighthouse" is a particularly interesting example of Bailey's quest poems—for the lighthouse is not gone out to. Instead it is very much like the unclimbed mountain in Robert Frost's "The Mountain," as well as reminding us of Virginia Woolf's lighthouse in *To the Lighthouse*, the eventual visit to which is so much less than the anticipation. In all three examples, the lighthouse/mountain exists more importantly as an idea than as a thing: in Woolf, the actual thing is less than the feelings about it; in Frost, the actual thing is less than the pleasures to be got talking about it; in Bailey, the actual thing need not, may not, exist except as a "concrete unit of mind"—something to measure or think by, "the middle point of the visible world" and a "focus of force," but possibly not real in itself, only a "copy of what they had in their minds," "whatever it was." The major facts about it are that it is believed "empty," that it is never reached, that it has a "name to leave alone," and that it "drew the eye, the questioning thought." For Bailey, the mind is the seeker, the name, the "unit of mind," that is sought.

Bailey's recurrent and characteristic questioning about the certitudes of ideas recurs even in such charmingly patriotic poems as "The Shadow of Mr. McGee":

> One thing is sure they could not thereafter claim
> to identify a phenomenon with other than a classified name
> drawn newly minted and whole
> from the vocabulary of the putative national soul.

A word to be drawn, newly minted, from the putative? *Supposed* is not *proved*; the lighthouse is not reached.

Bailey does not, however, debunk the quest. He shows nothing but reverence to the seekers, the founders, the ancestors, who have preceded us, and he insists on the value of thinking. The closing poem to *Miramichi Lightning*, "Reflections on a Hill Behind a Town," sums up his credo:

> knowledge was in itself a good
> and would bear issue
> in season.

That knowledge, like all things, should be seasonal, does not devalue its pursuit. Again and again Bailey's poetry reminds us of the search for knowledge as an inner necessity of our biological beings. Thinking, seeking for "nomenclature"—cogitations:

> it would not be well to abandon, (let us say)
> for a trip to the woods in Spring
> to admire the skill of the trailing arbutus
> in decanting its fragrance
>
> ("The Question, Is It?")

For, as "Trump" asserts:

> and so I will write down
> what I must
> or go to wordless fields of stuff
> beyond the nones
> cradled in the great stare

> unrocked   uncomforted
> so I will if I can
> I will write away the   emptiness
> make a firmament of words
> the Word
> name pain,   invoke an ark
> become
> if to utter is to live.

"Trump" may be taken as the voice of the word user, word maker; it may also be taken as the voice of God. God is certainly the speaker in "The Curve of the Ethereal," God in process, creating the "cellular," "coding my creations into multitudinous dictionaries, / and who will there ever be to gainsay my nomenclatures?" Like all makers, this God is within history, within flux; in "The Curve of the Ethereal," God has not yet created other word makers. But, as Bailey makes sometimes frighteningly clear, the Word contains its own destruction, as life contains its death: "the wolf that sleeps in every prayer / will slay the man-child as of old" says "The Blood of the Lamb." Both original sin and the holy ghost reside in the word, sleep in it, kill it—for the word lives within nature like a seed, or an ever re-forming idea. History, the story with ever changing words, is our medium.

And the other sense of the word "medium" also serves to describe Bailey's work—the *moderate*, the *un-overdone*. Bailey avoids the swoony passivities of Carman, Swinburne, Tennyson, or even Eliot. And, although Bailey's depicted nature quivers with vitality, his dandaical method of speaking about it reminds one more of Marianne Moore's witty proprieties than of the *sturm und drang* passions of Whitman, Jeffers, Crane, or Thomas. Bailey takes mythology and religion more relativistically, more lightly (though not irreverently) than does Eliot. And Bailey is far too Canadian to attempt the Grand Legendary Manner of Williams, Olson, and the American Dream Company. He differs from Marianne Moore in preferring imaginary gardens to the "real toad"—in preferring ideas to things. Even his decanting arbutus is nearer to being an idea than a flower. And although Bailey has a somewhat Frostian manner, in his relish for the ways we can talk about things and in the ambivalence of some of his reassurances about relativism (as in "The Human Form is Practically Resilient"), his darks are never desert places. Cheerfulness keeps breaking in.

I have an acquaintance who prefers the music of Charles Ives to the music of Beethoven on the grounds that Beethoven's work is "pompous." I find this remark Baileyesque, even if Bailey does not share her opinion. (I doubt he is immoderate enough to do so.) But the "wordiness" of Ives's music—its intertextuality, its echoes, its self-conscious references and artificialities, and its blatant, sentimental patriotism—its wit, its vigour, and its moments of sadness, tenderness—and its announced preference for interaction and conflict—make it a very good simile for what Bailey is doing in verse. Like Ives, Bailey likes unresolved and mutually interacting, mutually grating situations—gaiety and seriousness together; and the grotesque in preference to the over sweet to the over grand to the "pompous" certitudes and the great pronouncements. There is a kind of friskiness, like that of a small, lithe animal unobliged to make Great Pronouncements, that typifies a particular kind of Canadian verse I have grown very much to admire: I find it in Bailey, in Gustafson, Gotlieb, Macpherson—and in several others. I think of Bailey's muskrat, in his "The Muskrat and the Whale," as a figure for this moderate, medial, medium-conscious, poetic gaiety.

If one reads Bailey's "Statement of Persons Once Classed in Category 'C'" as a clue to an alternative reading of "The Muskrat and the Whale," one begins to suspect certain cultural, sociological, conflict-laden historical motives for the muskrattiness of so much of our best poetry, and of Bailey's poetry in particular. The persons "once classed in category 'C'" have left a nation of swelled-headed people (like Ahab and his whale? like the multitude-containing Whitman?) whose "self esteem was egregious" and whose "vanity and underhandedness were nourished by an outlandish local quirk in semantics." The un-swelled-headed people decide to abandon that vain, outlandish language; they cross "over the border" to a language that, they feel, does not easily lend "itself / to guile or evil intent." Or, at any rate, the category 'C' types think, a language less vain, less big-headed. They take a great deal of pride in not being quite so big-headed. Although Bailey is here, in part, making fun of Canadian anti-Americanism, he, too, dislikes big-headedness.

In "The Muskrat in His Brook," I spoke of Bailey's muskrat as a "humorous apologia" for Bailey's own poetics. The muskrat's gift is "seen as lying in his play," in "his natural medium" "liberated by reason." A muskrat, I wrote:

is unportentous and not uncommon; he is confined to a smaller habitat. Whales are huge, rare, frightening—and, the image implies, profounder of element—perhaps thus, indirectly, of subject. They surely write larger—and longer poems, and less playful ones. The Whale is the Great Poet and the muskrat isn't. But, as the poem truthfully asserts, the muskrat has his own dignity, and, even, the poem hints, a plus of liberty.

I have grown to see more motivational force in Bailey's favourite words, "mete" and "feat," as I have learned to see how much his sense of the medium—as verbal, as textual, as temporal flux, has punningly intertwined with his sense of the moderate, his sense of proportion, his sense of relativity. The "feat" insists on a sense of the medium.

All of Bailey's seekers, whether ship-wrecked swimmers or land-racked thinkers, are Maritime or fluvian, often "storm-bound" and "tidal" ("Guide") as well, but they are liberated and strive and live mostly, and perhaps only, in the exercise of their reason. The muskrat does not yearn for grandeurs greater than it can cope with intellectually—after all, it can not step twice into its same brook! Its featness depends on the meteness of its efforts, of its knowledge of and acceptance of—and its play within—its medium. And, while the muskrat has "bliss" in its blood (and we need not forget, here, Carman), the whale has only "sedate" fluids. The whale is self-consciously important. The muskrat is unconcerned with proof, portent, or self-image. He has the dignity of being a thinking being:

> even though his habitat is narrow
> and confined because
> of certain data of existence
> best known to himself and
> other frequenters of the shallow
> bed of gurgling water that he works and plays in.
>
> His reason
> liberates his nights and days in
> the medium this reason both foreshadows and reflects.

His medium is our context, our sense of proportion, our "putative national soul"—it is the language we found, or invented, "over the border." It is Bailey's language, Bailey's medium. Genius, Bailey has written, is

> regarded as a function of the social and cultural
> milieu, and as a supreme expression of the
> processes and impulses latent within it.[8]

The muskrat, having chosen his stream, having crossed the border, is no longer deracinated, but native. He has made his context his medium.

---

from *Canadian Poetry* (Fall-Winter 1986)

NOTES

[1] Alfred G. Bailey, Interview with M. Travis Lane, September 1985, for *Studies in Canadian Literature.*

[2] Bailey, Interview.

[3] Bailey, Interview.

[4] Alfred G. Bailey, *Miramichi Lightning: The Collected Poems of Alfred Bailey* (Fredericton: Fiddlehead Poetry Books, 1981). All poems quoted in this paper are from this edition.

[5] Bailey, Interview.

[6] M. Travis Lane, "The Muskrat in His Brook," *The Fiddlehead,* 100 (Winter 1974), 98-9.

[7] Lane, "The Muskrat in His Brook," 100.

[8] Alfred G. Bailey, "Literature and Nationalism in the Aftermath of Confederation," *Culture and Nationality* (Toronto: McClelland and Stewart, 1972), 61.

An Unimpoverished Style: The Poetry of George Elliott Clarke

Many of our contemporary Canadian poets have adopted for their verse a deliberately plain style, whose lack of ornamentation, allusion, and musical grace is intended, in most cases, to portray a sense of newness, of emptiness—what they perceive as the linguistic and cultural barrenness of the Canadian "landscape," the Canadian experience. This style conveys a sense of cultural de-racination, but, sometimes, also a kind of cultural inhibition—as if a turn of speech natural to an educated mind might be somehow un-Canadian. At its best (Atwood, Kroetsch), this style of heightened simplicity can be powerful, but, as in the comparable paintings of Colville, it is not so much a representation of reality as it is an artificial conventionalization of reality. The adoption of this plain style may have helped our poetry sever its colonial roots, and, as practised by its masters, it need never be rejected. But a mature literature needs to use the whole of its inheritance. The poetry of George Elliott Clarke, author of the substantial collection *Saltwater Spirituals and Deeper Blues*,[1] can help free us from a convention that sometimes, in some hands, seems to make of the sense of the Canadian experience, of the Canadian language, a sense of impoverishment.

Clarke does not write as if he feared being rejected by an audience imagined distrustful of educated reference. Instead he uses the full range of the cultural resources available to him as a Canadian, a Maritimer, a descendant of the black refugees of 1812. The art, music, literature, religion, and history of Europe, North America, and Africa are native to him. His being at home in this larger world reminds the reader of the respected, if unfashionable, poetry of A. G. Bailey and Ralph Gustafson. Like them, Clarke possesses a sense of history as continuous and present in his own context. But, and here again he reminds me of A. G. Bailey, Clarke also possesses a rich sense of what the Canadian found in Canada—of Indigenous history, of nature—as well as what the Canadian brought. Not even the Arctic tundra was barren. The emptiness of a field is in the eye of the beholder. For Clarke, to whom erased villages, abandoned homesteads, and lost nations are present in history, the "boulder-barren, stone-strewn soil" of Canada, like its language, is not naked. Consider, for example, Clarke's "Musquodoboit Road Church":

micmac windpoems sing
Spring's resurrection,
foretold by the sharp, fused fragrance
of jubilee roses,
and the appearance of shiny, new
blue cars of waves,
cruising the beaches.
knowing this sensual verse
we ensure fertility.
we prepare a path through the wilderness.
we prepare the Easter Sunrise Service;
blue-grass banjo jamborees,
sepia saints in ivory robes, and the flash
of fish, flapping and flopping,
the hooked close of a gossamer line
predatory poetry.
we prepare the way of the Lord.

The experience from which this poem is written, with all its specific celebration of the local, includes a sense of the richness of ancient Mi'kmaq culture. It includes European Christianity re-translated into Afro-American culture ("sepia saints in ivory robes") and the special Afro-American sense of "jubilee" with its remembrances of freedom lost and regained. Here, too, are the ancient fertility myths of Africa and of Europe, the heart of the resurrection myths. And here, too, the bluegrass jamborees, music original to the New World, not imported from the East, which represent the closeness to the black American South that makes part of Canadian "country" music, and of the Canadian black experience. And with all this is the modern and continually predatory world of commerce and of nature "making style" (as the West Indians put it) in new cars, new fashions, new poetry. The sensuous vitality and multiculturalism of this verse is as Canadian as those sharply fragrant beach roses.

It is good to be reminded of the richness of our world, as in Clarke's poetry we are. But it is primarily Clarke's technical richness that creates the excellence of his writing. He has a gift for the adjective and a good ear for consonance, assonance, alliteration, rhyme, and rhythmic stress. This textural richness makes his lines what in a painting would be called painterly—although to call a poem poetic nowadays is almost regarded as an insult. So much of what is called poetic, as technique, has been vulgarly poetic (see Aldous Huxley's famous essay, "The Vulgarity of Poe") that modern poets, scrupulously trimming technical vulgarities from their verse, can sometimes achieve a verse so purified of technique that there is nothing left in it but sentiment. Clarke, on the other hand, is still making art. Thus the repetition of consonants, of vowel and stress patterns, in poems such as "Musquodoboit Road Church" is far denser than prose and contributes directly to the sensuality of the reading process. Further, stressed associations of sound assist the hinting of nuances of meaning. "Prepare the way of the Lord" is thus linked to "predatory"—and thus, indirectly, to the predatory images of the blue, cruising cars, and to the sharpness of the fragrance of fertility, and to the hook on the poem's line.

Although Clarke is aware of the major traditions of English-language poetry, he mostly writes in rhythms that are, to my ear, typically Canadian. That is, he does not write in the complexly sinuous rhythms of the best West Indian verse, nor in the colloquial "loose iambics" of the best American verse, nor in the more cautious iambics of British verse. Rather Clarke tends to use the short-lined, loosely trochaic rhythms which at their best (Pratt, Marty) can sound Beowulfian, and at their worst, a trifle like brick-laying. In the "loosened trochaic" form most Canadian poets use, the strongest beats of the line are most often at the beginning of the line. The lines usually end with a weakened stress and often with a dropping of the voice. The verse is not usually constructed as a rhythmic paragraph (as in Milton or Hopkins); rather the structural sense is declamatory—the heaping or layering of one statement upon another. Reading this material out loud, the Canadian poet speaks with emphasis and, at times, a driving, pulpit force, rather a bob-tailed Dylan Thomas effect at its best, at other times more like dictation, or the delivery of one-line jokes. The total effect is that of a hammer rather than that of a dance. In a few poems, however, Clarke goes beyond this somewhat delimited rhythm, with magnificent effect. One such poem "The Emissaries," will be looked at in detail later in this paper.

Clarke's instinct for visually just but fresh imagery gives originality to the Old English or Dylan Thomas style of linking nouns and adjectives in strong stresses and falling rhythms: "incandescent angels / whirling in crayon blaze" ("The Stars are Winged Creatures Over a Blue World," section V from *The Book of Jubilee*). The physicality and the childishness of crayon colours suggest the peculiar, innocent brilliance that only child artists—and Van Gogh—can give to a representation of the heavens.

At his best, Clarke develops and connects his imagery. From "Signs," section VII of *The Book of Jubilee*:

> i saw the seagull, saint of harbors,
> grey pier-prophet, miles inland,
> burning, but not burning;
> i saw a book of stone through water-light,
> its words moved when read,
> scattering like tadpoles,

(Notice the *Beowulf* rhythms.) The readers' recognition of the force of these images deepens gradually. First we envision the tadpoles' tiny ink shapes as they scatter and vanish in a pond. Then we perceive the implied question—what happens to what we have read as we read it? Is the word static while our eye moves, or is it our focus, our attention, that is static, while life and the words which are part of the process of living move away from us into our past, into our memory, into the pond/context of our lives? Water-light is a reflected light—punningly, the light of reflection, and, here, a spiritual light. Light and water conjoined to that which burns but is not consumed, i.e. the divine bush of the Holy Spirit, and to a book of stone, carry a wealth of literary and religious allusions, from the Old Testament through Dante, Eliot, and Thomas. With these earthly elements is the creature of the air, the gull prophet. The gull's cry, warning, raucous, unflattering, dire, is suggestive of Old Testament prophecy. The reader who recalls that the saints and prophets were often querulous, mangy, wild-eyed, garbage-eating, can recognize a saint in a seagull. The gull is also a conspicuous white bird, and, like the equally vulgar pigeon, a symbol of the Holy Spirit. The bird/spirit/prophet/saint of the air is thus connected to the burning bush whose fire, also, is the Holy Spirit, and to the book, which does not decay, being written in rock, which is the book of the law, and the Word. The Word, of course, is also the fourth element, the water of life. But the Word is also alive—like the tadpoles, with all the ambivalences their scattering suggests.

The sequence from which this excerpt is taken, *The Book of Jubilee*, is supposedly spoken by Richard Preston, founder of the African United Baptist

Association in 1854. This beautiful long poem is not a simple narrative record of the steps toward the proclamation and founding of the African United Baptist Association; instead, it records the experiences, depressions, and exultations of the prophetic Preston, and how, not emptied of his mission in the founding of the African United Baptist Association, he moves on. The conveyed sense of a fullness of living keeps the historical facts from being dead issues.

That the spirit of jubilee still lives and struggles is evident in the preceding section of Clarke's collection, *Soul Songs and Blues Notes*. But the short poem for Clarke has a limiting tendency. Too often it is a lyric of a single mood, and the expression of the single impulse does not, as a form, demand the structure-risking complexity of redefinition or development. Clarke's shortest poems, especially in the *Soul Songs* section, are sometimes only collections of unexplored images linked by the general mood of the poem, but by no more than that. For example, "Guysborough Road Church":

> we are the black loyalists;
> we think of the bleak fundamentalism
> of a ragged scarf of light
> twined and twisted and torn
> in a briar patch of pines.
> and then, of steel-wool water,
> scouring the dull rocks of bonny
> bonny nova scotia—
> this chaste, hard granite
> coast inviolate; the dark,
> dreary mountains where sad Glooscap broods
> over waters void ...
> we are the world-poor.
> we are the fatherless.
> we are the coloured Christians
> of the african united baptist association.

Br'er Rabbit's briar patch is not organically connected to steel wool, which, though it can suggest both the colloquial reference to African hair and to hard labour, is casually dropped for an allusion to Nova Scotia's sentimentalized Prince Charlie. To none of these are chastity and the supposed inviolateness of the coast related—nor are any of these related to Glooscap (who is not a rabbit trickster figure in the Malecite tales.) While it could be argued that the failure of these pieces of cultural reference to cohere is part of the impoverishment and abandonment felt by the "coloured Christians," the impoverishment affects the poem itself. In this poem, at least, the inheritance is not yet owned; the material world not integrated.

But Clarke's second section, *Blues Notes*, has more poems with a minimal degree of narrative cohering the imagery. Too, the *Blues Notes* poems more often take as their structuring point not a subject but an image. A poet who works first from a subject may be tempted to use imagery decoratively, so that the images refer only to the subject, never to each other. (As for example, the "scarf of light" in "Guysborough Road Church" can not be connected to the "steel-wool" scouring pad of water a few lines later.) Where a poet takes the risk of allowing a central image/emotion complex to develop its own suggestions, without reaching for "subject," wholeness of effect is more often achieved. Giving a poem "its head" in this fashion is as risky as recording one's dreams, and as dull, if one does not, at the same time, exercise one's deepest understanding. It is a poet's emotional understanding of the images that insist upon coming to the poem that controls the poem's strength. Emotion is not a matter of imagery alone; it is, in fact, primarily, a matter of rhythm. One of Clarke's finest poems, "The Emissaries," shows what Clarke can do when allowing his understanding of imagery and emotion to create the poem, to become pure poetry, what Robert Frost meant by "poetry" when he called it what could not be translated into a different sound.

> red apples and brown coffee
> in the indigo dawn early
> paired, dark forms of ducks
> moving in water,
> seem like strange rocks
>
> or the breasts of my daughter
> as the motorway develops
> images of autos and truck stops.
>
> a motel sign glares blood-red,
> opposite a home of the freshly-dead.

the black body of a Bible,
lynched on the tree of a table,
is motionless as possible. i would read it if i were able
(if its words were not birds of prey
in a bomber-sky, olive and grey).

coin-operated lovers
exchange lucre in cold covers.
piercing lights of moloch lamps
hurl arrows of electricity
to drive out darkness where it camps
in the stock markets of the city.
i would alter if there was change
to alter what is not pre-arranged.

i have lost so much of what was nothing
(even the stars above the lakes are frothing).
have i said that my daughter's breasts
are like two, young, black swans?
that each generation of emptiness rests
upon my toiling for such futile funds?
going forth mornings to keep alive
the human doom, the too-human drive.

("The Emissaries")

Notice how Clarke does not desert the central location of his perceptions and
concerns. Everything is organically connected to the literal level; everything
relates, corresponds. The motion of life against the motionlessness of death
(and of the unreadable, killed Bible) is paralleled with the deep ambivalence of
the coin/change complex. The delicate queries about the possibility of change
(as alteration) is entwined with the knowledge of the malignity of human
drive, human change, human greed (coin). The frothing of the stars reminds
us that they, too, like the generations of man, pass and decay in futility. And
the movement of the bird imagery—from the black ducks, which are at once
rocks—hard, strange, unalive—and soft, pulsingly alive breasts of a young
girl, to the birds of prey, the bombers, and then back to the black swans, and
the daughter's breasts, again, is a movement from beauty observed through

the recollection of despair towards an assertion of beauty imagined and existing—the imagined swans, the existing daughter.

In most of Clarke's poetry, as in "The Emissaries," Clarke expresses an intense sense of the motion of time. He expresses a sense of a past whose pain seems not to have ceased to exist (the Bible, the lynchings) and of a present which, as it surges and yearns towards the future, feels rootings mounting within it—to use the wonderful assertion of Clarke's "Can't Seem to Settle Down" that roots "will mount with the shrink of time: / they will ooze through me / when i am still atoms of earth." Repeatedly in Clarke's verse the images of highways, railways, automobiles, ships, airplanes, flying, dancing, driving, and the motions of sea and wind occur. Even his fettered black loyalists are fettered to storm-winds and water, to the "revolving sea," to the surging motions of time and nature. This sense of being fettered to time, but to time which is change and motion, lies at the heart of "The Emissaries."

A second major theme of "The Emissaries" that is common to much of Clarke's work, and that is the prevailing theme also of *The Book of Jubilee*, is the theme of being sent out, of reaching out, of striving—and of being among things which also seem to have purpose, indication, and messages. Who are the emissaries of "The Emissaries"? The unreadable, terrible words of the closed Bible? The suggestive, paired, dark forms of ducks? The piercing lights driving out darkness? The human spirit, futilely, mysteriously striving? All of these, the reader feels. There is some sense in the word "emissary" of a secret message—something very important, but not spelled out plain. What we feel with the brilliant, moving forms of this poem, is Melville's sense that these things are "not without significance." These things portend.

One of the most interesting ways Clarke loads his forms with significance in this poem is through colour. His colour sense is always a painter's, and the colours of "The Emissaries" are chosen for their emotional and symbolic values as well as for their coherence to the literal morning-in-the-motel landscape of the poem's "place." Indigo is the colour of a dark Canadian dawn, literally, for in our short-day seasons the world of human commerce dawns while it is still night. But indigo is also the blue-black peculiarly Afro-American in historical suggestion—the indigo of the plantation economy and of "the blues." The red of the apples and the brown of the coffee, as colours, and as plain nourishment, support the colour history—as do the blood-red sign and the black body (breasts, Bible, lynching victim)—the same colours of body and blood, of Afro-American history, here suggestively sacramental. As the poem progresses, Clarke reminds us of the slow progress of morning light (and of history). The colours pale, but remain the colours of death, now the military colours of Moloch, god of war and greed. Against the bleak olive and grey of a cold Canadian morning, Clarke places electric arrows whose fierce commercial "drive" echoes the motion of the highways, mimics the glitter of the stars, and reminds us, subtly, of what has happened to Blake's Jerusalem, our modern world. As usual, in Clarke's verse, alliteration assists stress and colour patterns. (And it is, of course, splendid to discover that it is still possible to write rhymed verse in English without sounding awkward.)

But what I most particularly like about this splendid poem is the way Clarke subtly alters the rhythm of the lines as the poem progresses from the shorter lines of the opening stanzas, written largely in "loosened trochees," with major stresses at the beginning of the line and falling rhythms, towards the more beautiful, longer, and more iambic rhythms of the last stanza. There are kinds of meaning for which the trochee, however "loosened," is not appropriate. It is too crisp, too hammering a rhythm for some kinds of statements, for the ultimate, flowingly meditative affirmation of the poem. For it is not simply the image of the beloved daughter's breasts that contains the affirmation of this dark poem, but the piercingly lovely melody of the concluding stanza. Notice how, by placing the major stresses later in the line, Clarke affects the emotional tonalities. Notice how the last four lines grow into a paragraph, not as four units, but as a single unit strongly stressed. No brick-laying here, but organic form. The shorter, more trochaic lines of the opening stanzas convey just slightly that sense of construction and unmusicality that suit the opening mood. But the sense of constricted despair and hammering stress ("piercing lights of moloch lamps") alters to a calmer sense of having lost "what was nothing"—after all, even the stars are temporal. The relaxing of the mood is conveyed in part by the way the rhythm of the line swings away from the hammer-beat or the mechanical impulses of the highway and the motel sign. For the natural grace of birds, of organic nature, which the concluding imagery affirms, comes in a slower metre. The darkness of the opening perceptions of the poem remains, but the exploration of these perceptions has deepened the emotions away from the constriction, and the accompanying sense of incapacity and hopelessness, of the opening lines towards a stronger, more tragic, and more life-accepting irony, towards a greater dignity of expression, of sentence sound. The speaker of the poem has become the master of his mood. It is this change of rhythm, this gaining of expressive, melodic dignity, that is the poem's point, the secret message of the "emissaries."

We must, more of us, learn to write like this.

---

from *Canadian Poetry* (Spring-Summer 1985)

NOTES
[1] George Elliott Clarke, *Saltwater Spirituals and Deeper Blues* (Porter's Lake, N.S.: Pottersfield Press, 1983). All subsequent quotations from Clarke's poems are taken from this edition.

Maximalist Poetry: A Review of
Whylah Falls by George Elliott Clarke

Much recent poetry is written in an unornamented style almost austere in its modesty. I cannot deny the grave beauties of some of such poetry. Readers accustomed to so spare a diet may come down with a sort of aesthetic indigestion upon reading George Elliott Clarke's lushly ornamented poem *Whylah Falls*. Yet, to judge from the many I have heard praising it, some of us have been hungry.

Clarke is a maximalist. He celebrates the fullness of life and the wealth of our cultural and linguistic traditions. He does not simplify his writing towards a conventionalized norm. He does not put on a particular vernacular as if it were a team uniform. Instead he enlarges, includes, extends his language. He supposes no gulf between local dialect, with its own poetic traditions, and the various languages of the literary worlds, foreign, ancient, white, yellow, black, or red. Western tradition, which includes what he knows of Africa or of the Orient, are his to claim, to use, to be at home in. The people of whom he writes use naturally a language rich in metaphor and image, full of anecdote and "sayings," rich in Biblical, folk, and musical allusion. His major characters are as gluttonous for literature as they are for beauty, food, music, love—the whole physical and worldly world. Literature furnishes already furnished minds.

Clarke is also a maker of lists, a reciter of labels, a taxonomist of the ordinary. He reminds us, a little, of Joyce or Williams. (Whylah Falls is smaller than Paterson or Dublin, but as specifically loved.) Also Joycean is the degree to which Clarke's poem not only makes its own music but refers to music (specific tunes, specific musicians) as if music, including nature's, were as omnipresent to our attention as thought or sight. Smells, tastes, textures, weather, food, above all, sex, are detailed, celebrated. Clarke's character Amarantha remarks, "In school, I hated poetry—those skinny, / Malnourished poems that professors love." *Whylah Falls* is not malnourished. It is fat, extravagant, self-indulgent. It is what people who don't like Dickens, Puccini, or Dylan Thomas don't like about them.

Clarke's subject is the whole of human life; his instance: the black labourers, musicians, preachers, poets, lovers of Jarvis County. He brings us to his

"Beauty Town" with its poverty, its suffering, its meanness, its drunkenness, its envy, its hate, lust, greed, murder, religion, wisdom, folly, joy, love. The cover of *Whylah Falls* shows three young women, grouped like Botticellian graces, but the poem celebrates more than three women, and each is a distinctly portrayed individual. Clarke is unusual in his ability to distinguish one female character from another. If anything, it is his male characters who are less lovingly differentiated in attitude, speech, habits, and vision. In its character groupings and emotional gestalt, *Whylah Falls* is something of an *Under Milk Wood*, but it is more Dickensianly focused on social evil, more Williams/Whitmanesquely respectful of its characters, and lacks Thomas's kindly tinge of condescension. Much of the time it's splendid; at times it's a bit much. Maybe.

A major delight of *Whylah Falls*, and a contributor to the sense of fullness the poem conveys, is the wide variety of styles Clarke employs: from poet Xavier's imitation of Pound's "The River-Merchant's Wife" to the lyrics of Ma Rainey, from *The Book of Solomon* to a grocer's catalogue, from *The Canterbury Tales* to "Negro-natural, those green, soiled words / Whose roots mingle with turnip, carrot, and squash," from journalistic prose to ranting sermon and traditional ballad, all is relished. Clarke's chief heroine, Shelley, tells her poet lover, "We are responsible for Beauty." He replies, "Literature be the tongue you do your lovin' in." The underlining suggests Clarke quotes, I don't know from whom. But the belief is Clarke's.

Whylah Falls follows in the polynarrative tradition: Chaucer, Williams, Melvin B. Tolson (whose *Harlem Gallery*, insufficiently appreciated in Canada, has a vigour which reminds me of Clarke's). Of the many Canadians who have written such poems (e.g., Geddes, Gunnars, Gutteridge, Livesay, Ondaatje) the two to my mind who most resemble Clarke in their intention and breadth are Andrew Suknaski and Daphne Marlatt. Suknaski and Marlatt share with Clarke a desire to create for the reader a sense of the specific "world" out of which their poetry comes. They voice for us cultures previously little heard in our general body of literature. In a way, each revises for us a sense of the "centre." Suknaski's Ukrainian Canadian West is new to our poetry. Marlatt's Mother of Language is newer. Black Nova Scotia only now claims major attention. All three poets relate their particulars to the broader literary past, and all three relate their "new" present to our broad, geologic history.

Few other contemporary poets share so spacious a sense of time. Suknaski has emphasized the breadth and, as well, the discoherence, of the voices of his world. Marlatt has focused on the consciousness of the Woman/Writing. Clarke's poetry is the most traditional, the most romantic, the most (I think he will forgive the pun) highly coloured. But all three are important poets, if only because they are building floors to our mansions.

I think we are lucky to be living in a time when so much good poetry is being written.

No review is complete without quotations, by which you may judge the reviewer. I conclude with three:

I see the moon hunted down, spooked from hills,
Roses hammer his coffin shut, O stilled
By stuttered slander, judicial gossip,
And a killer's brawling bullet. Bludgeoned
Men, noosed by a loose law, swing from pines; judges,
Chalked commandants, gabble dour commandments;
Their law books yawn like lime-white, open pits
Lettered with bones, charred gibberish, of those
Who dared to love or sing and fell to mobs.
Language has become volatile liquor,
Firewater, that lovers pour for prophets
Who haul, from air, tongues of pentecostal fire—
Poetry come among us.

("Vision of Justice")

There's a black wind snakin' by Whylah Falls;
There's a river of blood in Jarvis County;
There's a government that don't know how to weep;
There's a mother that can't get no sleep.
Go down to the Sixhiboux, hear it moan
Like a childless mother far, far, from home,
"There's a change that's gonna have to come.
I said, a change that's gonna have to come."

("The Ballad of Othello Clemence")

The text is open.

There was a shining in the bushes
by the river, then I felt her.

Liana, Liana!

She is the Word, a code I read,
fingers caressing the braille she keeps
opening for my touch.

The river is archetypal, is deep;
her hair is a river.

I study her and sight African
violets, cassava, wild cherries.

Her true name is Oshun.

The text is open.

("Discovery")

---

from *The Fiddlehead* (Summer 1992)

WORKS CITED
Wyllah Falls. Polestar Press, 1990.

Say What You Can: A Review of Milton Acorn's *Whiskey Jack*
and *The Uncollected Acorn* and James Deahl and Milton Acorn's
A Stand of Jackpine: Two Dozen Canadian Sonnets

It is saddening to read these posthumously published collections of Milton Acorn's poetry. Acorn's talent was considerable. He was very much our generation's notion of what a poet should be: passionate, eccentric, personally identified with the "common man," and undebased by academic or yuppiedom. But he was never quite as good as we wanted him to be. Only in Acorn's 1982 collection, *Captain Neal MacDougal & the Naked Goddess* (Charlottetown: Ragweed Press), were his poetic excellences—his apparently inimitable rhythm with its "jackpine" iambic, forceful, supple, musical, and his brilliant, accurate, and sometimes astonishing imagery—gathered into a scheme worthy of them. He had planned, as he wrote in the preface to this work, to do more with MacDougal.

The three volumes under review have the strengths and weaknesses of Acorn's earlier work. All too often, Acorn's passion for justice and his lust for vitality translated into simplicities. In his quarrel with the wicked of the earth, he was somewhat disinclined to see "shades of grey," and perhaps too convinced of the rightness of his impulses to make poetry out of any quarrels with his own ideas.

Acorn's essential poetic impulse was celebratory and ethical. The technical skill which yields us so completely the sound of his generous emotions always appeals, but his verse is too often rant, slogan, or "occasional," without that "yet another level" which is the mark of great writing. In Captain MacDougal, Acorn created a self not his own, a self who could be viewed from without as a Character, as an exaggeration, as a myth. Myth, being narrative rather than imagist, obliges complexity because it is necessarily situational. It is at once specific and symbolic. Through MacDougal, Acorn was able to show poetic fire and human labour together, dramatically, rather than merely generalizing about them. And, too, Acorn needed to dramatize for himself the regal bawdiness of his muse, to "justify" her ways to man. Through the tiny "hardened" Captain and his gluttonous Goddess, Acorn was able to give his sermonizing impulse a situational wit, a sophisticating distance, and a metaphorical depth—all that a "crazy" Captain and his ship at sea can, as narrative and metaphor, provide.

Captain Neal MacDougal and the Naked Goddess are among the finer literary inventions of recent years. I am sorry I did not meet them to greet them as such during Acorn's lifetime, and it is a pity that their book has not yet been generally recognized as being such an original and powerful work. It is possible that the Captain, being in character near to Acorn's own poeticized persona (but wittier, feistier, more heroic, as the narrative allows him) was not recognized as being artifact, as a Character. Perhaps Acorn's peers had been too used to dismissing Acorn as "character" to read his art seriously. Or perhaps the Character (like the Author and like God) is dead for the postmodernists.

A Stand of Jackpine contains twelve informal sonnets by Acorn and twelve by James Deahl. Of Acorn's sonnets, one is reprinted from the MacDougal collection, and another, "The Naked Goddess," belongs in it. Two others, "Many Ghosts" and "Invocation," while not MacDougal sonnets, seem to have learned from them how to present intuitive feelings dramatically and how to charge metaphors with symbolic weight.

Most of the Deahl sonnets are in two sequences, "The America Sonnets" and "Pittsburgh." Deahl writes in the gentled "loose iambic" we recognize as being almost conventional in contemporary American verse. The assimilated ghosts of Lowell, Wright, Sandburg, and Benét are recognizable. All of Deahl's sonnets are well written, and a few, especially IV from "Pittsburgh," have an originality and a poetic power that makes me wish to read more of Deahl's poetry. Deahl hasn't the rhythmic forcefulness or the "jackpine" quality of Acorn; the bond between the two poets seems one of sympathy rather than of influence.

Whiskey Jack, with its charming introduction by Al Purdy, has a number of attractive, if mostly somewhat lightweight, poems. My favourites are "Hummingbird," "The Canadian Moon," and another MacDougal sonnet, "What Right Has a Gull." *The Uncollected Acorn* is largely a work of piety, but it, too, has some attractive poems: "Never Say It's All For the Best," "Sonnet Seeing with MacDonald," "Thawtime," "Eyes and This Man," (and "Many Ghosts," repeated from *A Stand of Jackpine*). I hope the editor, Deahl, will be asked to make *The Complete Acorn*. But I am sorry we will have no more of that grotesque immortal, MacDougal, to tell us slant that Acorn had to say:

"Poetry and sainthood ought to be
The aspiration of a man or woman,

Or they should ply some instrument at least—
I'm serious," said Captain Neal MacDougal.
"I myself used to manipulate the
Juice harp as I was brought up to call it
Before I found that talking was my bent.
I was meant to be a saint but worked too hard."

Seen by him alone, a being appeared
Who had the manner and grace of a woman,
A teasing look that challenged and afeared.
She stuck out a tongue to lick his whole head
Totally around, inward through his brain:
"Say what you can although your task's insane."

("Miracle with One Witness," from
Captain Neal MacDougal & the Naked Goddess)

---

from *The Fiddlehead* (Spring 1988)

WORKS CITED

Whiskey Jack. Introd. Al Purdy, HMS Press, 1986.
A Stand of Jackpine: Two Dozen Canadian Sonnets. Unfinished Monument Press, 1987.
The Uncollected Acorn. Ed. James Deahl, Deneau Publishers, 1987.

Summoning All That's There:
A Review of Anne Simpson's *Loop*

Anne Simpson's work fills me with admiration and envy. I don't know when I have read richer poetry, or a book I will want to read more often. Her earlier books combined much narrative and imagist strength with the kind of witty "conceit" we associate with the great metaphysical poets. *Loop* adds to these strengths remarkable skill in formal composition and experimentation and an enormous range of suggestive and emotional reference. In addition, she is one of our most musical poets, with a sensitive and appreciative ear for the cadence of our language.

Part of the reason why the excellence of her work is being so widely recognized is that at present there is growing among many poets and readers a great yearning for and admiration of formal poetic effects. In my youth poets were, by and large, reacting against what was felt to be the constricting and old-fashioned forms, with their closed and echoing rhymes, and what in lesser hands was their often over-regular metres. The open form reflected for us, then, our desire for our world—that it should open out, perhaps hopefully, toward new discoveries, even if this might mean, as well, new complexities and ambiguities. But the open form brought with it, along with many gorgeous poems, a mass of very dull, prosy poetry. At present, bored with openness and its now old-fashioned hippie connotations, and, as well, perhaps alarmed at the chaos and apparent formlessness of history, nature, etc., many readers and poets are returning to the admiration of closed forms. The tidiness of the classical sonnets, sestinas, etc., are less often seen as politically incorrect.

Anne Simpson has the ability to use closed forms while retaining the emotional and intellectual validation of the form—that is, she does not use these forms purely for their decorative or impressive effect. Instead the repetitiveness, the emphasis on closure, the echoes and returns, underscore and convey the meaning of the poem. The simplest of Simpson's closed poems is the charming "Möbius Strip," which enters and exists with the same lines. Each line is repeated, going in, going out. The central lines (the twist in the trip) read:

We're filled, yet we tip constantly. Goodbye. As for happiness—

it spills itself. The petal of a violet, a blue ear, listening. How easily

it spills itself. The petal of a violet, a blue ear, listening. How easily

we're filled, yet we tip constantly. Goodbye. As for happiness—

The sweet sadness of the emotion is emphasized by the form's insistence that nothing changes. The poem is quite powerful. But such a form should be unique to the skill and sensibility of Anne Simpson this one time. For anyone to imitate a form so self-enclosed, and, indeed, for Simpson to do it again, would result in underlining for the reader the form's unnaturalness. There are admirable works of art that should never be imitated. I think here of those enormous, pink plastic wrappings of islands, gorges, national buildings, etc., by you-know-who-but-I've-forgotten—the first time was an aesthetic effect of short, irreverence, illumination, and joy. No other was needed.

More elaborately and more interestingly closed, (and a more important poem), is "Seven Paintings by Brueghel," a corona sequence of sonnets meditating on the destruction of the World Trade Centre towers. 9/11 is shadowed against the disasters contemplated by Brueghel. Each of the seven sonnets begins with the last line of the preceding, and the sequence ends with the first line of the sequence. The iambic is attractively varied but adequately present, and each line rhymes without drawing attention to the rhyme. The only other poet I can think of who can rhyme so unawkwardly is Derek Walcott. On the basis of this sequence alone, Simpson is a major poet in English, not just Canada. Not, I want to stress, because she can do this skilfully, but because she can do this as part of the poem sequence's meaning and emotion thrust: "What goes around comes around."

Yet by universalizing our reactions to this material (which she does by making them personal, present, both Brueghel's past and New York's present), Simpson also manages to include a wisp of hope. We are, moreover, reminded that in Brueghel's great paintings the disasters depicted are always placed in the context of humanity's seasonal life, always only part of the general scene. Life goes on, his paintings assert—as do Simpson's sonnets.

In *Loop*, Simpson does not limit herself to one sort of poem. Many of the loveliest poems in the collection are not in the least closed. Simpson understands the use of closed form and does not use it where the poem's material does not respond to this tightness. The opening poem of the book, "Little Stories," is a charming example of a poem that continually reopens, questions, breaks up. The stanzas break illogically, mid-sentence, to emphasize that "things don't stay the same."

Among my favourite of these poems is "The Trailer Park," which, although avoiding closedness, has a wonderful layeredness. As in the corona sequence, small single circumstances are set up as parallel to each other, mutually resonant. The temporary visions, fear, and pain of a child hurt slightly in a fall from a bicycle are shown against a wealth of other lives, other stars, other visions, loves, deaths—things past and things present. The trailer park becomes the world; two loves become the universe "expanding." The poem is rich and rewarding and shares, with so many of Simpson's other poems, an affirmation of human love, a deep tenderness, and a sense of balance and measure—as if we read these "*sub specie aeternitatis.*"

One of the lines repeated to great effect in the corona sequence is the last thing said in "someone's cellphone": "Are you still there? *Are you?*" The answer, Simpson's poetry makes one believe, is, somehow, yes. Does everything vanish? Against the last sonnet of the corona sequence:

We turn; we sleep. But once there was a prayer,
a way to finger mystery. It floats,
one plastic bag, freed from the fence, that snare
with loops of wire. We translate into motes,
a glimmer in a shaft of sun. One glide,
we're gone. A painted scene: against this plea
is set in stone. An end. Each thing is tried.
A man makes notes in sand. The wind goes free.
One gust: his words are ghosts. The dust, absolved,
has vanished too. First kiss, last glance. *Tick. Tock.*
All goes to ground. We kneel down and dissolve.
Turn in. Turn out of time. Where nothing's clocked.

A touch so light. Love's breath. Things we can't hold:
these watches. Ticking. Still. Each hour is cold.

(whose last line is the first line of the sequence) we may read the last section of "The Trailer Park," which ends with the camping lovers:

Tent of skin. Pegged.

hard: breath: breath: breath:
a man's body deep
in a woman's, or
hers deep in his. She can't tell

breath
from breath. She sees
her own death and
his—even. now—
sees how small they are

and large, so large, at the same
time. Light
years between
her fingertips. Heat
inventing and re-inventing them: blazing,
stretched, almost invisible, but

expanding

expanding

expanding

It is the size of Simpson's universe, as well as her poetic skill, that so impresses me. To zero in on the couple in their tent, the hurt child, the cellphone unanswered (because the person called has died in the 9/11 disaster), the caught shred of plastic, the blue violet "ear," and the hugeness of the universe, its dissolving cold, and its small/ huge "reinventing" love.

---

from *The Fiddlehead* (Summer 2004)

WORKS CITED
Loop. McClelland & Stewart, 2003.

Haligonian Charm: Sue Goyette's *Outskirts* and David Hickey's *Open Air Bindery*

Both Sue Goyette's *Outskirts* and David Hickey's *Open Air Bindery* are admirable, amusing—in fact, quite charming. They have much in common: not just subject matter: fog, moon, sea, Halifax, domesticities, but, as well, a generally genial and playful attitude, and one marked similarity of style. They both use a form of description or adjectival reference that is non-visual, stressing emotional attitude rather than image—often with whimsical personification of non-human material. For examples:

Fog is polishing the street on its hands and knees.
                                                    Goyette, "Fog" (60)

The night waded into the ocean. Up to its waist, it looked back to us on shore.
                                                    Goyette, "Custodians" (95)

[the ocean] Lately it's been stalking us.
                                                    Goyette, "U-Pick, a Triptych" (44)

The moon actually dances off
from its own dinner party
                                        Hickey, "Footnote to the Book of
                                        Moonlight" (27)

Meanwhile the kitchen is
quietly studying its magic, its abracadabra of pots and pans
                                        Hickey, "Insomnia Drawings" (46)

[garage doors] wave solely/goodnight
                                        Hickey, "Suburbia the Beautiful" (22)

This style of description seems lighthearted. Indeed many of the poems in both collections are not meant to be taken, in Matthew Arnold's phrase, as examples of "high seriousness." The intentions, and effects, are charming, not profound—why should they be? Good light verse needs no apology.

Where the two poets are not alike is in their choice of cadence, pacing, and line length. Goyette likes to work with long lines, internally varied, but nevertheless stacked up against each other in equivalent equalities, like ocean waves continually arriving on shore, varied internally, but essentially similar. Hickey, on the other hand, works with short lines, and stronger pauses—a less accumulative effect, and less potentially weighty.

Much of Goyette's collection is taken up by poems written in the repetitive "litany" manner that is currently so fashionable, especially as performance poems for a listening audience. The most egregious is perhaps her "Mission" (48), which begins thirteen of its fifteen two-line stanzas with "We will" and includes "will" in the fourteenth, and three "we will" or "we'll" in the fifteenth. I am calling this manner "litany" because in the litanies and the psalms we first encounter it, but we also find it in political speeches and rants, chants, and other forms of public-directed writing.

Generally, a listening audience, without the words on a page in front of them, can rarely remember the beginning of a poem read to them by the fifth line unless the poem is strongly narrative. Listeners to poems that keep changing ideas, images, and syntax from line to line lose track. The litany manner, where the general subject is announced at the opening and not significantly changed, and in which each line repeats and reinforces the opening lines, with only minor variations, is not a form, however, suitable for private meditation, private reading, or subtlety. (Hickey presents us with at least one litany poem: "A Brief History of Human Longing," but the litany emphasis on simplicity of syntax and the avoidance of marked changes in subject, image, or rhythm affects a good deal of his verse.)

Goyette uses a more sophisticated variety of litany repetitiveness in poems such as "Erosion," "Clear-Cut," and "Aquifer." In these poems, each sentence is a variation on the announced theme with an intelligent and amusing "dead pan" comparison between the degradation of nature and human behaviour. Our sense of repetitiveness is enforced by Goyette's satiric use of the "plonking" style (see Stephen Potter, One-Upmanship—but an earlier example of plonking is the "dying" history lesson in *Alice in Wonderland*)—all too common in governmental or academic writing. An "outside reader" for a journal, reading an article in this style might suggest that syntax and rhythm be a little more varied, but here the essential dullness of the plonking style is part of Goyette's joke.

The habitat of Nova Scotia old-growth conversation has been greatly degraded by 400 years of privacy pirating, opinion redevelopment, and more recently, texting. Over the past two decades of conversing, the rate of interrupting has doubled in volume endangering all acoustic confessions. In the last decade alone, the number of conversations thinned annually at supper tables has doubled to almost 70,000 hectares of television and website soliloquies. In Nova Scotia, almost all misunderstandings (98%) are accomplished ... women older than 100 years have become reduced to scattered groves representing less than one half percent of the shade of our mothers.

"Clear-cut, two" (82)

The resemblance between Hickey and Goyette is likely to decrease with time. Hickey is working with discovering the subtleties possible within the appearance of simplicity. Even where he risks being a tad too simple, his sensitivity, his wit, and his good ear for cadence will continue to serve him well. One of my favourites of Hickey's poems is "Vespers":

Whatever arrives at dusk
    doesn't arrive alone:
there's a whole day huddled
    at its wings, and the hours follow
thereafter, faraway
    from the kingdom of second thought
where now
    there's just the first thought
repeated: evening, light
    traveller coming from market,
expected guest
    whose meal is always warming,
I'm remembering
    a story
that was told late at our door—
    it was
clothed in old
    tales from your village.

"Vespers" (53)

Notice how the shape of the poem and its subject hint gently at repetition (of time, of travellers) as a theme, what Hickey calls "the horizon's bedtime story" in "Message in a Bottle" (36). There is a similar effect in his attractive series "Snowflake Photography," a simplified language and gently playful but magically suggestive references, such as "the universe's tidy / store of time tucked inside / a snowflake" (62). These poems are well worth rereading.

I like Goyette's work best when she is neither trying to amuse nor trying to be sure we get her point. Nothing can be more effective than the combination of serious intention with an innovative and witty style. In poems such as the six-part-long title poem "Outskirts," she is still using largely non-visual means of describing attitude and emotion, and still writing with a touch of humour, but without the intentional whimsy of her lighter poems, and without the sometimes fatiguing repetitiveness of her litany poems. "Outskirts" combines a colloquial manner with extraordinary "images" and a Whitmanesque breadth of subject and depth of suggestion. The first section opens the poem almost wistfully:

> We dissolved in you like sugar and had no choice but to hunt for
> galaxies. Our hands
> disappeared before us. Planets, we were told, are one constant light;
> open for
>
> business. Have we always been too big for our boots? We forgot to
> ask exactly what you
> do. Do you fill trees with your shadow, blue leaves starched in
> moon? Is that your
> secret? Or do you urge them to branch out, an earth-filled
> mouthful? There was so much
> to explore. We were young and thought you were ours. We thought
> everything was.
>
> "Outskirts, section 1" (99)

Those last two lines are particularly touching. As the poem progresses, its cadences seem to increase in solemnity. Towards the conclusion of the fifth section the poet announces that "it's time we speak to our deaths as breathren" (103), and the poem concludes: "Darkness bears its own sight. The path is lit by the sound of / our footsteps" (104).

All of Goyette's poems are a pleasure to read aloud. "Outskirts," however, is a poem for the anthologies. It is a privilege to read it.

---

from *The Fiddlehead* (Spring 2012)

WORKS CITED
Outskirts. Brick Books, 2011.
Open Air Bindery. Biblioasis, 2011.

Review of *For and Against* by Sharon McCartney

Many people believe artistic form and truth telling are incompatible. Truth-telling, they suppose, will be spontaneous, unpremeditated, unrehearsed, impulsive, awkward, unpolished. We know from experience how such "truth-telling" sounds: the clichés, the self-justifications, the vacuous generalizations, the "you know" and the "like" of those who can't find words. Even reporters, like gossips looking for "grab-you" facts, don't try for "eloquence." But in such artless tellings there can only be facts. Only art can "make real."

In "So Long," Walt Whitman explains that "who touches this" does not touch a book, but, instead "touches a man." Only of very good poets is this true. But it can be said of Sharon McCartney's *For and Against*—who touches this, touches a woman. Not because it is "facts"—but because of this writing's formal excellence. Sharon McCartney is one of the few Canadian poets for whom "form" does not mean a grid defined without reference to content or the nature of English. Nor does she believe, as too many of us seem to believe, that rhythm and emotional eloquence are added to the text by performance. McCartney's poetry performs itself. It does not need to be enacted.

The poems of *For and Against* are written as complete paragraphs, each with a beginning, a logically traceable coherence of argument or reflection, and a musically and emotionally satisfying end. Her cadences are rapid but not monotonous, with a kinesthetic urgency and theatrically necessary pauses. She uses alliteration and assonance rather than rhyme because rhyme interrupts, however slightly, the cadence in which it occurs (end rhymes particularly). The minute pause at the end of the line, in addition to the pauses of meaning and punctuation, is all she requires. No unnecessary word, no dull word, no stock imagery, every new insight or description at once astonishing and just, everything at once new and yet polished, diamond hard. Her language is brilliant, sensuous, startling, sometimes relaxed and cajoling, sometimes savage.

Her subject is intimate, personal; an "I" subjected to an intelligence that seems like an omniscient/objective narrator, seeing the poetic speaker in context, in proportion—presenting "I" as a character responding variously in complex situations rather than seeking to "defend" or "confess" any single action or response. And what a range of responses! This poetry can be achingly funny, tender, sad, irritated, frightening, angry, wry, self-mocking, miserable, erotic. McCartney's erotic poetry is particularly effective because of its dramatic context, whether, as sometimes, in the long narrative of a breaking marriage or in the smaller contexts of a single poem. (Check out "Dorothy" on sex with the Tin Woodsman, or "Against Sanitation.") Eros without context is eros without focus, material for daydreams, not for theatre. These poems have the range and movement of theatre. They are not lyric.

Further, because of the intensity and depth of her imagination, McCartney is one of the few Canadian poets who can enlarge a metaphor into a symbol. (Most of our poets can not even deal with metaphor, preferring lively images—pictorial descriptions—instead.) Something of most of these qualities can be seen in "Against Coyotes," which moves among aspects of the canine: literal wild animal, traditional trickster, destroyer, unreliable, endangering, and as thief and betrayer, metaphor for cancer, disease, and, as hunter, trailer, metaphor for obsession, which "dogs" us. As wild and as pet dog, as shadow and shadower, the coyote symbolizes death and, as well, invasive male and embracing female, and as dog, pet and comforter, as aging friend, as shield and shelter, hiding place.

> Bushrats, ambushing unaware housecats, snipers
> reconnoitring their Leningrad of suburban sagebrush,
> asphalt and gravel, their alto bagatelles infiltrating
> late night TV. One worms into my sister's skull,
> scratches up a bed of ganglia and whelps a malign
> brood there. Another screws me behind the house,
> gets me stoned first, then lifts my shirt, lipsticks
> with foam from the creases of his chops.
> One dogs my Joan of Arc mother, dragging a leg,
> aping her pathos, her someday-my-prince-will come.
> I hate that one. As I do the one who shoots craps
> in Vegas with my father, claws clotted with caked-
> on lies, snores with him in a parking lot off the strip,
> both of them infinitely more at ease in the casino's
> cornucopia of tedium, oddballs, than they are at home.
> One's here with me now, arthritic, his calcified bones
> buckled in the warmth of a folded afghan, sorrow's

psychedelia tickling his siesta. I stroke his skinny
ruff and he shivers with pleasure, his mulligrubs
vanquished, as if he had given discontent a smooch
and a hug, hailed a cab for it, pitiless, turning away.
This one I suffer unto me. With a dagger I open
his belly, curl into the vaginal grasp of its cavity
and shelter there, sheathed in repudiation's regimentals.

"Against Coyotes" (49)

A sometimes debated question is whether the reader should suppose identity between the "I" of the poetic speaker and the "I" of the poet. The answer is usually "no," and, generally, "none of our business." The possibility that something might be "none of our business" has become increasingly alien these days. I have an acquaintance who tries to provide anyone she encounters with intimate information about people with whom she is not on intimate terms. At a recent Grad House poetry reading one member of the audience, waiting for the reading to start, informed a group of us that two Hollywood actresses had just quarrelled. The idea that this might not be interesting, or any of our business, was not in her imagination. It was not as if she cared—except this sort of celebrity gossip is where her imagination lives, and aren't we all celebrities these days, for our seconds of public attention?

The pervading themes of *For and Against*: grief, illness, betrayal, divorce, and the significant presence of Frederictonian detail suggest McCartney may well have made this poetry out of a loss of privacy and a socially published pain, but, however afflicted with the callousness of gossip, she has made poetry according to Yeats' dicta. "All that is personal soon rots," wrote Yeats, unless "it is packed in ice or salt."[1] The poems of *For and Against* are packed in salt. And, if, at times, we recognize in them the "look of agony" that Dickinson liked, it is the salt of art that has made that "look" real. This is a book that will continue to matter when all of us living now have ceased to be anybody's business.

---

from *The Antigonish Review* (Fall 2012)

NOTES

[1] W. B. Yeats, "A General Introduction for My Work." (1937) Reproduced in *The Norton Anthology of Modern and Contemporary Poetry* (2003): Vol. 1, 883-9.

WORKS CITED

For and Against. Goose Lane Editions, 2010.

THREE

Feminist Perspectives and
Reviews of Female Poets

Rare Mountain Air: A Review of
Phyllis Webb's *Selected Poems 1954–1965*

This beautiful and useful book contains forty-eight poems from *Trio, Even Your Right Eye, The Sea Is Also A Garden,* two previously uncollected poems, and the whole of Webb's tiny, recent *Naked Poems.* But before we reach these poems, we encounter thirty-three closely printed pages of introductory essay by John Hulcoop. Since the last fifty pages of the book are almost empty, the book appears oddly weighted towards Hulcoop. Indeed, his essay dominates the book. Hulcoop does read Webb's poetry carefully for us, and, despite his queasiness about "neurotic" art, his drawing of the relationship of Webb's thinking to the modern existentialists is valuable. But an essay of such length in such a dominant position ought to be better than it is. And, as the only essay introducing a selection/collection of one author's poetry, its tone of praising with faint damns seems out of place.

I have three quarrels with Hulcoop's essay. The first is the least; it over-documents itself with quotations from Webb's poetry as if the lead essay had originally been intended for separate publication. The effect is tedious and over-explanatory. My second objection will not be shared by many: Hulcoop consciously defends his assumption of an essential identity of poet with poetic speaker. This theory that art is true confession, inadvertent diary, ignores, in my opinion, the nature of art. Critics of Hulcoop's sort say a poet is maturing when they mean the poems he has written more recently are better.

Third, I can not agree with Hulcoop that the "naked poems" are Webb's "most mature" poems to date. Although most of them are quite lovely, they are, nevertheless, merely her most ordinary poems in the currently fashionable but somewhat overrated genre of tiny verse. This genre has simplified itself away from the surrealism of Stephen Crane and the striking haiku metaphors of early Pound to the red wheelbarrow simplicities Williams moved on from.

That Phyllis Webb is not wholly at home in miniaturist simplicity can be proved by observing that, of the five groups of "naked poems" in her last book, four are actually long single poems whose stanzas are given a page each, as if they were, as they are called, a "suite" of poems on related matters. But the stanzas are connected by structural meaning, described situation, language, and "plot." The musical term "suite" implies a sequence of more diversity than is possessed by these sequent stanzas. These separated verses do not possess that extreme simplicity of diction and brevity of expression (one to seven words a line, the shorter lines preferred; one to eleven lines a page) that is called "naked" nowadays.

Thus reduced, all poets with adequate taste sound much like each other. The following lines, for example, could be written (and may very well already have been written) by any member of any poetry group in North America:

> Then you must go.
> I sit cross-legged
> on the bed.
> There is no room
> for self-pity
> I said
> I lied

I am not saying these lines are bad. The voice of Everyman has an absolute dignity. But I have read these lines before this year, more or less, and I shall be reading them again.

Phyllis Webb is truer to her genius when she surprises us with our recognition of a truth we had not phrased to ourselves; in the third verse of the sequence "Some Final Questions" she admits that the "naked" genre is itself analogous to clothing—it is a protective, shielding, masking movement, a gesture covering the vulnerability of extended expression:

> *Now you are sitting doubled up in pain.*
> *What's that for?*
>
> doubled up I feel
> small like these poems
> the area of attack
> is diminished

Hulcoop praises these "spare poems which exhibit something of the quality of abstract paintings." I'm not sure what he means, since her poetry is lucid, representational, and (as Valéry reminded us) composed of words, not pigment. And Hulcoop deplores "hysteria" and "purple rhetoric" as something he is glad Webb has grown out of. But the difference of excellence between the two "naked poems" quoted above lies just in that tinge of hysteria in the second. If you want to call it hysteria. Is there a poetry without neuroses or eloquence? What we want is what Webb calls, in her great poem "Making":

this made-ness out of self-madness
thrown across their bones to keep them warm

And poetry is not the confession of madness; it is "made-ness"—it is artifice.

Reviewers and readers are very much at home with "naked" poetry these days, since most of us write it ourselves, just as Elizabethan wits wrote gentlemanly sonnets, just as cultured Japanese write socially acceptable haikus. (Mao too.) And there are still people ready to be impressed by any sonnet, by any haiku. But we ought not be blind to the merits of a poetry that is not being written by every Thomas and Richard. We ought not call "neurotic," and thus somehow inferior, what might just as well be called both profound and original. We should stop judging everything by the demands of a single, minor verse form.

How do we know that Webb's literary, highly rhythmic, often rhymed and, for these three reasons, unfashionable, poetry is good? The traditional tests, not entirely distinct from each other, are the test for structural integrity, the test for emotional effectiveness, the test for rhetorical eloquence, and the test for the unique and memorable, Arnold's "touchstones."

Since the illustration of the structural integrity of a single complex poem can take pages, I had better defend Webb's excellence in this field by a sketchy discussion of one of her simpler poems, "Rust on an Anchor," whose structure is not untypical. Repetitive parallels here (in other works, actual refrains) function as illustrative of the circular repetitiveness of life and thought. The "thoughts" in Webb's poetry are "insights," not "solutions," and she must, therefore, structure (like Pound) by metaphor rather than by argument; the climax becomes the "best" metaphor, or the most vivid, most pertinent, most inclusive illustration. Again, like Pound, she has not always any particular need, via the argument, for any particular number of images; the effect is of someone "finding" the concluding image, or of winding around the central issue from the edges of the central metaphor spirally into the point. In order to see the congruency of her metaphoric sequences, one must take her point fairly immediately, and, like Gustafson, she relies heavily on our having read other poets. At its best, hers is no work for an amateur, and possibly the turn to "naked" poetry was provoked by a sense of the limitedness of a literate audience. In "Rust on an Anchor," for example, the connection of "remote," "Chinese," and "sanity" relies on our being already prepared to associate a sense of cool sanity, of emotional and historical remoteness, of objective aestheticism, with the graceful formalities of Chinese art; we must be already prepared with a notion of Confucian properties and linear vigour. We must know already that traditional Chinese art is not, for example, Brueghel, Frans Hals, or Rembrandt. And in the same poem it helps to know that Japanese ballet combines the linear remoteness of the Chinese with grotesque, semi-comic violence. As again it helps to share certain thoughts about Venice in her prime and about neoclassic England.

"Rust on an Anchor" conjoins the suggestion of art as "remote" and as "touching"; it suggests the relationship to nature and to sanity of the antique, the exotic, and the artificial; and it reminds us of the undeniable rootedness of an art's "mountain air" sanity in humanity's grotesque comedy. And all this is stated as an aside to a description of a specific human relationship which touches, in its loving, upon this exhilarating sanity "now and then." Art and love produce similar emotions—"now and then." And the poem suggests all this without using the same metaphor twice, as if to "show off," but also to remind us of the brevity of these mountain moments by the brevity of the suggestions. The final lines remind us of Emily Dickinson's famous prescription for poetry.

If to be remote
                    (if only momentarily)
        as a Chinese poem

    is to achieve sanity

    then you and I
                    like a Japanese ballet

                touch it as if

between the acts
of a violent comedy
                    a way to say

now and then
                    the rare mountain air
        is caught
                        in a small

Venetian glass bottle
(used for a time

in early Eighteenth Century England

for snuff for the

pleasure of sneezing,

a mild and conscious apoplexy).

We also want from fine poetry an emotional experience, whether a "mild and conscious apoplexy" or a sense of "frugal sadness" (as Webb terms her dominant note). I find particularly attractive her dark gaiety, the tonic wit of works like "Earth Descending" or "Breaking," where the very vigour of the bitterness of life-asserting:

> We would not raise our silly gods again.
> Stigmata sting, they suddenly appear
> on every blessed person everywhere.
>   ("Breaking")

What a pleasure to have words for just that frame of meaning, that exasperated-with-despair offhandedness!

Of course the forcefulness of these lines depends not simply upon the emotion expressed but upon the emotion-qualifying artfulness of their expression: the colloquial propriety of "silly" and "blessed," the alliterative ingenuity, the half-rhymes, the pentameter's measuredness. For it is because poetry's rhythms are more concisely coiled around its sense, and because its metaphors must be of sound as well as of image, that poetic art can assert that "rare mountain air" we can "now and then" touch.

Finally, for the "touchstone" test—beyond intelligence and eloquence, beyond being merely good—to pass this test, a poet must produce something utterly unique and yet so meaningful, memorable, artful, that we use these lines in our thinking as permanent counters, no longer just part of our reading, but part of our literature. Let me summarize the first part of the poem "Making" before quoting its conclusion. In "Making," this "made-ness out of self-madness" is like a patchwork quilt that warms us, that includes the efforts of the imagination, of love, of doubt, of the will to religion "making the intolerable, accidental sky/patch up its fugitive ecstasies" until:

> From the making made and, made, now making
> certain order—thus excellent despair
> is laid, and in the room the patches of the quilt
> seize light and throw it back upon the air.
> A grace is made, a loveliness is caught
> quilting a quiet blossom as a work.
> It does.
>
> And do you,
> doubting, fractured, and untaught, St. John of the Cross,
> come down and patch the particles and throw
> across the mild unblessedness of day
> lectures to the untranscended soul.
> Then lotus-like you'll move upon the pond,
> the one-in-many, the many-in-the-one,
> making a numbered, floral-essenced sun
> resting upon the greening padded frond,
>
> a patched, matched protection for Because.
> And for our dubious value it will do.
> It always does.

Such a great poem should be basic to anthologies, and is worth a million "naked" poems.

Hulcoop tells us Phyllis Webb is now working on a major project, "The Kropotkin Poems." The depth of thought and extensive eloquence of poems such as "Making" give us every reason to be joyfully hopeful of her work-in-progress.

from *The Fiddlehead* (Winter 1972)

WORKS CITED

Selected Poems 1954–1965. Talonbooks, 1971.

Travelling with St. Theresa: The Poetry of Paulette Jiles

Travel, the perpetual flight of being, and the pursuit of a sense of self by the self are not new subjects for poetry in this existentialist century. But Paulette Jiles, who commands a matured, expressionist technique, develops these themes powerfully and originally. Her poems, without over-simplifications or faddishness, bring new material to the literature of feminism. The strength of her poems, in particular the two longer ones, "The Brass Atlas" and "Schooner Cove," makes it likely she may come to be considered as one of our best poets.

Paulette Jiles's poetry does not suffer from the romantic division between intellect and emotion; as a consequence, she can develop her themes intelligently and emotionally without the wobble between image and statement that characterizes our weaker verse. Her poetic speaker is never too "drunk" to make sense and never too "dry" to be moving. Her sometimes surrealist images are never mere Dada. But her originality, which is not a trifle of vocabulary, syntax, spelling, or rhythm but an originality of thought, makes her a somewhat difficult poet. It would be unfortunate if her contemporaries dismissed her work as surrealist, or hippie, or feminist, and failed to read it carefully enough to see what it is, and, perhaps, how much we need it.

Jiles's *Waterloo Express* (Anansi, 1973) is set in the universe of perpetual flight which, from Heraclitus through Pater to Einstein, has increasingly presented itself as reality to the philosophic temperament, if not, as yet, to the common man. The transport images in Jiles's poetry—train, boat, truck, car, horse—are not merely the means of travel but the travelling world. Movement, present or imminent, is mentioned in every poem: things are in flight, or about to "pop," about to discover the "endless possibilities beyond," to climb or to swim, to be thrown away, to be carried off. Even a character falling asleep sees "they are coming up the hill," and a dreamer, fasting, sees visions "emerge." The speaker, immobilized, dreams of escape, of evaporating or of ballooning to another place. More frequently, the poetic speaker is a traveller, a hitchhiker, a fugitive, or a moving machine.

The flight in Jiles's poems is not portrayed as from an unreal world towards a more real world, nor is there in most of these poems any sense of search for a more deliberated, more fundamental, more Thoreauvian lifestyle. Often the motive for travel does seem to be a kind of nervous crisis (nerves and nervousness are often mentioned) or psychical *angst*. But the crisis is not personal; nobody is to be blamed or excused in personal terms; the "mal" is of the world itself, a general ill, even, perhaps, a general sin. Restoration of some degree of psychic health to the speaker does not alter the world.

In Jiles's voyages the sense of the variability of the speed of time and the correspondences of exterior landscape to interior states of the soul remind us of the journeys into the psychic interior of Theodore Roethke, but Jiles possesses none of his phallic pantheism, parental obsessions, or amoral mysticisms. Nor does the sense of things being wrong that is associated with the motivating nervous crises of these poems have the appalling weight of Kierkegaard's "dread," Lowell's neurasthenia, or Ondaatje's "slaughter." "Nerves" may be the twentieth-century prompter, but the visions prompted vary: Jiles's poetic universe is not unmitigatedly awful. The travelling poetic speaker is sympathetic without heroism, without boastfulness, and without hate. She is no victim, and is intelligent enough to see more than one aspect of her own situation. Jiles's speaker can be serious and humorous at once. She is, perhaps, too intelligent to give us the saintly but somewhat inadequate version of the Levertov "authentic"—where what is truly realized will somehow always turn out to be holy.

Jiles's poetic speaker appears to be the typical, booted, Levi-ed hitchhiking youngster from whom we have learned to expect anarchistic protest against "The System." Jiles's traveller, however, speaks of suffering, the causes and, especially, the response to suffering. The experience is youth's, but the voice is adult. The adult use of juvenile material is perhaps most vividly seen in "The Tin Woodsman" [sic], where Jiles uses Baum's hollow-chested, metal hero to suggest that double sense we have of our own insensitivity and super-sensitivity. In the child's storybook, the tin man is mechanical, hollow; he has no heart but yearns for one (much as Jiles's speaker yearns for understanding in other poems, especially in the hollow-hearted "Fast"). In the Oz books, the tin man is the most feeling of Dorothy's friends. Indeed, his super-sensitivity is a danger to himself; his tears can rust him. Dorothy, that youthful, itinerant, female child, is, of course, a figure for the condition of Jiles's usual poetic speaker, and Jiles knows that the Tin Woodsman, like all Oz, was within Dorothy.

Jiles's tin woodsman, whose feelings cannot endure feeling, is within us. In Jiles's poem, the super-sensitivity of the hollow man draws him to yearn for his metallic sense of himself, to desire to rust rather than to feel. The poem opens not in Oz, but in a war area whose hills are numbered, as were Vietnam's: "This is Hill 49, an area for bad dreams" where, the woodsman says, he does not "harmonize"—he does not fit:

> I'm held up by an armature of nerves,
> for which I take pills.
> Mechanics come along and tender to my ills
> with oilcans and grease-guns.
> My eyes are red and full of thumbs.
> This is sleep falling on me; snow—
> It constitutes a resolution.
>
> And now, Dorothy, they are coming up the hill.
> If, like a shotgun, I blew my brains out,
> how many could we kill?
> Tough luck for you, you pink thing,
> all full of corpuscles and organs.
> The shotgun hollers in a big balloon of sound
> goodbye, goodbye.
> Rusting is painless.
> I will settle
> in the shadow of this red rock
> and be metal.

Two major children's sagas have been written about young girls travelling through an alien universe, yet neither Alice nor Dorothy have yet been taken as a picture of the female soul. The wonderlands have been attributed to the male authors, and the little girls considered as objectifications of childish simplicity and brutal common sense rather than as egos travelling through their own interior worlds. (The use of the female child in these books has been considered evidence of the authors' inability to handle adult sexuality, although sexual imagery recurs in both wonderlands.) It is possible, however, that Baum and Carroll shared with Hardy and James some insight into what it is to be feminine. Certainly Oz, witches included, is a fuller picture of a human mind than can be got from the macho or victim piffle presented to us as adult literature so often these days. There has been too much defining of "woman" merely by what she cannot have in common with "man," thus defining us as clitoris, no separate "self" at all. To discuss sexual definitions is to discuss social expectations and biological diversity, but it is not to define the "self." Yet we need to ask: "What is the Self?" and we have needed a woman's answer.

In "Inside from the Outside," the poet speaker recollects extrinsic definitions of self. Much of what constitutes the general notion of our identity, she reminds us, is neither chosen nor personal:

> this person's identity remains a mystery.
> One day sitting in an office waiting for an appointment I realized
> I had it on.

But the "self" is not the identity we try on:

> Novels drive us into stereotypes.
> What are we but denials of novels?

Most of Jiles's poems about the self in pursuit of an idea of the self emphasize in this manner the distinction between external definitions of identity and the active sense we have of the separate and observing "I." Her speakers move towards definition by separating themselves from the inessential, by paring down the extrinsic. They abandon the socialized self: jobs, clothes, relationships, particularized functions, and, of course, looks. The body is not the self, as many of Jiles's poems make clear, especially perhaps "Inside from the Outside," "Body," and "Tallness." So much of our identity consists in the perceptions and preconceptions of others. In the title poem, "Waterloo Express," Jiles's speaker says:

> Who do you think
> I am? I bet you think I'm running away from home or
>
> a man who never done me wrong. I bet you think
> I'm twenty, with the fragile soul of a wild fawn.

A similarly adventuring male young poet would have supposed himself to be envisioned, admiringly, as a "young dog." But the viewer in the quotation saw only his imaginings; the speaker's self is quite something else, and, travelling, she casts off the inessentials:

> There they go—a toe, a finger, my coat—honey,
> you'd hardly recognize me, pared down to one white eye.

> It has the cynical glint of a dynamite salesman.

The ego alone—no fawn.

Jiles's "The Brass Atlas" yields a similar revelation. Within the intelligent, sensitive Dorotheas of this world, our Middlemarch, lives St. Theresa—an aggressive daemon easily "too big" for the identity society constructs for her to wear. In "The Brass Atlas," St. Theresa has to be kept, with difficulty, under control: "St. Theresa keeps wanting to fight with them." In "No Days Off," "Discoveries," "He Beats Her Off With a Rake," "Mass," "Horses," and "Tornado," the self cannot be the fragile, feeble, passive "fawn"—it persists in becoming a natural force, "too big":

> I am a horse once in a while
> and run off like thundering barrels for whatever horizon
> offers itself
>
>   ("Horses")

And, as a whole, society doesn't like the St. Theresa, the salesman eye, the essential self of the woman this large:

> I have grown too big for you or anybody,
> a natural phenomenon.
> And I didn't even mean it,
> I didn't mean it at all.
>
>   ("Tornado")

Perhaps all of us feel gigantic occasionally, and the talented more often than most. The exceptionally talented creative artist often finds his or her talents exceeding the desires of the community, dismaying the kindly relative and sociable friend. But a male voice could not write the apologetic "Tornado"; that speaks a woman's predicament.

Theodore Roethke wrote disparagingly of women poets "stamping their tiny feet at God." Tininess, physical or intellectual, has been the expected lot of women. (Roethke is not on record as disapproving of Ahab or Melville.) But the self has no size. Either sex can feel as hollow as the tin woodsman, huge as a tornado; either sex can run off like a horse or a truck. Jiles is no chauvinist; the men in her poems are usually seen as equals, even when their regards or their memories are fallible. It is the human, not one sex or the other, that moves in her moving universe. In "We Are Like Two Tow-Trucks," the man and the woman are virtually identical:

> After an exhausting day of dragging wrecks
> and disasters after us . ...
> On the National Highway I see you coming
> up behind in my Superwoman rear-view mirror
> flashing coded signals . ...
> O Mr. Toad, someday I will call you on my 2-way
> radio to come and get me for a while:
> the blind leading the blind,
> a towtruck towing a towtruck home.

One of the difficulties presented by Jiles's longer poems is her expressionist structure. In "Schooner Cove," Jiles writes:

> The sea is the most nearly formless thing in nature;
> its order is complicated and profound, underlying
> all rhythms.

That is, the sea is *not* formless, only that it appears almost to be so. Dylan Thomas wrote to Henry Treece (Treece's *Dylan Thomas*, 37) that poetry, existing in the "living stream of time," must be constructed out of the diverse and fluid elements of reality, the images quarrelling or breeding with each other. A "complicated and profound" structure out of fluid imagery refuses decoding or paraphrasing. Such a poetry must think within its material, avoiding the abstractions of reasoned language but also avoiding the temptations of sentimental or self-indulgent not-thinking. Too many poets fear they will lose their inspiration if they think about their imagery. And too may reviewers dislike the intensities and complexities of profound and mediated art. Jiles's shorter poems are vivid and plain-languaged enough to attract the average reader, but the excellence of her longer poems may prevent them from becoming immediately admired.

"The Brass Atlas" is the longest and finest of Jiles's travel poems. The poetic speaker takes a train south along the Mediterranean towards Perpignan, then to Cadiz, where she embarks for Las Palmas, a lay-by she plans to leave shortly for Tamarit. The traveller speaks of herself as writing reports or letters to "you," addressed fondly, who may be masculine, who may be back home in Waterloo, Ontario, who may be the "him" without whom the speaker feels empty, and who is very much missed. The poetic speaker is travelling with St. Theresa, sometimes writing as one or two women, sometimes writing as one woman alone. As the poem develops, we learn that St. Theresa knows what only an aspect of the self knows about the self:

My brain, St. Theresa informed me, was at that point
a black tide ...

The saint is part of the traveller's self. So is the independent and insomniac "concern" mentioned as a character later in the poem. The speaker talks of and to herself. And the relationship of the addressed "you" to the self becomes suggestively complex as the poem unfolds. "You" had, to some extent, defined the self.

The motive for the trip is unhappiness. The "bitter" mail from home is dreaded.

"We'd better go on," I said, "the end is coming soon in a red
package"

They join a mail train. "Mail," as message, as communication of relationships, and "mail train" as means of flight recur prominently in the poem. The poem itself is a letter and a map, an atlas of its own spiritual trip:

I was determined to report back to you. I am lost on the road.
These silences jam the mind like radar; staccatto [sic] silence,
the holes between Morse Code ... containing a message.
That's the message.

The way the speaker feels is parcelled out among her selves. She feels lost and empty like the wind "that followed us on the mail train." Her shoes and, in a flashback passage, her "concern," exhibit her tension and nervousness, both insomniac, the shoelaces tying and untying themselves all night. The Night Manager "does a poor job with his dreams," and, moreover, wants them back in the morning. The "I" is empty, wistful, passive, mere baggage the customs officers inspect:

> The Guardia Civil destroys my careful packing ...
> They found out how empty, empty I was and the French said
> "If we'd known how empty you were without him
> we wouldn't have bothered."
> St. Theresa keeps wanting to fight with them and I have a hard time
> getting her out of bars.

The saint, unlike the poetic speaker, seems to be enjoying the trip; she is alert, observant, quarrelsome, and insufficiently retiring—the instinctual aspect of the feminine intelligence, the life-affirming non-ego.

> not been spotted by any of the numerous accidents that crept
> along this particular line, the conductor had not yet discovered
> I had no ticket, my destination was still unaware of my plans—

The sense of "self," so travelling increases our sense of its absolute freedom and its absolute vulnerability, which the sea trip to Las Palmas, the "thin, precarious surface" of the water and the thin, precarious personal relationships with the passengers on the ship, re-emphasize. The speaker meets a corporal who

> wrapped his rings up in my hair and put my Levis in with his khaki to be kept
> neat and clean. He assured me it was no trouble. "Just until we get to Las Palmas," he
> said, "then you're on your own."

Clearly the self's vulnerability is, to some extent, being taken advantage of. (Is he smuggling rings or being amorous? I think the latter, since long hair falls down too easily to be a secure wrapping, but I am not sure.)

The encounter with the corporal brings the speaker to reconsider "I," "we," and "you":

And now we are gone, I remember us, corporal, don't think I don't.
"—!" you wrote. Do you think I could bring myself to answer that?
Just because I have lately begun to remember a sailor don't think I am beyond
recall of our three days at sea

Who is "you"? Sometimes "you" is almost the reader, sometimes mankind in general, as when, speaking of the Night Manager's selling dreams: "You'll have to line up for tickets and they'll cost you," or when she warns whoever receives her reports against Las Palmas: "Don't come here." But in the second section of the poem, a waiter's "opalescent freshness / reminds me of you," and whoever, Waterloo friend or corporal, wrote her "—!" seems, also, clearly a man. "You" is whom she misses and to whom she writes.

Something of how the self feels, as woman travelling in a world full of men's attitudes towards her, is suggested in an image at the centre of "The Brass Atlas":

the effigy of a wax virgin lurching among the cheering victors …

around her feet were the eyes and flashlights of a thousand
regretful secret police

whose regrets are like embroideries on the wax effigy's velvet gown. The wax virgin, whose clothes are more splendid than her wax, suggests the insubstantial character the self feels in her self in her relationship to men, the inadequacy, perhaps, of her sexual condition. The blackness of the velvet parallels the earlier blackness of her brain. The lurching movement of the doll suggests again the vulnerability and the travelling of the speaker. The crowds that cheer the effigy parallel the crowds on the train and the "loonies" at Las Palmas.

The secret police are among the many often uniformed and always imperious men in this poem whose relationship to the speaker (or the effigy) includes sexual affection, some degree of bullying, and potential heartlessness. Earlier the speaker had claimed for her hand (only a part of her self) a probable "allegiance" to "Charlton Heston / cowering nations under his heel." The Guardia Civil, the corporal, the Night Manager, "him" and "you" are less glamorous but almost equally insubstantial emperors.

How I used to envy him and the way he could forget!
Sleeping without dreams, laid back on the cushion of my
    concern …
He forgot everything. He forgot my name, he forgot where he
    was
and where he had been.
I was his map.

Throughout the poem, the traveller has referred to memory. Her messages are records; her experiences are "reminding, reminding" and "hoping I'd remember you." She perceives her existence and her relationships in "devious lines, like a map, the grids / of longitude and latitude," but her memories and the speed with which she travels alter as the poem progresses. The mail train from Grindlewald had speeded everything up, but the sea journey slowed everything down. Now, at Las Palmas, the sheets seem to entangle her, almost to fasten her down. She breaks her travel to lay up, to record and to remember, and she remembers "him" as one who forgets. Was his lack of concern his health or his emptiness? The speaker has moved away from his forgetfulness. She is getting "fed up with these maps," these memories, these relationships, these entanglements. She seems, at the close of the poem, no longer insomniac, and less multi-personed. But she is still empty, lonely:

I miss, miss, miss you or somebody,
I forget when.

The poem ends there, mid-stream, the speaker having moved from bitterness and more vivid rememberings through greater despair and towards a wistful forgetfulness. Nothing is resolved. The wholeness is thematic, as in music— this is the way the feelings go; the tune fits in. The poem's title is taken from the mechanical figures of a cathedral clock. The "flushed, brassy messengers coming and going like an advertisement" remind the speaker of herself, constantly recording, moving—yet lifeless. "I was striking the hour," she says, marking time. The poem is an atlas because it records; it does not explain.

"Schooner Cove" takes a more conventional shape, but it, too, is about the nature of self. No lover is missed or remembered or addressed in "Schooner Cove," and the sense of "mal" that has triggered the flight to Schooner Cove seems less a crisis of the poetic speaker's personal life than the general "mal" of the modern world: jellyfish "come floating in from Vietnam like distracted brains." The self has removed to the simpler world of nature to be alone; she practises the essential rituals of survival. (In the non-heroic tradition of feminine realism she digs clams rather than wrestles grizzlies for supper.) The poem moves towards a sense of the essential being, "I" at the minimum, but returns to the idea of the self in its relationship to the desperate, ailing world whose messages still come floating in.

The opening section, "*The dawn sky*," begins the movement towards simplification. "I am an animal blackening into my natural colours," the speaker says, blackening as if from the individual towards the general, or as an animal takes on the colours of its environment, or towards age, death, or colourlessness:

> My voice is already unrecognizeable,
> having grown in strange ways
> around the noise of the tide and nicked fingers

and her clothes "are the only mirror" she has:

> I came here to practice being lonely, and ended up
> with myself, a complete stranger.

Again, the Jilesian split between "I" and "myself," subject and object: Who do I regard when I regard myself?

The speaker is not wholly alone with her self, but, like Thoreau at Walden, has visitors—whales, clams, and crows. Even a candle's flame is a visitor (like Coleridge's flame in "Frost at Midnight"). The tide's behaviour is also Thoreauvian in its domestic economy; it keeps the beach as if keeping house, laying out "a porcelain wash, bland and simplified." The speaker uses "we" and "us" referring to mankind in general, I and her self, or herself and her inhuman companions. No human joins her. But, housekeeping alone, simplifying like the tide, she discovers:

> Without clothes we burn like candles, our veins close
> to the surface, and weeks later we begin to shine.
> *"It's not myself, but something in the universe*
> *I have been left with."*

The speaker of Jiles's poem "Insight from the Outside" also feels her body "came to me like a suit of clothes," but in "Schooner Cove," the speaker grows into harmony with nature. The "raving" crows have ceased to resemble nagging people and she makes "peace" with them. The environment alters her perception of the relationship of the self to the universe, restoring proportion and spaciousness:

> Eyes cannon out great distances
> and things no longer smell like the inside of my nose.

Living at "such a pitch our skins / cannot contain us," the speaker asserts, the self, like the vision, enlarges. Everything has become more immediate and more meaningful. "The is a world of results," the speaker notes, relishing an oncoming storm:

> Outside the winds unwind a thousand miles of current,
> like the courses of planets they blow and blow.
> Only the candle flame, busy as a bird, circles
> around this shack. It lays a dry brush on my paper,
> yellow and shy.
> Is this loneliness? It is something bigger yet,
> it's an old fear of giants:

that nature, so quickened, would "take on speech," or that the soul, so quickened, would understand it.

> I have had to seal myself in ten times over with the nervous
> ferocity of an obsessed spider; a plant is growing, huge,
> frondy, the barometer of a wisdom needed nowhere else in the
> world.

What is the wisdom needed in Schooner Cove? The primitive wisdom of the camp dweller? The natural sympathy with storm and calm of the self reduced to essential being? Is the huge, growing, frondy plant an emblem of the renewed, storm-quickened soul?

It is not during the storm but after it that the essential nature of the self is defined by the issue of survival. Jiles takes advantage of the traditionally alleged sexlessness of the singular masculine pronoun to make her subtle point. A swimmer is being "carried away in the undertow," but the self is determined to survive, even as it recognizes the narcotic appeal of extinction: "He fights and will always fight to get to the shore."

> Eventually his feet have touched bottom.
> He has been left with nothing but his life: his suit was a size
> too big and it was the first to go.
> He staggers onto dry land, his hair snaking itself into long ropes
> around his shoulders,
> recovering his femininity. After losing everything but an idea
> of staying alive, she had become a beginning point. Her social
> imperatives of passivity and sweet remorse had drained away
> like an undertow, leaving only a terrorized body
> which sheared a path through the retreating sea.

The suit and the social imperatives of femininity are not the reduced, quintessential self—only the will to survive, the beginning point. Male writers have often supposed that what they knew as human was male, and that, therefore, what was female must be what is not human. James Wright gives an extreme example of this thinking in his poem "In Shame and Humiliation":

> That fire, that searing cold is what I claim:
> What makes me man, that dogs can never share,
> Woman, or brilliant bird,
> The beaks that mock but cannot speak the names
> Of the blind rocks, of the stars.

Within the context of traditional folly, Jiles's truism, that to be human requires only humanity, is original.

The epilogue of "Schooner Cove," "*The Holes in My Shoes*," returns us to the theme of travel that unites the book *Waterloo Express*:

> Now that I am mending their laces,
> how close they are to my heart

says the speaker of her boots:

We have travelled so far,
from indifference to discovery.
We have become larger and more desperate
than the government itself.

The book that began with an image of the travelling self reduced to a glinting eye, choked with the sense of falseness, lostness, hollowness, suffering, and sin, now closes with the self still travelling, still desperate, but stronger, bigger than ever, a "natural phenomenon" and bound to survive. Travel with such a self would refresh anyone. We are fortunate to be able to tag along.

---

from *Essays on Canadian Writing* (Spring 1978)

WORKS CITED

Waterloo Express. Anansi, 1973.

Self-Conscious Art: A Review of Daphne Marlatt's *How Hug A Stone*,
Andrew Suknaski's *Montage for an Interstellar Cry*, E.F. Dyck's
The Mossbank Canon, and Geoffrey Ursell's *Trap Lines*

In all four of these well-designed books from Turnstone Press, a self-conscious
artfulness pervades the writing. All four of these books insist that the reader
be aware of the author as artificer, as artificializer. In all four, poetic method
or form is emphasized by the authors as independent of and almost irrelevant
to what normally would be thought of as the subject or content of the poem.
Like many other contemporary poets, they have rejected "organic form," the
fusion of style and content, as old-fashioned, and they have adopted as poetic
language a style of discourse that is very far from the "ordinary speech of men."

On the back cover of E.F. Dyck's *The Mossbank Canon*, Robert Kroetsch
is quoted as saying that this "is what happens to literature after postmodern."
Whether this is postmodern I do not know. But, of course, it is not new. What
has happened is a resurgence of interest in the experimental artificialities of
early-twentieth-century poets in combination with late-twentieth-century with-
drawal of interest away from the "outer world" of nature and society towards
the "inner world" of self-consciously formed, artistic verbal patterns. Three
of these poets, Daphne Marlatt, Andrew Suknaski, and Geoffrey Ursell, have
their loyalties divided between the organic world and the world of artifice.
But in none of these four books is the language and imagery new.

Daphne Marlatt, in *How Hug a Stone*, writes with Joyce's interest in con-
textuality, in Joycean rhythms, and with Joycean word-savourings and puns.
Andrew Suknaski, in *Montages for an Interstellar Cry*, uses, like Pound and
Eliot, non-European languages and recondite references from little-known
aspects of archeology and anthropology with Eliot- and Pound-like ambition
of theme. E.F. Dyck's chinoiserie in *The Mossbank Canon* is Art Deco; his
language is Sandburgian. And Geoffrey Ursell, in *Trap Lines*, offers us material written in the modern medieval manner, with quaint spelling. However,
although these contemporary poets are not making it new, their elaborately
constructed poems are interesting, and worthy of respect.

Making it new according to artificial or inorganic devices is to date oneself precisely. Organic form can never be new, because it is locked into the
chemical shapings of the universe. There can be no life without form. The

effort towards formlessness of the recently fashionable "naked" poetry often produced unlively verse, yet it was an understandable rebellion against the life-suffocating construction of artificial forms. The Maritime poet William Bauer has a poem about a minute and labyrinthine building constructed of toothpicks and tightly sealed; from it, a tiny, imprisoned voice seems sometimes to cry out. So, too, from the extremes of post-modernist or, as Kroetsch implies, post-postmodernist verse, a living voice cries out.

Canadian postmodern critics of poetry have much interested themselves in Marlatt's statements of poetic theory, rather to the comparative neglect of her often superb poems. She has developed for her poetry a highly self-conscious style. She writes as if self-consciousness about words and the sounds of words were as necessary to her and as constant to her as breathing. The speakers of her poems are always listening to their own inner voices, self-absorbed, self-listening. But Marlatt allows voices and personalities to interrupt her constant self-listening, and her genuine interest in and affection for other people usually prevent her poetic manner from being alienatingly narcissistic.

At one level, Marlatt's *How Hug a Stone* is about how to be a poet constructing a poem all the time. In real life, such pervasive self-listening could make for bad driving and burned toast. But the second and major level of *How Hug a Stone* is familial love. And, although Marlatt's linguistic style is "arty," very unlike ordinary speech, her narrative of order (or, as a less postmodern poet would put it, her perception of order) is organic. Marlatt has always had a naturalist's sense of the community and wholeness of the created and living universe. She thinks of her poem-making as analogous to the swimming of a fish or the flying of a bird. The details of nature interest her as much as the details of language, and the movement of her poetry is always towards understanding and towards natural harmony, or the order of truth, rather than toward the arbitrary patterns of radically inorganic verse.

In *How Hug a Stone*, the speaker, a mother herself, is visiting relatives and remembering her dead, beloved mother; she is accompanied by a young son who becomes frighteningly ill. Neither the child nor the dead mother become generic figures; each is uniquely individualized. The poet represents herself making a poem of her perceptions, recollections, and thought processes, as if this way of constant poem-making were a way of "not being lost," of not succumbing to fear, death, mystery. She also records the spontaneous interruptions and antithetical concerns of the people among whom she is thinking. Chief interrupter is the son, who breaks into her literary musings with his own reactions to an unfamiliar environment of reminiscing adults and to his growing education into the fear that is part of adult knowledge. He has come from childhood into a world of adults, and it seems to him drenched with fear. As the poet muses, in her Joycean manner:

> how hug a stone (mother) except nose in to lithic fold, the
> old slow pulse beyond word become, under flesh, mutter
> of stone, *stane, stei*-ing power

the child yearns to go "home" where it is "nice and boring," unreflective, free from the voices of the dead. He wants to move towards simplicity, towards life. The lithic mother/mutter, an Earwicker-ish murmur, is only the half-life of self-conscious art. It is the child who will be hugged, he who will fly out from the "squat, stone others" of Avebury towards an unselfconscious freedom, like a wild bird.

Marlatt relates her maternal fears to the symbolic world for which she has been constructing a narrative. The stone Avebury "mothers" are like her mother, now stone too, and like the earth itself, a stone mother, beautiful, tomb, womb, present, and repossessing. She allows her theme a double ending: the enduring stone, the free flight of the child.

Like *How Hug a Stone*, Andrew Suknaski's *Montage for an Interstellar Cry* supposes the constant presence of an artist self-consciously constructing the poem. But Suknaski has not got Marlatt's sense of pattern. Indeed, the apparent patternlessness and meaninglessness of the existing world is his point; patternlessness is his process. Suknaski offers us a montage with Michener-like sweep from Paleolithic times to the present, shown through a disconnected litter of contemporary intellectual interests and proletarian remarks. Although Suknaski insists upon the reader's recognition of the artificiality of his process, and describes the artist as making and as discussing the making of his constructions, Suknaski does not let the poet-as-thinker, or as point-in-time-and-space-process, control or organize the poem. Rather it is as if Suknaski wishes to represent all levels of earth's condition as crying out confusedly and at once (with a slight, but understandable emphasis on the voices of the Canadian pub). This has much strength. But there are, for me, marked weaknesses in Suknaski's poem.

First, Suknaski includes in his poem allusions to archeological matters about which little is known and from which he gains little emotional or descriptive resonance. In addition, he frequently refers to mythologies, which are not as presently meaningful as historic reference. This second point needs, perhaps, elaboration. Our use of the term "myth" obscures the enormous differences between different kinds of myths. The Christian religion makes mythic use of what can, in the gospels and in most of the Old Testament, be taken as historic material. The cross is a gallows. The disciples encountered letter-writing, papyrus-preserving Romans. Peter, Pilate, and Pinochet have an equivalent historicity, which Perseus does not. In Suknaski's poem, the inhuman gods of Olympus or Asgard are feeble, decorative figures, like highfaluting poetic language among the plebeian outcries of Suknaski's humans:

fuck off dud!
go roost somewhere else ...

hey! gee
is that a ceebee? ...

yeah man
just sat there like a puppy ...

Christ, whether God's son or not, lived among such human voices. Baldur did not.

But, for me, Suknaski's rejection of organic form is the most serious weakness of *Montage for an Interstellar Cry*, in spite of the power of many of its portions. The rejection is illustrated by Suknaski's choice of frontispiece, a photograph titled "The Mike Olito Box," by Michael Olito, which shows a nude man artificially enclosed in a magician's trick box; the man's genitals and legs have been replaced by what appears to be a tiny dollhouse. Our astronomers, understanding that only organic form can be understood between stars, have sent chemical formulae and a picture of two nudes as earth's "message" to possible life forms elsewhere. "The Mike Olito Box" trivializes the organic nude. Suknaski's over-decorated style trivializes the sufferings of earth.

Fortunately, Suknaski's *Montage for an Interstellar Cry*, as it progresses, moves away from the archeological and the decorative towards the movingly recorded speech of living humans. Suknaski allows earth's cry to drown out the poet's perturbations about how to write; it drowns out even the artist's self-consciousness:

> all i wanna say
> we've all got the right
> the right of the cry
> that pregnant women
> the voice an i humiliated
> needlessly
> she has
> the right of the cry ...

Here life, weary and drunken life, rather than artifice, speaks. The quality of life, as we perceive it, may indeed suggest very little pattern, and perhaps very little dignity. But Suknaski has, by instinct and affection, principles and perceptions that make it impossible for him to represent the human condition as wholly without rights or value. It is not simply that the trick of boxes of postmodernism is unsuitable to an interstellar cry; they are also unsuitable for Suknaski.

Marlatt's *How Hug a Stone* is basically an old-fashioned organic poem about "truth" with a surface of postmodernist self-consciousness about poetic construction. Suknaski's *Montage for an Interstellar Cry* adopts aspects of the deconstructed and of the inorganic effect, and combines this with postmodernist self-consciousness of the artificiality of art and with an old-fashioned concern for the condition of mankind. Whatever his style, his aim is to speak the "truth." But E.F. Dyck, in *The Mossbank Canon*, has little interest in the "truth." What concerns him, deeply, is his order of the words on the page. As a way of de-emphasizing content, "truth," and emotional reference, E.F. Dyck goes deliberately against the traditional advice given writers: Dyck does *not* write about what he understands from his own experience. He does not let his form and his rhythm be suggested and shaped by the human subject and the natural syntax. He does *not* use as symbols and images things that can be felt by his readers as emotionally meaningful. And he does *not* invent or describe new images or characters.

As plot, Dyck uses the lives of two generic, de-individualized Chinese, the hero Mao Tse Tung, as legend, and an immigrant to Saskatchewan, Jong. Both lives are described in the highly stylized manner of tourist souvenir art:

> After walking at dusk under a red sky
> Mao swam in the red waters of the pond
> A white lily was his pledged child-bride
> Closed, her flower   :closed, her eyes
> Red were the eyes   :of his weeping mother
> as her star swam past the white budded lotus

and

> The red star rose slowly in the dark sky
> a model of control   :a model of courage
> as Jong rode a steel belt to the great wheat
> buckle of the world, *Wheat City* of the prairies
> *Mecca of Investors*   :*Commercial City*
> *He rode a steel belt to Chicago-in-the-North*

Dyck's combination of the Sandburgian style with chinoiserie, and with a modish interest in the ancient book of divinations, the *I Ching*, is distinctive:

> each of the sixty-four stanzas has its lines based on the form
> of the *I Ching* hexagrams, and each line is either *yang* (un-
> broken, virile, active, nominative, indicative) or *yin* (broken,
> muliebral, passive, imperative or subjective, prepositional.)

But the polarities of *yin-yang* thinking deny logic and realism for decorative form. Fortune-telling also denies logic and realism. Any system of divination relies on a tacit agreement about cultural conventions between teller and customer. The customer believes the generalizations and conventions to which he has been trained. The formulae and the conventions behind the *I Ching* are more exotic and unnatural to the Westerner than the formulae and conventions of the tarot, but both tend towards decorativeness and away from biological and historical reality. It is perfectly possible for a Western writer to use Eastern philosophy meaningfully. But Dyck's sixes, eights, and lotus buds are not matters of philosophy, truth, emotion, or experience, and they are related to his characters' lives only insofar as they are Chinese motifs rather than European motifs. That the imagery of each section is suggested by a hexagram suggests an exercise in poem-making so purely artificial that it can be excused only by the pleasure it must have given E.F. Dyck to write it.

Indeed, this sort of poetry, written by formal decree rather than by expressive impulse, can be fun to write. There is an extravagant, seriousness-defying folly about *The Mossbank Canon* that would make it forgivable in any world where serious art received the attention and support it deserved. It will be interesting to see what Dyck writes when he has something to say.

Also amusing is Geoffrey Ursell's small book *Trap Lines*, whose first section, "Love of Beaver," is a lightweight romp with the fashionable trappings of medieval lore and modern erotica. In this section, content matters little. But the second section of Ursell's *Trap Lines*, "The Art of Pulling Hearts," is serious and very fine. The first few of the poems in this short section are grouped around the theme of trapper and trapped, victim and victimizer, and share with the poems of the first section a certainty of rhythm and a traditional formalism that is very appealing. The few remaining poems are also good, but less thematically related to the trapping theme of the chapbook. Three of the second section's poems, "Trappin'," "A Self-Explanatory Place," and "The Bends," suggest that if Ursell can bring himself to abandon the chic emphasis on artificiality, he may become a poet to be seriously regarded. Poetry atrophies too far from emotion. In "The Art of Pulling Hearts" section, Ursell does not appear to be afraid of emotion:

> *When they come ta check my lungs*
> *the Doctor says, "No need to worry about these,"*
> *an I tell him, "Those are trapper's lungs,*
> *from runnin my line all winter."*

That night I phone the Coast, tell my mother

He's in fine shape, came through really well.

She has already spoken to my uncle's wife.

You're wrong, she says.
That's cancer.

("Trappin'")

Daphne Marlatt has achieved her poetic voice and intention. She is, for Canada, a major poet. Andrew Suknaski is still struggling for the excellence that is surely in him. E.F. Dyck and Geoffrey Ursell are still beginning. I wish them all well, and hope they may all fly free from the constrictions of avant-garde verse. May Ursell desert the quaint *beastes* and G-string beavers and stick to the expressive lyric of human concern. May Dyck's muliebral muse finish her sentences and discover flesh-and-blood reality. May Suknaski escape from the Mike Olito box. And may the interruptions of love continue to urge Marlatt out of her self-imposed disciplines of internal reverie towards the vitalities and harmonies of the living world.

---

from *The Fiddlehead* (Winter 1984)

WORKS CITED
How Hug a Stone. Turnstone Press, 1983.
Montage for an Interstellar Cry. Turnstone Press, 1982.
The Mossbank Canon. Turnstone Press, 1982.
Trap Lines. Turnstone Press, 1982.

Imagining a Hero: A Review of John Barton's
West of Darkness: A Portrait of Emily Carr and Douglas LePan's
Weathering It: Complete Poems 1948–1987

John Barton's narrative sequence and Douglas LePan's forty-year collection are both primarily concerned with representing an idea of the hero. Barton's work is biographical; his hero is the painter Emily Carr, specifically, her imagination. To call Carr Barton's "heroine" would not be, as our language at present speaks, to say that she was for him an image of the heroic. There is no condescension or protectiveness in the attitude of Barton's book towards its hero. Barton does not write as if he thought Carr needed his help.

Barton structures his book with Carr's words, quoted or adapted, and with her paintings, described. For the headnote to his first section he chose from her journals:

> You come into the world alone and
> you go out of the world alone yet
> you are more alone while living.

Yet in loneliness "Carr" finds kinship, and in the darkness of loneliness, clearer vision.

LePan's poetry is self-expressive and much of it, including the title sequence, avowedly autobiographical. LePan's hero is the soldierly male imagination:

> The effect of bronze and the effect of water,
> that is what my art would capture ...
>
> All male, the sea writhes like a serpent ...
>
> Lashed to a froth, the armed and armoured sea
> can crush whole armies. Valour of bronze
>
> is forged from salt inconstancy,
> veined with the sea's sway, riddled with sea-myths.
> On a warrior battling with the waves
> a warrior battling with himself ...

Splendour again ...
that broad deep gulf, a man.

("Interlace")

Most contemporary poets are like LePan in their self-regard. Indeed, most of our contemporary verse biographies, usually written as fictional autobiographies (as is Barton's), describe their ostensible subjects less than their poet authors. Through the masks of historical reference Atwood, Geddes, Gutteridge, Ondaatje, Sherman, etc., make themselves more visible. But there is nothing visible to us behind the mask through which Barton speaks but the "Emily Carr" with which we are already familiar through Carr's own writings and paintings. When Barton's "Carr" speaks of one of her own paintings, we feel we are hearing how Carr would speak, to herself, about it, and we recognize the painting:

Age hangs over me
like bones

of an arm
articulate

in its lack of flesh
the tips

of its fingers
softened by feathers

of cedar
floating on the wind

like chimes.

("Cedar")

Appropriately for his subject, and perhaps reflecting Carr's own prose style, Barton's poetry is aurally neutral: poetry written for the eye rather than the ear. When not describing the painter's images, he invents painterly images for the painter's emotions: in "Lizzie's Death," the two sisters stitch a shroud:

141

"soft linen yielding to thread, / gleaming needles joining panels of absence."
(Some of Carr's paintings show this white-on-white effect, but the shrouds/
absence/white-on-white is more familiar to us from contemporary abstract
expressionist painting; Barton's own eye is painterly, informed.)

For his "Carr," Barton uses three levels of speech: compact, pause-weighted,
and rhapsodic short lines in which the painter tells us the feelings and ideas of
the imagery in her paintings, as in the above-quoted "Cedar"; a prose shaped
by recollected or implied conversation, which structures and clarifies the narrative. And a slower line, set as poetry, in which Carr speaks as much to herself
as to others in half-letters, half-diaries, with the simplicities and awkwardnesses
and occasional gruffnesses we associate with her published writing voice. In
"A Sunday Afternoon (A Letter to Lawren Harris)," a diary-like awkwardness
relaxes into a painter's vision of reflected light on yellow flowers:

> Have not slept well all week,
> kept waking to the wind
> chastening branches that screen my window.
> Was Lazarus chafing at insomnia,
> its hand clammy on my brow.
>
> Thought this morning what the use—
> rose early and walked to church,
> found comfort in the responses,
> the prayerful bond God contracts with Man.
> Bunched humbly on the altar
> daffodils—those immortal flowers—
> drank up light the organ spilled
> from its pips, their thrilled faces opened wide.
> My heart burst its dam, sang and sang.

Barton handles with considerable sensitivity and subtlety Carr's sexual and
social vulnerabilities. Particularly well done are the passages which elaborate
on Carr's relations with Father and Mother figures, the protector and pro-
tectress, who are also D'Sonoqua the devourer and Horrible Rapist, powers
of nature and of the divine, terrible and entrancing, death and life together.
Also excellent is Barton's ability to show us how "Carr's" sense of herself as
the child Small makes of Small a secure place, a sanctuary:

Quiet fell the evening inside me,
my life striations of cloud
at last lifting away from the moon.

The heart of the forest thrown open before me,
I approach overwhelmed,
myself a daughter of prayer
conceived by Father in Mother
for God's pleasure
at the edge of the world.

("Portents")

There are, in fact, as Barton shows us, two safe places for "Carr": the lost Eden of Small, who has not yet heard of the terrible darknesses, and the ultimate essence of nature, into which she wishes to be absorbed: to be buried "deep in the forest, / as the Indians would, in an unmarked grave" ("Last Letter to Baboo") or in the "endless conduit of essence" ("Jack in the Pulpit, Remembered,"—a painting by Georgia O'Keeffe).

Barton's understanding of Carr's work and his sympathetic and plausible interpretation of her inner life make his poem sequence valuable as biography. What his writing would be like without the controlling images, sensibility, and speech-style of his hero, Carr, I cannot imagine. Barton may well be Keats's "camelion Poet"; or, he may have to invent a new voice. At any rate, I can heartily recommend his *West of Darkness*. (I wish, however, that someone with no love for our language had not written on the back of the book that Barton "has authored two earlier volumes.")

Neither Barton nor Barton's hero are primarily concerned with exploring or expressing their personal identity. But for Douglas LePan, the self-image is all-important, not just as subject, as in the autobiographical sonnet sequence "Weathering It," but as style itself. Style is the man, as the saying goes, and, for LePan, the man speaking must be romantic, glamorous, scholarly, and a gentleman.

LePan is a better poet for the ear than for the eye, for his high-coloured images are at times somewhat clichéd, but his control of assonance, alliteration, vowel sequences, cadence, and metre give the reader immense pleasure.

Aware of the normal tendency towards the iambic in the English language in meditative or lyric speech, LePan is careful never to over-stress or over-regularize. He writes melodically, rather than to the metronome. Although most of his lyrics are end-stopped, with variable line and stress lengths, his sonnet sequence, the most interesting metrically of his work, is essentially pentameter. Here LePan counts meaning stresses (which may be groups of words or stressed pauses) rather than counting syllables or long vowels. By over-running his lines, even sometimes spreading his stress across one line into the beginning of another, LePan delicately underplays the measuredness of the pentameter beat and emphasizes the integrity of the sonnet-paragraph as a rhythmic whole. In the following quotation "mild / May" is an example of the stress carried over the line break. Notice how LePan heightened the iambic effect in the concluding line (in which the five stresses are: *birds thought, gun-fire, morning, started,* and *sing*).

> A tunic hanging in a closet ... a dome blue with eternity ...
> a face glimpsed in battle, frightened, passionate, resolved ...
> these quicken, and will quicken till the day he dies, all
> the artillery positions from Cassino to the gates of Rome,
> when they moved almost every day, and every day was taut
> and blue and lustrous as the last, and every day jewelled
> with the danger of death. Death close as a comrade, moving
> as they moved. From that first position, with the guns camouflaged
> among the olive trees. There at eleven o'clock on a mild
> May night the trees were cut through and a thousand guns
> opened up, scaling the dark ramparts of heaven with licks
> and ladders of flame. Coming out of the command-post, he remembers
> there was lodged in his brain a fragment both brutal and lyrical:
> the birds thought the gun-fire was morning, and had started to sing.
>
>   ("Campaigning Weather," Sonnet XXII)

In his poems, LePan likes to make literary references, some "stock" (dome of eternity, ramparts of heaven), but at the same time to centre or weight the poem on a naturalistic detail, such as the birds singing at nighttime above. Nature provides his strongest images, literature his romantically jewelled battle scenes; but neither nature nor literature helps him with imagery for the politics of war. For his "years as a diplomat" leave no glamorous memory:

> The torrents of paper
> that is what he remembers as much as anything else,
> the despatches, the telegrams, the endless memoranda.
> And the endless meetings ...
>
> the clammy mist that rises from impossible choices.
> Across his desk the sludge and sewage of a ravaged
> world. He felt tired. He needed to wash his hands.
>
> ("The Despatch Case," Sonnet xxx)

I don't think a reference to Herod is intended, because none is extended. Rather, it is that the "impossible" and sometimes morally ambiguous choices of diplomacy make the speaker feel dirty as merely killing people (as a soldier) did not. He does not feel guilty; he is doing his job. It is proper to be "something not too easily shocked, not too strenuously virtuous" with "the smile of those who do the world's work but who don't / take the world at its own valuation" ("A Conversation Piece," Sonnet xxxix). What is admired is style—to be, and seem, a gentleman.

LePan likes to hint what in other poets would be either stated in greater detail or concealed, rather as if LePan were calling attention to his own discretion and lack of hypocrisy in sexual and political matters. The effective is worldly, graceful—a bit as if the author, recollecting in tranquility, no longer cares "who/what/when/where." It seems also a form of showing off. For example, no second person is mentioned in Sonnet xv, "A March Day," which concludes with the boy making a choice "that came from the core / of his being. He chose. And he read no more that day." The reference to Dante's lovers is the hint. Without hypocrisy, discreet.

LePan's poetry is full of the hero worship of the soldierly ideal which was and may still be upheld in the "good" British boys' schools, a world in which to be a gentleman (and thus an officer) was the definition of honour, and in which male-bonding forms the definition of love. LePan's soldierly ideal has never felt Biggles's romance of the machine. Rather it is the classical, medieval, or Renaissance knights (and their ladder-stormed ramparts, their castles and swords) which colour LePan's imagination, to such an extent that LePan's war scenes contain no references to twentieth-century artifacts, however clogged they may be with mementoes of antiquity.

Equally unmodern is LePan's caste sense. His gallant soldiers are imagined as if carrying swords (a gentleman's weapon) rather than the enlisted/conscripted man's pike or bayonet. Indeed the sombreness—and the democratic vistas—we associate with military writing from the nineteenth-century masters Whitman, Melville, Crane make their work seem far more contemporary than LePan's. The emphasis on raunchiness, moral corruption, and distrust of the ruling class, which figures in most twentieth-century war writing, is largely absent from LePan. Where noted, not dwelled upon. For, to LePan, individual heroism and gentlemanly honour overshadow the cruelty and futility of war, and indeed make futility and cruelty an aspect of natural beauty.

"Reconnaissance in Early Light" praises an officer whose men, including the poet-speaker, "hate his guts." But this officer is seen by the speaker to show heroic magnificence: "He might be mated with the lion sun," rhapsodizes LePan. "Through all his veins the sacrament of danger, / Discovering secret fires, runs riot." We, the children of Falstaff, can only understand LePan's sort of hero-worship through remembering our own pre-adolescence when we played at being D'Artagnan, the world where there is no distinction between honour and glamour, where to be heroic is to be swashbuckler, all dungeons and dragons. Emily Carr's ability to see Sophie Frank, caring for her children's graves, as heroic, and Barton's ability to see Carr's unglamorous and undangerous life as heroic, are maturer gifts.

LePan's 1987 sequence "Weathering It" follows the poet from childhood to old age. He recollects the adolescent decision to "take the hurdles" and live his life fully, and to fully serve the sexual "prince" and "nest of rattlers" within him, and recalls, with tenderness and discretion, his years of public service. As age brings with it what Peter Pan called "the greatest adventure," LePan's hero, like Tennyson's Ulysses (as possibly suggested in the concluding line of "Wild Cyclamen," XLVIII) continues to strive nobly, and to retain a gentleman's style:

> The intolerable struggle against the bitterness of old age
> and its malice, envy, jealousy. He hadn't guessed how hard
> it would be to keep tempered sweetness as physical
> strength unravels; and doubly hard in a heart still riddled
> with contradictions; and hardest of all, almost impossible, in
> a world where there's so much shit, not only violence,

cruelty, oppression, but greed, ingratitude, hypocrisy.
Yet there are still sweet burgeonings, as rare as love or loyalty.
He's thinking of Ortona. Of the mud. Of all the poor sods
buried there, Tedeschi, Canadesi. (He's searching for something).
Of the door of the command-post. (Yes!) Of wild cyclamen
blossoming there that spring, the buds springing serpent-
like from the earth and breaking open in delicate annunciations.
Their flowers float like tiny sails over deep-sea-green leaves.

Even although the reader recognizes that for LePan, "greed, ingratitude, hypocrisy" are worse than "violence, cruelty, oppression," because these are ungentlemanly sins, the beauty of this verse attracts.

---

from *The Fiddlehead* (Spring 1989)

WORKS CITED

West of Darkness: A Portrait of Emily Carr. Penumbra, 1987.
Weathering It: Complete Poems 1948–1987. McClelland and Steward, 1987.

Other Tastes: A Review of R. M. Vaughan's
Invisible to Predators, Margaret Christakos's *wipe.under.a.love*,
and Elizabeth Philips's *A Blue with Blood in It*

That tastes differ all agree. As a reviewer, I try to recognize excellences in poetry that is shaping itself according to tastes other than my own. Thus I can find in these three dissimilar collections of poetry a great deal to admire—in spite of Vaughan's obsessive emphasis on semen, balls, and cocks, Christakos's deconstructivist experimentalism, and Philips's plain, overly moderate style.

R. M. Vaughan's *Invisible to Predators* is beautifully written. Vaughan has a marvellous ear for the place, timing, and emphasis of our language. His poetry is passionate, vividly detailed, and often narrative or with narrative implications. His elegies and mourning sequences are particularly dramatic, multi-layered, and moving. The sexual affairs described are personal, intense, unsafe:

> Now you've gone   out to shine the day-off sidewalks
> pop cheeked with morning air, a gum-snapping boy
> walking delivery men and slow cats   a minstrel,
> 3 centimetres taller for every itchy minute you spend inside me,
> your white mammy songs make rhymes off my body, our adventures
> as much as your vocabulary allows   On the heated bus, my
> burnt-wood soap from India dries to white crackles along your neck, lacing
> your brown hairline like tidal foam   this, too, causes no concern
>
> I'm bleeding   Or, you left your blood inside me   Or, both
> Or, it's only tomato peel and cooking oil, drawn ghee and cherry essence
>
> Call this passing, call this dribble of shit and brighter proteins   anything
> but blood, because blood means a deal, a handshake
> with slit palms; a throughline, a plot   one of us must outlive
>
> ("In a Year with 13 Moons," section 5)

In two of the strongest poem sequences of the collection, Vaughan "reads" French revolutionary history in terms of the danger, passion, and political vulnerability of his own sexual circumstances:

my atrocities, sweet politico, to bring us closer:
a trickle of white seed, spent into defenceless muscle
like snow muslin, fractions of lace stripped from shoulders
of dukes, later kings; the suggestion I was less than stricken
by a finger cookie cock   delivered with Robespierre's warning—
"daggers are waiting for me too"
a trick of breathing fast into selfish chests, to prevent alarm
with pants, short huffs—ticks any animal hears as boredom
as song for older ears;
promises let loose without pruning; the misuse of the verb like;
squares of money pinched under balls, with teary indignation—
how thieves mark triumph—5's and 10's never spent
on bills or food or lesser boys; whatever passes for love
in quiet homes, in lives set on harmless volumes   on puttering
into the millennium;

                                       forgive me
I was birthwrit, palmed   a deadly time   I chose paper, not scissors
    not stone

                         ("Six Love Poems for Georges-Jacques Danton")

Vaughan's poignant conclusion reminds us that in the game of chance, "Scissors, Stone, Paper," paper "wins" over stone only because it can "wrap" or contain stone—(a sexual image), but that in real life, paper—the poet's choice—is too feeble to cut or bruise. (We recognize, too, that "stone" tends to mean, in our verse, unfeeling, dead; that "scissors" connote both censorship and the blasé/guillotine—excision.)

The language of Vaughan's poems may not be to every taste, but the power and originality of his verse is undeniable even by those whose "lives (are) set on harmless volumes   on puttering / into the millennium."

●

Like Vaughan's collection, Christakos's *wipe.under.a.love*, as the title implies, rejoices somewhat more frequently in body fluids than has been, until recent years, at all common in poetry. She does not, however, have Vaughan's obsessive interest in these stuffs—they are mentioned and present simply as part of her credentials as a contemporary, rather than "old-fashioned" poet. I think Christakos may have been urged to the wipe title because of its appeal to the fashionable consumer. The title has little to do with the general attention of her work.

What interests Christakos is the defamiliarizing effect of disintegrating the syntactic connections between words as they are used in normal communication. In short, her subject is form, or, rather, dis-forming. Conceptual poetry, if you like. And it is this that makes her work initially fascinating.

Except in the first sequence, "Orange Porch," Christakos begins her poems with an experience, situation, or a reference to an item in the newspaper, which she sketches in fairly conventional language—(she doesn't always bother with complete sentences). Most of these are experiences of a middle-class housewife and poet: housework, kids, jobs, loves, schools, kitchen, computer. There is nothing newly observed in her material, probably because referentiality is not her point.

Then, after the opening scene-setting, rather as if she were playing 52 Pickup with the words from a set for refrigerator poetry, she shifts, rearranges, omits, or more rarely, adds to the same words she began with. Christakos scrupulously avoids narratives or argumentative elements. The effect she produces somewhat resembles the disintegration of thought that attends our falling to sleep, as our thought processes seem to unknit themselves and drift into illogical combinations of words and images. But our dreams are influenced, and perhaps urged, toward meaning: personal, cultural, archetypal. The slumbering self strives for a story line.

Christakos is not interested in dreams, self, or subconscious. What she is interested in doing is recombining a set group of words, repeating, re-sorting. Her idea, one gathers, is to make these words *as words* (not as ideas or references or images) "fresh" to us by presenting them newly broke out of their original referential context.

The opening sequence, "Orange Porch," and the closing poems, which refer back to it, dare further. The opening is already incoherent:

> porch view on sinews or possibilities. her out reminiscences shoulder laughing
> recently distance literature writing

The sequence later expands to include minor segments in normally referential manner, (something about a dog; the neighbours, sexual experience) but narrative is ellipsed or avoided. The sequence ends sixteen pages later with:

> I view coat possibilities. literature orange
>   up shoulder girl or longer porch
> muscle on laughing blanching writing written:
>   …
>   I muscle up all to sinews
> him where appealed among again, among
>   came breasts in cresting parks written:
>   porch orange

The poems in the section of the book also entitled "*wipe.under.a.love*" begin less distractedly, and almost uniformly conclude with a "Therefore," which represents not the distillation of the opening words, but the dissolution. "Grounds 2B" concludes:

> THEREFORE:
> twins answer sure body
> evaporates nothing

from which the opening images of the poem can not be deduced. "Grounds 3B" does rather better, beginning like a chatty diary:

> low bowl of spiral pasta, squash, white beans
> and succulent field tomato any restauranteur
> would be proud to serve: another ten-minute
> wonder dinner, pan-tossed. so what: i eat
> at the computer the food is lyrical, the writing less so
> and so what again i am ground down by the unsleeping
> toddlers, …

and, after a due process of rearrangement and disintegration, it ends, amusingly:

> THEREFORE:
> Soaked idea decapitated keyboard

wipe.under.a.love should be valued as an extremely careful working out of an experiment; those who love conceptual art will find Christakos's method provocative and witty.

❀

Elizabeth Philips's *A Blue with Blood in It* is in many ways a very typical book of Canadian poetry: rural, moderate, accessible, undisturbing, and sweetly tender, affirming generally shared values, a sort of neo-Georgian for our times. But her poems are appealing, and sometimes quite moving.

Philips has little truck with symbols, level of meaning, or complex ambiguities and ironies. High modernism is as dead for her as it is for Christakos. Instead, simplicity of language and a moderated vocal pace allow temperance and clarity. The basic poetic attitude is calmed. Perhaps typically, the bear that *might* be in the blueberry patch, in the title (and opening) poem, does not appear, and the "blood" turns out not to be real blood, but the effect of the poet's trying to describe the intense (un-red) blue of a gentian. (It is, as a matter of fact, one of the few weak descriptions in the book—used as a title, I fear, because of the belief that the word "blood" has a sort of mana, and that a nearly-there bear is, sort of, scary.)

Yet Philips's gentle, conservative manner can produce great beauty. And when she allows herself the occasional non-literal images, the surrounding simplicity seems to glow like an opal:

> I walk out at sunrise, early light throwing blue
> shadows over knee-deep snow, the air
> cold, fragrant with smoke
>
> from the house stove. A horse trail leads
> into the bush, my boots huge
> beside the stitches a shrew has made
>
> circling the high drifts, whimsical
> fringe along the cutline. As I walk
> the light grows tinged with sulfur, though blue

lingers under the tall spruce. Far off,
a woodpecker drills in deadwood. A raven
flaps overhead, her call

a swallowed bell. In the old swamp, dry reeds,
struck by wind's vibrato, have etched lines
in the snow, a calligraphy

subtle as the first brush of age
around the eyes. The last storm's heavy fall
has loaded down the scrub, wands of high-bush

cranberry bent into ribs, fresh arcs of snow
lashing everything into place
for the long moment that is winter.

A lightning-felled spruce, its cracked trunk
held up by neighbouring branches, shrouds
the path. Here, the light is blue
on blue. A mist along the ground, it fades away
when I dip my hands in it,
a blood of colour so ephemeral

it can't be gathered in, but must be known
aslant, like time
or love.

("Blue")

❧

Some of Philips's poetry strikes me as *too* plain. Like Philips, I, too, walk about
my garden reciting flowers' names. But this sort of recitation, however "accessible," or congenial, is not art. Perhaps her simplicities represent a reaction
against the extravagances of the romantics and the high modernists; they may
also arise from a desire to speak for, and to, the "community" rather than just
to the highbrows. I prefer it when Philips moves beyond literal referentiality
and startles us with a non-quotidian image. In "Sleepwalking," an old man
lies in bed:

He lies on his side, hands holding his ankles,
and thinks how small his wife is, her memory
a tiny doll in the basket of his ribs, a stitch
in his side almost a comfort.
During the first years of grief, she flooded his cells
like a drowning, water
in his lungs.

Note how powerfully Philips renews the cliché "drowned in grief." But note too the multi-layered first image: a doll, a baby, an Eve (Adam's rib), in a cradle, rib cage, womb, coffin—a wound, now healed, that had been "like a drowning, water / in his lungs." This image is as densely emotional as Vaughan's, and, by packing a plain sentence richly with multi-references (all the things "she" refers to: wife, memory, doll, baby, stitch/pain), more innovative than Christakos's. When Philips writes more often like this we may find ourselves less "at home" in her work, but more with the sense of the uncanny presence of art.

---

from *The Fiddlehead* (Spring 2001)

WORKS CITED
Invisible to Predators. R. M. Vaughan. ECW, 1999.
wipe.under.a.love. Margaret Christakos. The Mansfield Press, 2000.
A Blue with Blood in It. Elizabeth Philips. Coteau, 2000.

Poetry for the Ear: A Review of Jeanette Lynes's
Left Fields and *The Aging Cheerleader's Alphabet*

Nearly (but not all) good poetry is designed as much for the pleasure of the ear as for anything else. But some poetry is particularly well-designed to appeal not only to the ear but as well to be emotionally effective and intellectually graspable at first hearing. Of this sort of good poetry two new books by Jeanette Lynes are exceptionally fine examples. She has an excellent command of pace, stress, timing, and knows, as Frost has said, "It's how you say a thing that counts." The work must be marvellously suitable to the radio, requiring no more "performance" than the language itself provides. And this poet is funny, with that vigorous but modest irreverence I think of as almost peculiarly feminine: as in Bishop, Moore, Gotlieb, etc. I heartily recommend her collections.

Jeanette Lynes's poetry is somewhat colloquial. She has a stand-up comedienne's manner: a sort of deadpan throw-away demeanour. Her work has many literary references and often becomes humorous commentary on freshman English.

Of her two collections, I like *The Aging Cheerleader's Alphabet* slightly less, because the image/idea which largely controls the book, charming as it is, seems at times not large enough for a whole book. Many of the poems can stand quite well on their own, without the mildly narrative frame of the aging cheerleader's self-references, her past victories, her pom-poms, etc. Nevertheless, the metaphors that derive from the cheerleader's self-description give colour and shaping and wry humour to the whole. The cheerleader is a point of view, not a protagonist. Once I stopped wanting a short story or a novel, I enjoyed this collection immensely. One of my favourites, "Musing on Names While Driving During an Official Storm, Listening to Johnny Cash, Then Joan Osborne":

A hurricane named Karen. Boy named Sue. Whatever.
What's in a nom de pom? we're just winging it, here.
Mounds of dulse, tangles of purple moppery
dishevel the beach—why not call them cast off

merleader poms? What if the sirens were
us, singing to diver the enemy waterbacks?

The rainy season, someone trying to tell us
something? This road, ricking the brink
of sea (this hobbling path, this blundering trail, this
this, this) renders
dictionaries runnels, sad
gee-tars on stilts, wet despite. The names of things
topple. I'm less sure God's a ravening old man
with void issues; perhaps God's the torrent that humbles
or, as in Joan's tidal wail (cusp)
just a stranger   one of us.

Cash, Osborne, Arnold, Eliot, a bit of Anglo-Saxon, wonderful!

Lynes is well-known and praised for her ability to make us laugh at ourselves. But her jokes are not denigration, rather they are amusement at the
human condition. It is possible that the shallow listener may perceive many
of her poems as a sort of romp, and indeed they do read aloud as if they must
have been fun to write, but there are remarkable subtleties running along just
beneath the overt simplicity.

Among my favourites from *Left Fields* are Lynes's redoing of Browning's
"My Last Duchess." Next is "Duke"; "Brave" (about her grandmother's now
curving spine); "Shooting the Little Bear" (a date with Heraclitus); and the
amazing "This Can't Possibly be My Life," in which the poet juxtaposes her
affection for an elderly and dying cat and her concerns about the unrespon-
sive students she teaches:

Back at camp, drugged puss, having grown
smaller, warms another spot of time on the bare mattress.
"You won't believe the daydream I had," I tell her:
"I was a truth-dispenser, the awake ones
were dropping coins
in my mouth like
          a pop machine. As each coin hit
the pit of me, it said, in its tinny
coin voice: *drink this—*
this is your life, this is what it costs."

"Drink this!" *Alice in Wonderland?* The Eucharist? The English professor, the poet, as both? These are the poems I am not going to forget.

---

from *The Fiddlehead* (Spring 2005)

WORKS CITED
Left Fields. Wolsak and Wynn, 2003.
The Aging Cheerleader's Alphabet. Mansfield Press, 2003.

A Rare Originality: A Review of
Hannah Main-Van der Kamp's *According to Loon Bay*

There is an absolute sense in which all of us, as unique humans, are "original"—but originality in poetry, as in conversation, is rare. And since I have not read, and indeed could never read, all the poetry there is, I can not absolutely say that what Hannah Main-Van der Kamp has done in poetry is unique—only that I have never seen it elsewhere, never read about such a thing, and never thought of such a thing. In my experience, she is doing something new, original, and I find it very exciting.

Style, whether experimental or not, should and usually does not reflect a method of thought, and some thoughts do require unorthodox styles. But some new thoughts can be written in ordinary sentences. *According to Loon Bay* is a collection of nature poems written by a religious poet whose stylistic excellence does not seek to astonish us by its novelty. What is new in Main-Van der Kamp is not style, but her way of thinking, her perception, her approach.

Most contemporary nature poetry differs from traditional nature poetry. In the past, however ephemeral natural phenomena, Nature itself was regarded as reliable, its patterns permanent; Nature had a Presence, a kind of flowing stability. (Never the "same" river but always the "river.") But most nature poets nowadays are very much aware that the inhuman world has ceased to be stable, and their sense of the vulnerability of the "wild" has caused many to feel that nature needs to be more acutely observed, more precisely recorded, more relished and written about for its own inhuman condition than it has been in the past.

The main "point" of most contemporary nature poems is observation, recording, a kind of reverent discipline for what matters—and for most of our new nature poets what most seems to matter is less the poet observer than the thing observed.

While most nature poets record their pleasure in observation, many add reminiscence to observation. Others become intrigued with a particular quality or capability in the thing observed (the soaring of a bird, for example) and play with that quality in relation to their own emotions and desires; they empathize with aspects of their subject, and their poems become more lyrical, more like traditional nature poetry in which birds, plants, stones, or weather could stand as symbolic references for human feelings. Other contemporary nature poets become entranced by the words they are using or the images they are painting, so that their poems become more sound-oriented, a kind of "language" poetry.

And there are many contemporary poets whose basic reaction to nature still reflects and records a sense of an underlying Presence, strength, spirit or life force, which the poets communicate by reference to myth or religion or by emotional heightening. However vivid their description of natural phenomena, they appear to look through nature towards a deeper reality. (For example, Tim Lilburn's wonderfully vivid poems, in which some sort of Life Force divinity, almost more geologic than theologic, is envisioned as thrusting and moving beneath, through, and within the earth, scrub, grass, deer, water, etc.)

Traditionally, religious poets tended to "read" nature as a metaphoric or symbolic text: sermons in stones, parables in running brooks, eternity in a grain of sand. But the new Canadian nature poets do not use objects or creatures as symbols, or even as metaphors. The weight and value of most contemporary Canadian nature poems is outer-directed. Birds as birds. And here Main-Van der Kamp agrees. Her birds are not metaphors, not symbols. She does not "read" nature to uncover a greater theologic truth.

She does it the other way round. Deeply informed by the stories, parables, metaphors, and rituals of the Christian Church, she "reads" this religious material as metaphors for nature, as parables about ordinary life. For Main-Van der Kamp, stories about Pentecost, the doves descending, the tongues of fire—lead us to real birds, real flowers:

All-black sea ducks scrawl
ciphers over the bay,
cryptic speech unreadable in any language.

In the ditch among chokecherries and rowans
wild columbines proliferate. Little Pentecostals
essences of airiness, their Elizabethan prettiness
chirping in luscious tongues.
Dear holy rollers, you make us glad
by your yearly inflorescence,

quintet of flames arranged in a ring
and carried with a slender droop.
Flames neither Holy Ghostly nor hell
but herb beloved of hummingbirds.
Not cloven at all,
en pointe as ballerinas.

Here is the universal tongue:

arched sepals spurred,
energy of breezy doves.

("In Quivering Tongues Similitude" *from a fourth-
century hymn for the fiftieth-day after Easter*)

Non-gardening readers may need to know that columbine is so called because its flower heads look like a circle of tiny birds (the Latin *Columbidae* —doves). The sepals also resemble tiny tongues of fire—or small feet, deer hooves, ballerina's slippers. The point of this gorgeous and epiphanic poem is not that plants can lead us to the truths of the Bible, but that the Bible can lead us to perceive the "universal tongue" of natural beauty.

Main-Van der Kamp's rhetorical technique is unusually good. In the poem above, her ear for attractive alliteration is almost Anglo-Saxon. And her rhythms are always just right for her subject; the columbine poem is lively, even chirping. But contrast the long deep-breathed pace of the meditative poem "To Dwell in the House of the Lord Forever," in which our thoughts about heaven become a way of perceiving "now." Here again she reads through the texts of religion for reality, rather than, traditionally, the other way round:

To dwell is to breathe deeper,
to abide in slowness. *Dwell* as in to walk the length and width
of a room as still as a glass vase, the room
where the light comes through the walls
and the walls become grass. As still as that.
To desire intimacy with that grass,
to slide into it as into slumber.

…

Forever is only now
and now and now and now.
How frivolous time is. To pass away
is the body becoming earth again.
Worse things could happen.
The only thing I desire is to desire
the house, temple, shrine where intimate breath
is not metered out. To desire is to receive it.
The more implausible, the more sense it makes.
To inhale *forever* is more than neurons retrained to fire slowly.
All the days of my life
I will go there without knocking,
because it is already mine
and was long ago and will be
and is and is and is.

("To Dwell in the House of the Lord Forever")

There is so much to praise in *According to Loon Bay*. The prose poems of the section Tremolos will last me the whole of Lent. The long poem "Sliammon Sam and the Man Who Fell Among Thieves," a serious parody of much of the New Testament, seems designed for public performance. It is tremendous fun, and reminds me, just a little, of Dorothy Livesay's long poems for multiple voices. Just an excerpt from the section "A Certain Lawyer Stood Up, *A Dialogue*":

Concerned about surge channels at the seashore? Rip tides,
Stinging creatures, what is edible and what is toxic?
You're a lawyer and know when to ask an expert.

Lawyer: *What must I do to guarantee safety for me and mine?*

Of course the rabbi answers a question with a question:

Rabbi: *Consult the book. What is written in the field guide?*

It turns out the Good Samaritan must understand nature. Well, if you are not a naturalist and not familiar with the New Testament, *According to Loon Bay* may not appeal to you as much as it does to me, but I am quite happy to take it as one of my "field guides" and I will recommend it to anyone. I think even naturalists who are not religious would enjoy it, and for the religious—it is a new and renewing way of dealing with the old, still Pentecostal stories.

---

from *The Fiddlehead* (Spring 2006)

WORKS CITED

According to Loon Bay. St. Thomas Poetry Series, Coach House Books, 2004.

What She Saw: A Review of Karen Solie's *Pigeon*

Karen Solie's subject, environmental degradation and humanity's failings, is a subject important to us all. Of the many poets who tackle this theme, Solie is at once the wittiest and the least cheerful. Her most accessible poems are primarily descriptive of "objective" events, but nearly all of them also cue us in to the human—often selfish or irresponsible or unkind—response. A beautiful hawk? "Soon, we will have to have him" ("The World of Plants," 30).

Most of her poems are grimly funny. The long, opening poem of *Pigeon*, "Pathology of the Senses," describes a hot smoggy day in big-city Toronto so vividly it is almost unbearable. As is often the case in Solie's long descriptive poems, the speaker's observations are interrupted by words and noises the speaker is not herself making. Notice in this excerpt from the poem how much more effective the colloquial apology for profanity is than would be mere profanity, and how just that remark, "Pardon my French," summons a social context. It is one of Solie's particular strengths that her poems generally provide us a social context.

> Heavy cloud, colour of slag
> and tailings, green light gathering
>
> like an angry jelly. Pardon my French. The
> city
> on rails, grinding toward a wreck the lake
> cooks up ...
>
> (5)

Solie's black irony and stylistic flair are untainted by wistfulness. Rather, the prevailing tone of Pigeon is sombre, "noirish" (her term, from "The Ex-Lovers," 53), even angry. But within these dark tonalities she can create for us a remarkably wide range of emotional voice. "The World of Plants," for example, ends with a wonderfully complex sequence of tone: first tone of drab realism "objective," we might call it, which she follows with a bitter mocking of the futility of city ordinance and useful suggestions from environmentalists, then she gives us two lines exhibiting the sullen, resentful obstinacy with which the pathetic suggestions of those who would save us are generally received, and then concludes with a cry of bitter exasperation:

> The lake accumulates what is given it,
> until gradually, though it may not appear so,
> its constitution is changed. One thing dies,
> another takes its place, and an unknown
> potential enters the world. Anyone
> who spots the alien invader Asian
> long-horned beetle in the neighborhoods
> is asked to report this immediately
> to the city. Without our efforts no tree is safe.
> It's as if everybody always wants us to do something.
> I'd like to see someone make us. Please,
> someone, come on over here and make us.

(31)

Although much of the poetry in this collection bears witness to human inadequacy, there is as well plenty of compassion—(and that, too, "noirish" veined with sardonic wit). The speaker of "Prayers for the Sick," waiting in "emergency," using lines from the *Catholic Prayers for the Sick* says:

> Remember Ronny, who came home from a night shift
> at the birdseed factory north of Lethbridge
> to find his effects on the lawn of his rooming house?
> He'd secured nothing in writing from his landlord
> and got it. Jesus, make haste to save us
> from all those smug, nasty, overpaid with dumb
> nicknames, who would see us depart and be no more.
> For the very light of our eyes is failing. Our iniquities
> have overwhelmed us, and it is clear now that no one
> is getting out of here by noon.

Continuing in the confessional mood, the speaker goes on to say:

> In this present of enforced leisure, we consider
> the record of our own bad form, the bonehead plays,
> mean streaks like marblings in meat,
>
> ("Prayers for the Sick," 60)

As the Protestant *Book of Common Prayer* similarly says, "There is no health in us." Nor in the landscape. Or, Solie seems to say, at least not much. But there is tenderness in her poems toward neighbours, lovers, family, children. Little is totally black. Nevertheless, nothing is all that good either. Solie's peculiar excellence lies in her ability to render for us what it is like when we are not really having a very good time.

Although Solie declares that "beauty and reality are the same" in the poem of that name, (63), she is not very good at describing beauty. "Bow River Preludes" is a failure for that reason.* "In New Brunswick" reveals for us something of her problem: "The forest, / with its long hallways and concealing furnitures, / is not for me" (29). The forest, like the intensely beautiful Bow River, is too far from the human. Solie cannot describe an inhuman beauty. She writes as if more at home in the slightly damaged, the injured, the ugly. But where she is describing a human experience, as in the marvellous poem "Archive," which layers context upon context, Solie succeeds:

> the past, the immediate past, the moment, the about to be and is now
>   happening—even
> what is about to happen—the personal, the impersonal—the sense living in
>   flux, and
> of the desires and intimate fears of the writer/artist/photographer.

Ah!—extraordinary poem, and very beautiful.

In the title poem, "Pigeon," Solie reminds us that our attentions are always divided (as are our brains)—we attend to our own wants, and only half see what surrounds us. But, she asserts:

> My attentions were divided.
> Nevertheless, I saw what I saw.
>
> ("Pigeon," 33)

I read this as a declaration of intention—the poet as bearing witness, telling the truth. As part of truth-telling, she declares that she (and the rest of us, too) are limited in what we can pay attention to, in what we do pay attention to. Witness. "I saw what I saw."

Solie's poems are best when her attentions are shown to be divided. The purely descriptive—i.e., "objective" poems are the weakest. The best are the poems where she allows a degree of introspection and self-knowledge to affect her humour. I am particularly impressed by "An Acolyte Reads *The Cloud of Unknowing*," which is perhaps the least impersonal, and, as well, the least ironic of the poems in Pigeon. Here the speaker rejects the mystic's ideal of losing self (with its human fears, desires, memories, etc.) in the intellectually/experientially, reality-annihilating whelm of the divine "mystery," while at the same time admitting that there are moments in which the self does dissolve—the mystic's insight is not rejected, but the dissolution of self, among ordinary us, is temporary, and in terms of how we live: "nothing to do with me."

Throughout "An Acolyte Reads *The Cloud of Unknowing*," the speaker, while meditating on religion and philosophy, is shown as aware always of her social and environmental context: neighbours, noise, the news, distresses and disasters not her own. She is not meditating while surrounded by beauty. Her context is urban, her attentions divided. She is never out of context. Which is one of the reasons I so much admire her:

> I have dissolved
> like an aspirin in water watching a bee walk into
> the foyer of a trumpet flower, in the momentary
> solace of what has nothing to do with me, brief
> harmony of particulars in their separate orbits,
> before returning to my name, to memory's warehouse
> and fleet of specialized vehicles, the heart's
> repetitive stress fractures, faulty logic, its stupid
> porchlight. If virtue is love ordered and controlled,
> its wild enemy has made a home in me. And if
> desire injures the spirit, I am afflicted. Rehearsing
> philosophy's different temperaments—sanguine, contrary,
> nervous, alien—one finds a great deal to fear.
> A lake-effect snowstorm bypasses the ski hills,

knocks the power out of some innocent milltown.
The world chooses for us what we can't, or won't.

(84)

This is a very sad poem, "noirish," and as well a very beautiful poem—and very truthful. "Beauty and Reality are the Same," Solie has asserted. In poems like this, she proves it.

---

from *The Antigonish Review* (Autumn 2013)

NOTES

*Among other things, she gets the colours wrong! I really do not think Solie is a visual poet, rather a poet who observes with her mind, heart, and ears, but not her eyes. In "Bow River Preludes," she repeatedly calls the waters "green"—well, the Bow River is not the St. Paddy's Day virulent green we see in lakes and ponds, over-fertilized and infested with great swags of brilliant algae! The water of the Bow River has no colour at all. The minute glacier silt is invisible to us—but is massively and gloriously reflective—which would mean the water is "white"—i.e., all reflective—except weather and context, the grass, rocks, etc., are there, too, to be reflected, so the colour varies.

On a brilliant day, spilling ferociously, glacier silt water will beam gloriously with that strange blue/fluorescent light we discover in great bergs or deep glaciers. But mostly the river reflects what there is about and above it. On a grey day it is mutton fat jade, a whiteness only faintly discoloured by the environment. Often the water runs pale celadon—and sometimes cream of pea soup with yellowish overtones. And when the sky above flames red at dawn or dusk, these white reflective waters do what snow does, what the rocks do, what even the trees and the grasses do then: they reflect pink.

(The Bow River Valley is one of the most beautiful places left on earth, and we have not yet ruined it, even if the glaciers are in retreat.)

WORKS CITED

Pigeon. House of Anansi Press, 2009.

The Necessity of Re-vision:
A Review of Al Moritz's *The New Measures*

There are several excellent poems in Moritz's *The New Measures*, but, about the book as a whole, I have reservations.

Much of Moritz's writing in *The New Measures* seems to rise out of the familiar conventions of yesteryear, untainted by feminist or modernist criticism. For Moritz, the "poet" is a man who "sings" in "measures" (7). He is not troubled by clichés and is particularly fond of the traditional image of rain (or weather in general) inseminating the earth (indeed, this image of continual sexual penetration is something of a "King Charles's head" in Moritz's verse). As well, Moritz's Biblical allusions are not always pertinent to the poems in which they occur (e.g., "Farewell to Lake Michigan," 35).

The prevailing theme of this collection is moral: the necessity of re-thinking, revising, starting again, taking—and making "new measures," in writing, yes, but as well, in our lives. Of his poems on this subject, I particularly admire the poem which introduces The New Measures, "The Book to Come," and, as well, "Full Circle, i.m. Northrop Frye."

Moritz's most ambitious poem on taking "new measures" is the long concluding sequence "Open House." The sequence presents itself as a process, not as a finished result. Each of the thirteen sections presents a question, a concession, or implication that the process of poem-making must be revised or started again, six of the sections opening with "that" or "it" or the "question" is "not right." I much admire Moritz's innovative idea of presenting a poem in this manner.

"Open House" is also innovative in that it appears to have been originally shaped as an allegory, by which I do not mean, here, a personification of an abstraction, but a narratively extended metaphor in which the literal level of reference means less than the ideas metaphorically represented. The allegory is not consistently maintained, but this, it could be argued, is part of the idea in presenting the poem as illustrating the process of writing, re-writing, and, necessarily, re-visioning.

That "Open House" is an allegory became clear to me as I pondered the opening sequence:

They started with a question:
how could they unlock their door
and give to everyone who asked
and still be anything themselves, still work
and have a place to offer, not fade away in the swarm
of everything that enters, driven
or simply leaking, spreading,
to wash away their outline, erase their face?

(i, 62)

Initially this passage presented me with two closely related problems: the notion of a self that could be erased by the demands or behaviours of others, and the idea of regarding as desirable virtue what, on the literal level, would appear to be an irresponsible, unquestioning, and passive generosity (do you lend your car to a drunk, or paraffin to an arsonist?). Once I had figured out what sort of "self" could be endangered by showing generosity to a swarm of requests, I could see out what sort of generosity was being discussed.

When/how does a human being lose his or her "self"? (All we mean by the term "selfless" is that someone has not valued their own interests above another's, not that someone has no self.) Mystics and contemplatives write about losing their self (and their concerns with the material world) in a moment of spiritual illumination (with God, in nirvana, immersed in the All). They return to their selves enlightened, changed—but still themselves. Saul's self was not erased on the road to Damascus: Paul existed within Saul as a tree exists within a seed. We remain our selves in dreams. (As for the loss of "self" in insanity? This is not Moritz's topic. His subject is a "self" that can be endangered by the swarming demands of "everything that enters"—especially the neighbours.)

Thinking of invasive neighbours led me to realize that "Open House" works as a political allegory. We speak of neighbourhoods or of nations as having a specific character, a "face," an image of itself. An old woman living alone in a neighbourhood that used to be middle class will not lose her sense of her self when her neighbourhood "goes downhill" and fills up with vandals, drug addicts, beggars, and foreigners. What changes for her is her sense of "us" as a neighbourhood, "us" as a nation. We can suppose as a virtue a generous immigration policy: "whoever dared to come in would have what he wanted" (63), and yet, at the same time, fear the cultural results. (Later, section v illustrates what we fear.)

In the third section of the sequence, Moritz, visioning an ideal of absolute hospitality, presents the "open house" in terms of weather as sexual penetration, gentle at first, later violent:

> They started with some friends.
> Newly married themselves, they imagined
> a house all unlocked. Many doors.
> A body constantly penetrated
> by lovers like a summer rain,
> the kind that lightly quivering the petals
> erects a wakeful night
> stiller than deep sleep ... also the kind
> that shivers the house and tears with its nails
> to fissure the earth and work in,
> and rolls over like torrential sweat
> down, a back about to break
> so that house and ground whirl
> on a current, threatening to split in fragments
> and dissolve, be part of the mire
> suspended in a world of flood.
>
> iii, 64)

In section iv, Moritz's protagonists revise the image:

> That's not right. These friends of theirs
> were other boys and girls, newly women and men,
> not a storm or a stream of sperm.
> The house was an apartment, complaisant, yes,
> but not a temple whore. The dream
> of infinite permission and entry was a thing—
> as a dream is a thing—
>
> (iv, 65)

In section v, the "open house" ideal is shown to have, along with its pleasures, its disadvantages:

> They hadn't yet even unlocked their doors
> but it seemed a riot of tribes

ate everything, howling without truce
and sometimes they too joined in and displayed
their own crests, dances, and intricately carved throwing sticks
with three deadly blades. They loved
the moment of tired calm, the night, the variously tattooed heads
breathing together asleep, though somewhere
a voice could be heard muttering; someone drawled a story
before morning uncovered
the piles and scraps of filth, the breakages
of goods and bodies, a corpse or two,
a maiming cut or two, the wreckage of carnival, they saw
all brought together by their house, a world
of bodies permanently entering and accepting other bodies ...

(v, 66)

Some party! The image of primitive savages seems to be related to the problem of open house immigration. Constant sex continues to be seen as a good thing. (I am inclined to admire the morning-after insouciance of the house couple, but I can not imagine such a party—"a corpse or two"—as other than allegorical.)

By section vi, the protagonists, revising their ideals, but not abandoning them, continue to value the gesture of giving all they have to "whoever asks," but reject the idea of the open (and expensive) party house. For hospitality they substitute charitable thoughts:

Now where is that dead beggar?
who lets, who brings him in? What human wall
permeable but sheltering, lets him enter through it ...

(vi, 68)

What new openness, they ask:

might penetrate the closed, confused
walls of the word love
and rebuild it.

(vii, 69)

The next sections imagine the destruction of the house in terms of the natural change in houseless nature ("it has no home," 71). Natural erasure seems less threatening to the protagonists than social pressure. Indeed, the non-urban world now seems to them highly attractive.

And, once again, the couple re-vision their ideals. They recollect that they had begun as children, open to experience:

> They don't know generosity but see it
> being newly created
> each time
> they close a hungry fist on what they want.
>
> (x, 72)

> They started with the child—an eagerness
> a selfish anarchy admitting all. Later
> it became a word they found
> and pronounced: I love you ...
>
> (xi, 73)

Revising their understanding, taking "new measures," they envision openness as a form of perception, an openness of mind. The political allegory, with its concerns for the material demands of strangers, and the problems this causes to the ideal of open-hearted generosity, is abandoned. By the end of "Open House," the protagonists are content to be houseless and no longer inconvenienced by the demanding presence of other people. They set out on a spiritual quest:

> So later they went out. Left the house open.
> On the path through the fields alone together
> they'd live forever with the amber dragonflies,
> the black moths mating in air
> above the brome nodding, near the birch flickering,
> a fountain of constellations, in the go and come
> of light wind. They'd walk with their absent friends
> alone together
> trying to open,

each in the house of a body
that would be all doors.

(xiii, 75)

To some extent, the "open house" of Moritz's imagination resembles that of Oliver Wendell Holmes's "Build thee more stately mansions, oh my soul!" But Holmes's image aims to eventually lessen the distance between soul and God. Moritz is concerned to lessen the distance between one self and another self. And the emphasis on penetrability is entirely Moritz's.

Allied to Moritz's favourite image of incessant sexual penetration is his second favourite image, that of the beautiful naked and always obliging young girl, who reminds me of the naked blond on the cloud who floats through the daydreams of the young private in *Lipstick On Your Collar*. She is a masturbation fantasy, perpetually "open," always willing to be "penetrated." She is sometimes contrasted (e.g., "Eve," 18) with unattractive old women who have become disgusting with age. And she is sometimes seen as a "daughter":

> a daughter's hair
> brushed and parted perfectly and woven with pearl
> and diamond threads—a daughter otherwise naked,
> except for the light that resurrects the wall,
> dress of a deeper nudity. The daughter: she is safety
> and desire under the guardian trees, although
> there are no trees in the dusty downtown,
> no vines, no flowers, and the women,
> not young, not slender, waddle
> muffled up against paralyzing light
> along the frying barrenness of the wall.

("City Centre," 48)

The under-clad, very young girls who peddle their penetrability are, indeed, our daughters. They should not represent "safety" to their clients/fathers. The clothed, plump, waddling, middle-aged women are our mothers.

According to Moritz we "don't have the adequate verb":

> —not fucked, not made
> love to, something between—by the shafts

of sunlight that penetrate, and the marble
presence of the child god. Father and son,
light and sculpture, rapturous in the garden
of self-proffering femininity.

("In the Food," 55)

One gathers that real women, feminine women, don't say no.

---

from *The Fiddlehead* (Autumn 2013)

WORKS CITED
The New Measures. House of Anansi Press, 2012.

FOUR:

Books in Translation

Two Translations: A Review of Marie-Claire Blais's
Veiled Countries/Lives and Eugenio Montale's *The Bones of Cuttlefish*

Veiled Countries/Lives by Marie-Claire Blais and *The Bones of Cuttlefish* by Eugenio Montale, both by well-known authors, and both presented to us in competent translation, have little else in common. Blais's book, first published in 1964, is from a world that has to be approached by the reader through the efforts of a historical imagination, while the Montale, although published in 1925, presents us a world that is still familiar. To some extent the familiarity of the Montale, and unfamiliarity of the Blais, reflect the presence in the one, and the absence in the other, of the historical awareness and literary tradition that colour our sense of the present. But primarily, I think, the difference is that Montale's voice is very much the voice we have grown to expect from a major poet: deeply feeling and deeply thoughtful, intellectually and passionately authoritative. Blais gives us, however, a kind of feminine voice that has not been heard much in English literature (and, I think, not much in French). The major women writers mostly write in what, until recently, I had come to think of as the distinctive voice of the woman writer: a voice of great intellectual wit, passion, irony, realism, and strength—a very "characterful," "individual" voice. Women, I had thought, do not write in the submissive "female" voice male critics often ascribe to them—or so I had thought until I read Jean Rhys, until I had read Marie-Claire Blais.

Blais's *Veiled Countries/Lives* is a book curiously without any sense of individualized women. The women in her verse are a faceless, indistinguishable "we"—sisters or mothers interested only in the brother/lover/soldier/son (not in daughters, not in each other), who represent themselves as patient refreshers of the glamorously doomed (and often polygamous) males who so briefly resort to their solicitudes. "Mes enfants" turn out always to be "mes fils."

In "The Friend," for example, one is struck by the plural-ness of the mothers, and the single-ness of the man who, as god, as a fertility figure, as returning *paterfamilias* of a huge household of sexless children and women (Blais's men are always away at or coming home briefly from soldiering), is seen by his women as an impersonally caressing "well loved stranger." Blais's image of the "well loved stranger" occurs often in her verse, while some-times a much absent (or mysteriously present husband), the stranger may be merely a passing trooper. The young girls of the household will grow up and be servants and quiescent refreshers of these glamorous, doomed young soldiers. The deaths these young men discover are as mysterious and as quiet as their lives and their brief homecomings—for these men are figures from heaven, and die as quietly as Adonaic sheaves of wheat. None of these men is seen in a realistic, social, or political context, but rather are savoured in a kind of masturbation reverie, each as a "murderous dove" ("War"). Blais's women lack glamour without attaining realism; even their washing-up is but vaguely, dreamily described.

Typically, the raptures of Blais's long, concluding poem "Desperate Times" have narcotic fragility, and identify the female with the sexual neuroses no doubt rooted in a world where women never had the "face"—the individu-ality, the dignity, the imaginable mental health that they had been granted, however partially, in Chaucer, Dante, or the Book of Ruth. The poem con-cludes, after mourning for the "miraculous child," the "wanted" sin, with the following lines:

A duel, in the dream—but the blood flows a bit,
a cut from the reaping-hook on that quiet breast—
and from this wound, the she-wolves
will follow the tracks in the snow

That the unreal blood from that so quietly wounded breast should be pursued only by female wolves is a distinguishing trait of Blais's poetry. If you like this sort of thing, it is very lovely.

Harris's translation of Blais's book is mostly good English poetry. His faults primarily consist in his choosing to shorten Blais's lines, making them conform to the typically short-winded Anglophone Canadian pattern, rather than leav-ing them in the long breaths Blais gives them. And he occasionally reorders her lines, with a resulting shift of emphasis that, to my mind, slightly alters the appropriate meaning. In "The Return," for example, he ends not with her "die, little by little, in my two, too-living arms" but with "in my arms, too loaded with life, little by little, to die." But his lines are euphonic, and he has had the good sense to retain the French originals parallel to his own work, so his readers can have the double pleasure of reading both.

Although Antonino Mazza's translation of Eugenio Montale is, for the most part, exquisite, there are faults. The major fault is the absence of the Italian original. The sound of Italian is accessible, if only through the familiarities of opera and the Roman alphabet, and one yearns to sound out the original lines. Secondly, Mazza does not seem to have thought of having his manuscript reread by someone for whom English is a native tongue rather than a learned one. It is not native for Mazza. I am going to quote and comment on the following errors because I think Mazza is so fine a poet in English that I cannot bear for him to make these sorts of errors again, and I am not sure, without detailing his faults, that I could convince him he had any, given the general excellence of his command of language.

From "Falsetto," page 25: (Addressing a swimmer) "Submerged we will see you"—(who is submerged, we or you?). From "The Bones of Cuttlefish," page 36: "it was the horse fallen off its feet"—(only possible in English if the horse has been first detached from its feet and then set up back on them). From "Portovenere," page 47: "The hold-hands dance on the gravel shore was / the life"—("hold-hands" is not listed in the Oxford English Dictionary). From "Mediterranean Sea," page 56: "I am petrified in your presence, sea"—("petrified" is now a comic adjective when used in this manner). From "Mediterranean Sea," page 58: "the stretch / of the sea was a game of ringlets"—(the O.E.D. lists "ringlets," but as a dance, not a game; it is not in current usage). From "Mediterranean Sea," page 67: "that like women prostitutes / offer themselves to whoever wants them"—(unnecessary retaining of gender).

The resonances of Montale must make his work curiously hard to translate, yet much of Montale's tradition is nonetheless ours, even by this "distant northern sea." The final lines of "Mediterranean Sea," for example, draw deeply in our shared understanding of Dante and of the Greek philosophers, with an unmistakeable echo of Giordano Bruno ("What though the longed-for end be never reached, and the heart consume itself utterly in the violence of its striving? It is enough that it burn nobly!") Gathered with these is the burning bush of the Old Testament, the candle of the New Testament, and the ancient idea of the soul as immortal fire. Such poetry sets itself as part of the great conversation among its contemporaries—one thinks of the fires of "Le Cimetière marin" and of "The Waste Land."

There is, interestingly, one similarity between the poetry of Marie-Claire Blais and Eugenio Montale: both poets use as essential stance the attraction of and their rejection of (or partial rejection of) "swoon." The Blais swoon is towards the unthinking submission of sexual tenderness and dreamy eroticism; the rejection is only partial, vague. The Montale swoon is towards the inhuman realities of nature: sun, sea, unhuman life—the rejection somewhat firmer. But both poets speak of feeling the appeal of the swoon as a drawing-away from the human relations of the political or domestic community, and also as a drawing-away from the most individual or strong aspects of the poetic personality. In both, the swoon is towards death, whether it be towards the death-in-life of erotic dream, or the life-in-death of temporal flow.

Montale is very much a poet of what can perhaps be best called a non-metaphysical mysticism: i.e., there is no deity, but the larger whole towards which ephemeral life moves has something of the divine and annihilating glory for which "sea" and "sun" can be only metaphor. Nature in Montale is primarily a nature of the large cyclical forces, of time and weather; he has little of Jeffers's emphasis on the fierce beauty of the animal or avian world. Indeed, for Montale, the seahawk, because it does not arrest its dive (its swoon to death), is inferior to man who, thinking, can resist ("Bones of "Cuttlefish," 31). Jeffers' seahawk, being purer, less corrupt than man, would be nobler— and would not be "drawn in" by the heat to a drowning plunge anyway. (I feel the need to ask a naturalist about seahawks, heat, etc., but the matter may not be pertinent to either poet's vision.)

In general, Montale's speaker makes little of human relationships, or, as in "Portovenere," writes as kindly and perhaps elderly-bachelor friendly with an Alice-like child. Romantic or sexual love is absent. In "Falsetto," a youth, Esterina, is seen as combining the vigour of both female and male; she is a diver, a strong plunger into (but not drowner in) the deep, a conqueror of the potentially engulfing element. She is a type of the soul, the feminine as psyche, Diana, virgin huntress: a type of female unimaginable to the Blais consciousness, but for Montale a figure of human mental energy, the quint-essential fire of the body. If Blais's often erotic poetry seems almost mindless, Montale's poetry seems almost incorporeal. Yet Blais's corporeality is curiously abstract, almost dirtless. Montale convinces one of the corporeality of his world, of the reality of his dirt—although it is not his poetic speaker who will be doing the washing up.

Montale's great strength is his taking of a commonplace circumstance and, in representing it freshly, expanding its nuance of meaningful sugges-tion—rather like building a cathedral from a grain of sand. For example, from "Portovenere," page 49:

> The pulley of the well squeaks,
> the water rises up to the light and merges with it.
> A memory trembles in the brimming pail,
> in the pure circle an image is laughing.
> I approach my face to vanishing lips:
> the past grows deformed, it becomes old,
> it belongs to somebody else ...
>   Oh how already the wheel
> is creaking, taking you back to the black bottom;
> vision, by a distance we are kept apart.

Water and light merge with memory and margin. They well up from the ripple (distortion) of cyclical change (time, history, loss of memory) and of the loss of the ownership of the memory. And vision becomes re-understood as that which can be lost, and that which can, itself, separate.

This image occurs in a long poem dealing with the problems of loss and detachment from reality, about naming (or word-using) as representing such a detachment, about the thinness and fragility of happiness, vision, and memory, about the death of the instant, the approaching void (and the sinking black water) and about the storm of life, and about the future, moored as a cold landscape in fact, and still flowing. I am reminded of MacLeish's "Einstein," a poem that also reflects on the relativities of time and self-awareness.

The fashion that has moved us away from philosophical poetry and towards the sometimes trivial word games of the poet-philosophers has lost for us the majesty of serious poetry, has blunted our ear for the "sublime," which depends not merely upon a poet's ear, but also upon his or her depth of intelligence. I welcome the translation of Montale as perhaps indicating a return of interest in this sort of poetry. It has never been more pertinent.

I have in the past been powerfully moved by what little Montale I could read in anthologies. This magnificent collection, so beautifully translated, is a book I shall be reading with pleasure and gratitude for many years to come. It belongs in any serious reader's collection.

---

from *The Fiddlehead* (Summer 1985)

WORKS CITED

Veiled Countries/Lives. Trans. Michael Harris, Vehicule Press, 1984.
The Bones of Cuttlefish. Trans. Antonino Mazza, Mosaic Press, 1983.

Heart on Fist: Three Translations. A Review of Anne Hébert's *Selected Poems*, Knut Ødegård's *Bee-Buzz, Salmon Leap*, and Tarjei Vesaas's *Selected Poems*

Translation is necessarily simplification. We cannot transplant without breaking roots. Similarly many associations are necessarily lost when a meaning is plucked out of one verbal context and carried over into another language. But, even granted the simplifications inevitable to their labours, these translators, Poulin, Johnston, and Barnett, have done excellent work in conveying to us as much as possible something of the excellence of the originals. Hébert and Vesaas are major writers. Ødegård is younger; this brief selection suggests he may have considerable merit. All three books enlarge our lives. I had known of Hébert's excellence before, and I hope Poulin's work will make her writing more influential in English-speaking Canada. The Norwegian poets are new to me, and I find the discovery of Vesaas as exciting as my earlier encounters with Montale, Quasimodo, Neruda.

All three poets, Hébert, Ødegård, and Vesaas, write direct, uncomplicated syntax, and can thus be translated into straightforward sentences. Neither Poulin nor Barnett tries to imitate or to make up for the music of the original. George Johnston, however, has found in Ødegård's material (and possibly in Ødegård's style, although we can not judge, since the Nynorsk originals are not given) a marked parallel to a body of literature we know in English. The references to Nordic gods and Roman Catholicism, priests, seas, poverties, Mary, and whiskey, along with the glowing reveries of rural, green, and rainy weather are pure Celtic. Johnston uses a British vocabulary ("byre," "oxen," "kiosk") and the rhythm of Ireland. The most marvellously Irish of all are from Ødegård's "October, Orkney" sequence, which suggests the possibility that Johnston is quite right in showing the Norwegian's Irish hand:

> At last the tires shrieked high among cobbles and crooked
> streets of Stromness. The poet was awake and I
> pulled the cork: "I sit and call folk up
> from the grave," said he, "from the quiet churchyard:
> Andrew, I call, who was married
> to eight dry women and buried seven and then
> had his eyes closed at last by cold

girl fingers. Jeems, I call you, you
who flew over our five islands and fiddled dead drunk
with you [sic] bow over every last heart for weddings,
burials and births. And on Winterbride
I call, who put on her black shawl
when they came and said, "A wave took your beloved,
Jock" and forth she went with a fish-knife; Lay and washed
in the same waves, the black bride flung herself from cliff-side
into white waves at night. Did she
strike knife and its fishguts into her heart as she fell? I
call on you, cry you out of your graves!"
said George. "And on you all with Biblefingers
and fish blood in your beards under stones here
in Stromness!"

Even where Ødegård is not inventing an Irish poet he still sounds Celtic:

The big cows come swaying
out from my childhood with full udders, spread-legged
planting hoofs firmly in the greenness. Graze a little
at grass tufts and gaze at me with their wise eyes ...

But my childhood cows are dead, gone to the skies
to their cow heaven ...

                                    ("Cows and Turtles")

This is lovely stuff, and reads aloud much better than the prosy translations of Hébert and Vesaas. Johnston has in no way shortchanged his author. But the material—like the sound—is very familiar! No harm in that. Some things we like to have lots of.

The poetry of Anne Hébert is less familiar. The sonorities of her French do not exist in our language, and her crowded, wrenched, and often grotesque imagery is not common in our verse. Poulin makes no attempt to create a poetic imitation, preferring accuracy and logical clarity to eloquence. Indeed, he sometimes goes out of his way to change the elegant order of Hébert's rhetoric towards a more pedestrian sound, as in his translation of "Les offensés":

Par ordre de famine les indigents furent alignés
Par ordre de colère les séditieux furent examinés
Par ordre de bonne conscience les maîtres furent jugés
Par ordre d'offense les humiliés furent questionnés
Par ordre de blessure les crucifiés furent considérés

which he renders:

The poor were lined up in famine's order
The seditious were examined in anger's order
The masters were judged in good conscience's order
The humiliated were interrogated in offense's order
The crucified were considered in mutilation's order

At times Poulin does not seem to consider the particular associations of the English word; for example, "dreadful" does not work for the conclusion of "Small Towns," in which he translates:

Comprends-tu bien le présent redoubtable?
Je te donne d'étranges petites villes tristes,
Pour le songe.

by

Do you really understand this dreadful gift?
I give you strange small towns
for dreams.

But it is possible that one could wrestle for years and still not get those strange little towns into English. To what extent do they depend on Catholicism and rural Quebec winters? (Is perhaps "small town" too English? Too instantly provided with Protestants? Preachers instead of priests?) When reading Hébert I am always aware that her ancestors are not mine. The imagery, especially those clustering around female sexuality, psychic restriction, and the ancestral passions, are exotic, and, as such, seem not merely exotic but even alien when reproduced in the language rhythms of us anglophones, who mostly write as if with our hands in our pockets and our exhalations clipped.

But perhaps we have not wanted to look where she is telling us to look. We have not placed our hearts on our fists; we have not descended to our "dead kings." In fact, most Canadian poets and readers seem to have abandoned the visions of High Modernism before High Modernism took root in our culture. The shuddery dawn achieved at the conclusion of "The Tomb of Kings" is not for those who did not descend to their inner darknesses, "heart on fist." Belief in the existence of a root of being that poetry may explore is impossible for some. For Hébert, however, poetry must enter, and come out from, our inwardest being.

In her essay, "Poetry: Solitude Broken," Hébert warns against letting our fears and inhibitions keep us from that adventure. Poetry, she urges, must work "at the heart of the first six days of the world, in the tumult of undivided earth and water, in the struggle of life searching for its sustenance and name." In this generation, where unadventurous and unimpassioned writing is praised, Hébert still reminds us of what poetry can be.

The expressive sonorities of Hébert's tonalities are muted in Poulin's English, but not the high colouring of her images. She writes as if, like Thoreau, she could only regret not writing "extravagantly" enough—as if what she calls the "salvation of all right words lived and expressed" requires the largest possible out-reaching. She writes within the tradition of French symbolism, which has always been more hospitable to a rapid succession of emotionally charged and highly coloured imagery that has been the bulk of symbolist poetry written in English. (And surrealism, English *or* French, is tepid in comparison.) Thus, even in translation, Hébert sounds foreign, exotic. Reading her might correct the miserliness of our anglophone imaginations.

And perhaps we should be grateful for the plainness of Poulin's translation, for it turns us towards her text, on the facing pages. There can be few greater aesthetic pleasures than that of speaking out loud the poetry of Anne Hébert.

Tarjei Vesaas, like Hébert, is a major poet of our century. I find his numinous simplicities and dark undercurrents at once new and familiar—what Edmund Wilson called the "shock of recognition." Vesaas is the master of understatement, more laconic, even, than Robert Frost. None of the poems reproduced speak of the effort of poetry-making as directly as Hébert, and his vision seems somewhat darker than hers, oppressed not by living in a new land or in strange, small towns or by the metaphors of a sexually concerned religion, but oppressed rather, one feels by the weight of life itself, by history.

Anthony Barnett translates Vesaas into the same de-rhythmed cadences that Poulin uses for Hébert, and with the same conscientious search for accuracy, but the effect is controlled by Vesaas's short, blunt lines and the simplicities of his structure and vocabulary. Of the hundred poems Barnett gives us, eight have with them the original Nynorsk (modern Norwegian), a language which, we are at once convinced, was designed for Vesaas. It reminds us of the strong rhythmed oar-beat of Anglo-Saxon, which we can no longer reproduce in contemporary English. English has become frilled out with extra syllables and tiny words. Halfway between the extended cadences of French and the hammer stress of Nynorsk, we can make the sound of neither.

So laconic is Vesaas that some of the shorter poems in this collection don't translate—i.e., carry over. Without the fullness of their cultural context, translated out of their phonetic, they fade. For me a poem such as "Ketil's Place" has vanished altogether. But most of Vesaas's poems, however plain their surface, carry across their meaning powerfully, even in translation, at a "little lower layer," as Ahab calls it:

Your still boat	(Din stille båt
harbours no name.	har ikkje namn.
Your still boat	Din stille båt
has no harbour.	har ikkje hamn.
Your hidden boat ashore	Din gøymde båt ved land.)

For this is no harbour—
The leaves shimmer on spring nights
over the waiting ready boat
strewing yellow and wet
onto its thwarts in October,
and no one has been here.

But there is a pulling here from endless
plains of sea,
where suns rise from the depths
and the wind blows towards the harbour beyond.
But this is no harbour either,

only a place with pulling and calling
from far wider plains,
heavier storms along the coast,
and a larger boat in the evening.

Your still boat
settles slowly.
Your hidden boat ashore.

("The Boat Ashore")

Such a poem could inspire book-length manuscripts. This boat that is "ready," and that yet sinks into its hidden non-harbour aware of the calls and menaces "from wider plains," coastal storms, and larger boats, is our secret self. The burden and effort of life colours all things. The Nynorsk can show, as the English does not, the importance of not giving in, the importance of "measure," of strength, of responsibility—all to be carried by stress and kinesthetic syntax. We feel as we recognize Vesaas's point. "Rowing, Rowing" scarcely translates the heft of the title "Det Ror Og Ror":

The day is over
—rowing, rowing.

The dark rock
darker than the evening,
leans over the water
with black folds:

A flattened face
with its mouth submerged.
No one knows everything.

Rowing, now rowing,
in circles,
because the rock is pulling.
Bewildered splash in the deep.
Broken creak in wood.
Bewildered faithful soul who rows

close to going under.
He is there too,
the other,
him in the folds of the rock,
in the blacker than black,
listening out ...

In "Live our Dream," Vesaas writes again of the death that accompanies us
before we die, and asks "To whom do we talk / when we stay quiet?" Vesaas's
poetic concerns rise not only from living close to the sea and to Nordic culture,
but also from his having experienced two world wars—experienced, not just
read about. He writes as one "acquainted with the night," in Frost's words.

Those uneasy with high seriousness, and with words that point beyond
the literal and the literary, may be uneasy with the poetry of Tarjei Vesaas.
Yet where we are most alive cannot be described by philosophers, defined by
critics, or lexigraphed. Poetry can speak beyond words, and can quicken our
sense of life, can touch our innermost being. What Ødegård, Hébert, and
Vesaas have in common is their belief in the "sublime," and the power to
recreate for us a sense of it. They tell us what life is like, what it *feels* like, the
truths only art can say:

We row our boat
in the black night.
We feel the sea is here.

How well we know
nothing as black
as the sea's depths.

So limitless
our abyss below.

And someone starts shouting names,
far out into the night, seeking reassurance,
but each and every name on earth is here
and answers in terror from the same boat.
We are all in the boat.

We row our skimpy boat.
Our only boat.
And the sea is sea.

("In the Boat," Vesaas)

from *The Fiddlehead* (Summer 1990)

WORKS CITED

Selected Poems. Anne Hébert, trans. A. Poulin, Jr. Stoddart, 1988.
Bee-Buzz, Salmon-Leap. Knut Ødegård, trans. George Johnston. Penumbra, 1988.
Selected Poems. Tarjei Vesaas, trans. Anthony Barnett. Allardyce, Barnett, 1988.

Death-in-Life/Life-in-Death: A Review of
Tomas Tranströmer's *For the Living and the Dead*

Don Coles's translation of Tranströmer's *For the Living and the Dead* is beautiful poetry. Coles's own verse has distinguished itself by its sensitivity to emotional nuance, its near-aching tonalities. Coles has a natural affinity for Tranströmer's work, what seems almost a Nordic sensibility: both superb poets respond to the ambiguous half-lights of our weathers, and both use similarly plain but deep-drawing language. And Coles knows how to use what Saxon heft remains in English to translate Tranströmer's Swedish. (Swedish is perhaps easier, for an English translator, than a more open-ended, multi-vowelled language such as Italian.) But the blunt *sound* of Tranströmer does not come over. It can't. Swedish has more end-stops than English; it uses more compound nouns than we can, and uses somewhat fewer weightless words and syllables. "The" is less common. Our colloquial language is, in comparison, more dilute, more relaxed. Compare, from "Madrigal," (48-9):

Jag har examen
från glömaskans universitet

to

I have an exam
at oblivion's university

or weigh, from the same poem, "tomhänt" against "empty-handed."

The translator also can not echo the sounds of the Swedish poetry to which Tranströmer may be making allusion (poetry in general builds on other poetry), nor can a translator expect to find a reader well-read in Swedish who could catch allusive images. I necessarily respond to this gorgeous poetry more thinly than would a well-read Swede. But the majority of Tranströmer's images have such broad resonances that we feel at home in his world. His "mork skög" (dark woods) reach further back than Dante, and remain immediate, present, in our experience, part of our own, inner landscape.

The tremendous power of these poems lies primarily in the associational groupings upon which Tranströmer insists, associations to which we do respond with a sense of recognition, but which confute our preferred diurnal attitudes. The poems of *For the Living and the Dead* seem to group all experienced phenomena under two rubrics, titles for which I will borrow from Coleridge (and, to a lesser extent, Arnold) for whom such perceptions were not alien: Death-in-Life, and Life-in-Death.

Examples of Death-in-Life are the numerous images of confinement, restriction, imprisonment, illness. A ship is confined in locks; an invalid in bed. A city is seen primarily as walls, stones, cement; its trampling crowds are seen as confined by labour, hardship, fanaticism; scarcely alive, ghosts of themselves (like the crowd in Eliot's *The Waste Land*). The soul itself seems like the dead, its sight, like a submarine's periscope, controlled by icy darkness below ("Flyers," 27) and by the wall that is:

> a part of yourself—
> you know that or you don't know it but it's like that for every body
> except small children. For them no wall.
>
> ("Vermeer," 37)

Wordsworth's "shades of the prison house" indeed!

> Earth-vault,
> Often, that's half my life.
>
> ("Yellowjacket," 55)

Again and again Tranströmer speaks of us as sick, as sick souls confined like Anderson's sick emperor, yearning for the free song of the wild nightingale:

> I was sick
> and it visited me. I didn't notice it then, but I do now.
>
> ("Nightingale in Badelunda," 15)

But the tremendous vitality of the nightingale's song, because it is part of natural process, goes hand in hand with death. Nature, with its wild bird song, its freedom, its daylit woods, its restoring springtimes, is associated with the death of our personal, artificial, individual selves. Repeatedly Tranströmer indicates that the seductions of Nature, its wholeness, its freedom, its absorbing beauty, is Life-in-Death.

> We who live are nails hammered down into society.
> One day we'll be freed from all of this.
> We'll know death's wind under our wings
> and grow milder and wilder than here.
>
> ("Flyers," 27)

The bedridden invalid of "Indoors is Endless" (31) "knocks vainly / on the iron-bound day ahead" and:

> And the deep's God cries out of the deep
> "Free me! Free yourself!"

Death also frees the captain dying "in a hospital in Cardiff" who:

> got to lie down at last
> and became the horizon.
>
> ("The Long Forgotten Captain," 9)

Death puts away our pain, and rejoins us to natural process, to the innocent, selfless Life-in-Death of the wild, inhuman world.

But Tranströmer refuses to make absolutes out of his associations. "How I loathe the expression 'a hundred percent!'" He mocks people who are sure, "who cannot see anything except from the front," who "never open the wrong door and get a glimpse of the Unidentified." ("Yellowjacket," 53). We don't have to die to open that door, to get a whiff of freedom. Sometimes, he asserts, even as adults, temporarily rinsed of the moment, fresh-handed, we can lose ourselves to the thoughtless happiness of Nature. Nothing's cleared up, he assures us, but the happiness, however brief, is real, really there. It happens, now and then. We can feel it too, experiencing Tranströmer's poetry:

> I inherited a dark wood where I seldom go. But there
> comes a day when the dead and the living change places.

Then the wood sets itself in motion. We are not without hope.
The worst crimes are not cleared up in spite of the assigning
of many policemen. In the same way somewhere in
our life is a great uncleared-up love. I inherited a dark
wood but today I'm going into another wood, the bright one.
Everything living sings stoops waves creeps.
It's spring and the air's potent. I have an exam
at oblivion's university and am just as empty-handed
as the shirt on the laundry-line.

("Madrigal," 49)

No wonder many believe Tomas Tranströmer to be the best poet writing today.
We are fortunate to have Coles translating his work for us.

---

from *The Fiddlehead* (Spring 1997)

WORKS CITED

For the Living and the Dead. Trans. Don Coles, Buschek, 1996.

Speech as Machination: A Review of Nicole Brossard's *Installations*

Since I have read only two of Brossard's books, and one of these without a translation as trot, I cannot claim authoritatively that Brossard is a major poet, though this might be so. What I can say is that this superb translation of Brossard's *Installations* by Mouré and Majzels is, for me, a major piece of writing, which rewards in-depth rereading.

At first glance, *Installations* seems a collection of brief, compacted utterances, longer than haiku, less narrative than *lieder*, minimalist in appearance. (Indeed, many of these poems would be superb as lieder: emotional, evocative, and sufficiently lucid so the words would not dissolve in music.) But the prismatic gestalt of the "installation," or collection, as a whole is more intellectual than that of a song cycle.

Brossard builds these poems upon the idea that the site of language—of both perception and communication—is the tongue (and with it, of course, the mouth). Even in English "tongue" can mean language, as does "langue" in French. But Brossard emphasizes that the tongue can perceive (taste, feel, probe), that it can shape (whether licking an ice-cream or smearing paint), that it can stroke and caress. The vehicle of speech can hold, bite, kiss. By mouth we receive nourishment; from mouth, information. And, Brossard reminds us, women's genitals can be figured as tongue, mouth, reception, perception, embrace. Woman's mouthy genitals, her sexually responsive tongue, her *langue*, are, says Brossard, the *origyne*: originating, oral, the site of creation:

> I think of it out loud high fever
> a succession of mirrors and senses
> for plunging into matter and questions
> clandestine in dimension and intimate in exception
> memory emerges stirred up by the origyne
> the mouth demonstrative

("Private Parts," 38)

Brossard asserts a connection between sexual energy and the imagination, for it is the erotic imagination that perceives, relishes, speaks, holds onto, and works out our place in the universe:

> because it is with the mouth
> speech is an ultimate machination
> around the belly
>
> a flux of tenderness and fear
> that makes unfathomable the verb to be
> recto verso speech licks all
>
> ("Tongue," 29)

The excellence of the Mouré-Majzels translation shows in their Brossardian puns: "machination" for the French "manège," thus allowing an echo of the French "mâcher," to chew, and "licks," which allows "lécher" its cry of supremacy, while reminding us, with Brossard, that speech is a form of perception. The translation is almost richer than the original, but it does not betray the original. The point is what a tongue can do, and, as its ultimate machination, poetry.

Poetry, because it is speech at its most perceptive, is described by Brossard as involving some degree of frightening intensity: intoxication, panic, high fever, a "flux of tenderness and fear." We can't always live like that; sometimes we need prose.

> we need prose where it belongs
> to keep the body warm, fulfill
> minimally the I and others like it
> without neurons darkening
> intoxicated with what's lived and constant panic
>
> ("Tabloid," 124)

But, Brossard points out, the panic-filled intoxication of perception and desire at their most acute is our life at its most intense, most imagined, most expressed, most valuable. In "juin la fièvre" (from *Amantes*), Brossard writes that "le cerveau produit ses drogues qui sont nos utopies." We think up our

intoxicating utopias, our myths, our imaginary eternities. Says Brossard, in
"Eternity" (14), "all forms of eternity have been / invented." This is the great
power of poetry, not that it is durable, but that by it:

> I think we can
> remake the source of rapture
> the universe is so slow
> and we have the ambition of mortals
> to live a long while every afternoon
>
> ("Terrace," 116)

Brossard's affirmation of the pleasure life has for us, for all its mixtures of
fears and panics, and her confidence in the shaping imagination, the speech
of desire, the *langue*, are wonderfully exhilarating:

> every morning I take an interest in life
> huge detours and proofs
> the tail end of century as the heart of language
>
> icons, silks, often manuscripts,
> the odd-numbered body of women
> great quakes
> visible from afar
> I settle into my body's installation
> so as to be able to respond
> when a woman gives me a sign
>
> ("Installations," 49)

The French, "je m'installe dans mon corps," is well translated by Mouré and
Majzels's choice of "Settle," because the English "install" is too redolent of
metal tools. "Settle" has a ring of choice and comfort. But we want here also
the idea of the artist's installation: the display, the physical manifestations
of a shaping imagination, of invention, of the myths we desire and make.
The impulse is love, the goal, for the poet as for the lover, must be response.
How could the poet respond without a body, a mouth? Brossard beautifully
describes what, as a poet, she does:

I play energy against death
with a woman's musical mouth
on the mythical side of desire

("Continuity," 107)

---

from *The Fiddlehead* (Autumn 2001)

WORKS CITED

Installations. Trans. Erin Mouré and Robert Majzels. The Muses Company, 2000.

Deep Time: A Review of Hélène Dorion's *No End to the World*

No End to the World by Hélène Dorion is a profound, and, as translated by Daniel Sloate, beautiful book composed of two long poetic sequences: the title poem and "The Walls of the Cavern." Both sections are philosophical and deal with the questions about our relation to life that a computer can not answer.

"No End to the World" is primarily concerned with the problems of "definition"—the extent to which any noun is defined primarily by what it is not, the degree to which nothing can be defined "purely." "The Walls of the Cavern" is more concerned with our sense of place as physical as well as spiritual bodies within a very contemporary understanding of the geophysical/astrophysical movement of time/space. Both poem sequences are about the soul, but not about the individual. Dorion emphasizes that we are travellers in common, sojourners, pilgrims:

> Fathers, mothers, brothers and sisters walking
> along the same paths of distress
>
> ("Walls," 98)

But for her, there is no one strait path. Her assertion is more Zen, more existentialist:

> There is no path;
> the quest we are on
> lies in each thing we approach
> in each moment that releases its brightness.
>
> ("Walls," 130)

The Romantics' belief that poetry can and should cope with the largest imaginable philosophical subjects has lasted longer, it sometimes seems to me, in French poetry (including the Acadian and the Québécois) than it has in English. When I think of poems on Huge Philosophical subjects in English, I think of poems by Pound, Williams, etc., built up out of thousands of small bits and pieces, like monumental mosaics. Dorion does not use the tessera approach; she keeps her *gravitas* and her focus large, and yet without vapid generalization. Furthermore, her lines tend to be short—not for her the expansive lines of Hugo, Claudel, Saint-John Perse. Instead, her lines have such brief, evocative simplicity that they seem close to the effect intended by the Japanese and Chinese haiku (as opposed to the haiku in English, which is, because of the nature of our language, necessarily less resonant).

Dorion's work reminds me variously of William James's *The Varieties of Religious Experience*, and of some of the teachings of Buddhism, Taoism, and, at times, even of Baha'i and Christian mysticism. I know of few contemporary poets who can write so vividly about the sense of mystical presence without reference to the specificities or religious myth.

> Where is beauty
> untouched by absence?
>
> ("No End," 8)

The poet assumes that we do sense ourselves as living souls aware of a larger context which sometimes seems also to be seeking us, or to be realizing itself through us, or within us. From the title section:

> My steps begin in other steps
> like islands offered to the infinity
> that lies within us
>
> (31)

> There is no beginning.
> Love, silence, light
> have been here forever.

> The beginning has been within us
> forever.
>
> (67)

> Was a soul offered to the world
> through us?
>
> (27)

None of our perceptions are distinct from their flexibly indefinable opposite. "Edge," "end," "God," "other," etc., are all processes in which we are enmeshed, for Dorion time itself is, as the Lord's Prayer concludes, without end:

> Counted in vain, time travels
> from one atom to the next, passes through
> then closes the garden gate.
>
> Suddenly I fall, the way a bird
> falls into the perfect chaos of the world
> —exact measure and cadence of the dance.
>
> I have been that mass of atoms and broken threads
> since the beginning of time
> with my steps the universe pulses: fire, stones, dust
> —through them I know God.
>
> ("Wall," 125)

No End to the World is a hymn and a contemplative prayer for this modern and secular age. Dorion may be one of our finest religious poets, and her work should be better known. I would like to read this poetry in the original French, and I must order the earlier translation, by Agnes Moorhead, in 1995, also by Guernica, *The Edges of Light*. Her present translator, Daniel Sloate, has a fine feeling for English cadence, and his own book, *Dissonances and Shadows*, (Guernica, 2001), should be worth looking up.

---

from *The Fiddlehead* (Winter 2007)

WORKS CITED

No End to the World. Trans. Daniel Sloate, Guernica, 2004.

Identifying Greatness: A Review of Nichita Stănescu's
Occupational Sickness

Stănescu, who was nominated for the Nobel Prize in 1973, may have been one of the best poets of the last century, but English-speaking nations, North Americans in particular, have paid very little attention to the poetry of Eastern Europe, nor do we respect or encourage translations as much as we might. The excellent 1977 collection *Modern Romanian Poetry*, edited by Nicholas Catanoy, and translated by several excellent Canadian poets, first drew my attention to the importance and beauty of Romanian poetry, but, since it only included one of Stănescu's poems (quite lovely), I had no sense of his complexity or general poetic stance. Avasilichioaei has translated forty-one of his poems into a very lucid and ear-perfect English, and conveys Stănescu's penchant for brevity and simplicity, as well as the considerable tenderness of his love poems.

Romanian's Latin roots make it less opaque to the anglophone reader, than, say, Finnish or Navajo, and we must be grateful to Avasilichioaei for including the Romanian original. But since I am not able to read Romanian, nor knowledgeable about Romanian poetic traditions, I can not base my claim on language, nor would it be intelligent of me to base the claim merely on his nomination to the Nobel Prize. (After all, didn't Pearl Buck get it?) How can anyone judge the greatness of a poet on a translation? Well, if the greatness of the poet is almost entirely based on his use of language (as, say, Tennyson), I don't think we can.

But Stănescu certainly has one of the identifying characteristics of greatness: an imagination which creates for us new and powerful cluster-associations of meaning/image/metaphor/symbol.

I am not happy with any of the terms for what Stănescu does. "Image" for me always has to be visual, and not all imagery is particularly meaningful or "symbolic." (The best image-maker in our language is probably Marianne Moore, but most of her imagery can only be read as literal description.) "Metaphor" tends to be used for saying one thing in terms of another; "metaphor" does not suggest a grouping of meanings. For those of us to whom "symbol" does not only mean "sign" (like "&" for "and"), "symbol" nods towards those culturally traditional, possibly archetypal cluster-associations of meaning that we inherit. For example: the rose as vagina (and thus by association the Magna Mater, Mother of God, Sexuality and thus, in our cultural tradition, Sin, and, as well, the brevity of youth, life, joy, etc.).

But the great writers can, by poetic invention, represent meanings we did not have accessible to us before their inventions, but that we recognize as containing truth. Consider these three:

1. Sir John Falstaff
2. "luxe, calme, et volupté"
3. Celan's "black milk of daybreak"

It is absurd to call Sir John an image, a metaphor, or a symbol. The meaning of the French can not be said in English, and the phrase is no image, not a metaphor, and not really a "symbol." The "black milk of daybreak" has recently become a powerful reference to the Holocaust experience, no culturally traditional representation or allusion; it is Celan's gift. Each of these three things carries a weight of associated meanings, and, whatever terms are applied to them, they are, essentially, the same sort of thing: the perception and invention that is the mark of poetic genius.

Stănescu has just that ability to represent complex meaning in brief terms and in a unique and memorable manner. I have no room to do him justice. But I would like to mention three examples from *Occupational Sickness*, and to begin by talking about one of the most shocking: his redefinition of the word "soldier." Not the "image," the thing.

Stănescu writes of a world for which war is the normal condition. When a woman gives birth, she gives birth to a soldier. Every child is born a soldier. In "My mother and her soldier," we understand that mother was wrong when she screamed "painfully birthing me; / life isn't made for killing / life isn't made for killing!" But the baby, the "stifled soldier said":

"What blood and no bullet
so much blood
and what smells, what screams
a woman makes when giving birth"
this, the stifled soldier said

hurling his gun
at a butterfly …

(33)

The title of Avasilichioaei's selection comes from the short poem "Longing for man" (51) in which the Creator admits that in making man, He made man a sword; the sick-making occupation is God's. The child is born a soldier. The child is, of course, also a poet (and demi-creator). But, primarily, the poet, the child, the man, is a soldier. Cannon fodder.

And what is it to be born a soldier? It is to be not fully human, but "horse." In "Giving up the hearth," a child interrogates a sleeping soldier:

> "What are you dreaming of?" the child asked
> the sleeping soldier.
> "A horse, a horse, a horse, a horse,
> a horse, a horse, a horse, a horse."

(25)

The soldier never wakes. Whatever the child asks, the soldier mindlessly responds, "a horse." In Romanian his response (the repetition of "un cal") sounds like coughing; as if the response were unmediated, involuntary:

> —Acum ce visezi, l-a întrebat copilul
> pe soldatul adormit
> —Un cal, un cal, un cal, un cal,—
> un cal, un cal, un cal, un cal.

(24)

What is to be born a soldier? It is to be born vulnerable, mortal, dangerous— and not in command. The horse may be a means of survival, and represents animal strength. Like the soldier, it will do what it can to survive, instinctively, brutally. The soldier without a horse can't move as fast. But neither horse nor soldier is shown as thinking, or as in "control." They are not victorious, not in Stănescu's poetry. Here there is no Flanders Field sentimentality, or "take up the torch" bit. There is no "torch," no "cause," in these poems. War is just there. Stănescu's "horse" reminds me of Picasso's, as in "Guernica," a suffering monster. The soldiers and the horses just get killed. In "Soldiers in bas-relief" (53), the young soldiers in the window case sit "as they were found, shot through the brow." In "Sleep full of saws" (57), "Everywhere, / blood of headless horses / flows at will." To be born a soldier is to die as one. And everyone, the poet, too, is born a soldier, in a world at war.

In "I fear," the poet addresses his mother,

> I fear even you
> that you will leave me with no army.
> Heavy, I dismount and on the field sink
> in time with time the idiot
> who wipes my bleeding nostril
> hurls me toward Olympus.
> I fear I was born
> half horse, half babe.
> Mother, I fear words!
> when rays of stars give me drink.
>
> (31)

The human, half horse, half babe, is, whatever else, also a soldier. (Even in the comic poem "The poet like the soldier" (107), the two are conflated: neither "has a private life," and both, in order to survive, will steal and lie. Both, too, are dangerous to mess with.) Why has this happened? The answer comes from the angel of death:

> "Why?" I yelled. "Why?"
> "For no reason," the angel said
>
> ("Psyche," 29)

A second powerful complex of associations in Stănescu's poetry is the wing and the stone, especially the stone wing, with which, of course, you can't fly. Wings, stones, (and stone walls), are all continually related to the act of poetry writing, and to powerlessness. "Transparent Wings" is the longest and fullest elaboration of this complex of ideas. Here the "bird king" can't fly because he has no wings. He is impotent, insane, "unborn." (No winged horse, no poetic Pegasus. The "bird king," too, must dream "horse"?) Stone wings don't fly well, flap "faintly."

Stone is also what the poet is working on or against. Again and again in Stănescu's poetry "stone" is represented as both text and barrier. In "Transparent Wings," stone is not just text but also context; the barrier is the egg of possibility. The wingless "bird king" is not only the poet, he is also the possible Creator (see "Longing for man," above). Stoniness declares both potentiality and impotence. Where the past no longer exists and the future can not be imagined, can be read, I suppose, as now. But all this could be read as before the Big Bang. Or as a sad theology. Or more simply as a "poetics":

Here in stone where all is severe,
where time can be stroked,
where the past is nonexistent,
where the future is unimaginable,
lies the hall of the throne.
Here lives the bird king—
blind, mute.

Lame, deaf
ravenous, parched.
Unmoved, he's unborn.
Insane, unwise,
         unhappy.
unprotected, he's unborn.
…
Stones flap their wings the faintest.

Stones hold within them the bird king.
Stones fly standing still.
…
The bird king is inside.
Inside the bird king
are birds,
inside birds are their guts and mouths
in the birds' wattles are seeds.
Whoever wants to sow seeds
must first break stones.
…
Stones flap their wings the faintest—
inside them is the bird king—

The bird king sits on an egg-shaped throne.
The very world we live on.
The bird king is hatching it.

(79-81)

The "bird king" is perhaps the most complex of Stănescu's symbolic images. But perhaps the most powerful of all is the simplest, an image that needs no comment.

I am nothing but
a stain of blood
that talks.

("Self Portrait," 103)

From *The Fiddlehead* (Summer 2010)

WORKS CITED

Occupational Sickness. Trans. by Oana Avasilichioaei, Buschek Books, 2006.

Seul on est: A Review of Serge Patrice Thibodeau's *One*

Jo-Anne Elder's translation of the internationally acclaimed Acadian writer Serge Patrice Thibodeau's *Seul on est*, which won the Governor General's Award in 2007, is a must-have book for anyone who loves poetry but is uncertain of his or her French.

One (title abbreviated from the original, *Seul on est*) introduces itself with a quotation from Paul Valéry:

> Total embrace of the good and the better, struggle that swells,
> Mixing alone, one returns, alone, one rises
> Alone one thinks no more, alone one has will, alone one is.
>
> (*Cahiers/Notebooks 2*, translated by Stephen Romer)

Whether or not we accept Valéry's sentiments, we do not ask ourselves what "alone one is" might mean. Is one most entirely oneself when alone? Certainly most writers, thinkers, artists, contemplatives value the intensities of solitary meditation. Solitude assists concentration. Also perhaps true, when alone, do not we dissolve more readily into the general, become "one" with the universe? The religious tell us that God is with us when we feel most alone. And, as we are daily reminded, in the news and art (see *Everyman*), we are born, suffer, and die—alone. What do we mean by "alone"? The contemplative's chosen solitude is very different from the starkness of aloneness.

On the basis of Thibodeau's poems in this collection, there is no One with one when one is alone. The poet is translated as referring occasionally to "the good," which might mean virtue or comfort or beauty, and sometimes refers to "mystery" (the existence of which even materialists and atheists accept), but not to the "divine." However Thibodeau has introduced other of his collections with epigraphs from the Sufi masters, and readers who come to One with an awareness of Thibodeau's previous writings may find this collection less secular than I do (see Émile J. Talbot, "Serge Patrice Thibodeau and the Sufi Encounter," *Studies in Canadian Literature*, 31.2. 2006).

One is poetry that "goes with the flow," it engages us with the cyclical and recurrent movement of the river, the Petitcodiac, with the ocean, with seasons and dawns. The formal shaping of the collection is not linear or narrative, but repetitive, circular:

> everything repeating and rebounding
> —tirelessly—
> in the circle of mystery,
> mad with the most precious complicity.
>
> (17)

The intensity of "is-ness" in these poems tends to erase the individual, affirm the general. Thibodeau's oneness seems to be with nature and time, rather than with community or with spirit. Although the poems are sensually beautiful as writing, they are curiously impersonal. These poems celebrate weather, travel, return, roots and uprooting, and, in particular the immortality and brevity of dawn. They remind us that "dawn does not grow old" (53).

In the first half of *One*, Thibodeau's stanza form, as reproduced by Elder, seems to imitate the effect of the *mascaret*, "the tidal bore, or little ridge of water that, as the tide comes in, runs up river across the water, even as the river continues to flow." All the poems in the book are divided into two stanzas, and in the first half of the book the first stanzas demonstrate the long flowing lines of the river, while the third stanza, with much shorter lines, seems to represent the *mascaret*, the apparent turning back of the water:

> The snow falls without ceasing; behind all the white, the sun
> dazzles one again as if for the first time, as if time is moving backwards,
> so that one's gaze surrenders to its exquisite majesty; time catches the light,
> the shape of the house across the street has shifted, windows keep watch;
>
> > the tree, motionless
> > a mountain ash,
> > —a white sound hides within—
> > and encircled above,
> > Cygnus, the constellation of the swan.
> >
> > (26)

Although Thibodeau's poems are, in a sense, nature poems, they are not walking poems, in the sense that McKay's, Bartlett's, or Frost's often are: there is no sense of things come suddenly upon in the process of a walk, nor is there any sense of something being looked for, on the walk. There is little biological detail. Nevertheless, the joyous serenity of the poems and the gentle pace of the stanza form do give a sense of "spirituality" in the contemporary sense of the noun (which means, as far as I know, not crass, not commercial, not uncongenial—with some stress on nonmaterial, indefinable values, such as "beauty" or "the good" and, with this, a sense of unity or wholeness with nature).

> Everything connects, nothing keeps the dispersed bodies from reuniting,
> earth is left a legacy of love for the exquisite, even if one is reborn alone;
> at night, especially, knowing that sight stretches out, alone, from within,
> going back over one's steps, musky leaf-mould along the shore,
>
>> making a bed in its own nest,
>> underbrush, undersea, undergrowth,
>> —at night, one can see nothing but the whole—
>> for as long as it takes to gather
>> goodness.
>>
>> (15)

Gathering "goodness" here is not arduous. Indeed, the book is very comfortable. "Goodness" seems to be more aesthetic than ethic. In the forty-three double-stanza poems in the collection, there are only four references to ethical questions: two brief references to Acadian historical grievances:

> to the island that holds the horizon
> —against the current of the Deportation—
> high on the cliff ...
>
> (14)

and:

> Who stole the horses? Who savaged the land? Who burned down the barns?
> No matter, those brash enough to raise their heads received the brand

of history; now, the silhouette
of a god so fictive and naïve
—set to the chants of formless winds—
emerges, brazen-faced, from the fog,
frightened by its own reflection.

(20)

The third example leaves the poetic speaker very comfortable, but the reader unconvinced:

Here, the ice brings a memory to the tip of its tongue, chestnuts roasting
on charcoal in Barcelona, on Las Ramblas, in front of a bookstore,
a few euros in a pocket, a hunched-over woman given a yogurt,
a baguette, a piece of cheese and a coffee; thank you, she says

to the stranger
and she walks off
—anything but indifferent—
without a worry
about her next meal.

(23)

The "goodness" of this strikes me as bourgeois complacency. The last example of the unparadisiac refers to the general, sinful nature of humankind rather than to any specific occurrence, and fails to resemble any imaginable reality. (The stripes and the yellow eyes seem particularly unhelpful.)

It is said: man is born to betray his own,
to sign the confession of his acts, to contemplate nothingness,
his unique creation, another way to stick out his tongue, kneeling,
black stripes knotted around his neck, a serpent in his fist,

eyes thick with yellow,
mouth ready to utter the last judgement,
—soul stranded on the sandy floor of the arena—
weapon aimed and ready when the time comes
to fire on his neighbour.

(35)

Yet "goodness" does exist, and Thibodeau's best poems, recreating beauty for us, and demonstrating the health of serenity, and of a faith in beginnings and "world without end," in the immortality of dawn, and in the value of contemplating wholeness, rather than nothingness are, as celebrations, well worth celebrating.

---

from *The Fiddlehead* (Spring 2010)

WORKS CITED

One. Trans. Jo-Anne Elder, Goose Lane, 2009.

FIVE:

Widowers and Orphans

Review of Robert Frost's *In the Clearing*

The reviewer of Frost's latest book is tempted to treat it as an epilogue to the *Complete Poems*, and is, accordingly, tempted to review the *Complete Poems* as well as *In the Clearing*. We haven't the space here for so heroic an attempt. Frost has been publishing excellent poetry for over sixty years; his latest poetry is no exception. The urbane (though not urban) verse of *In the Clearing* stands easily among the best poetry written these last few years. Perhaps, as Landor and Frost both illustrate, an urbane muse serves poets longer than a more impassioned one. Frost told his friend Sidney Cox that he "almost never experienced ecstasy"; perhaps consequently, the tenor of his poetry is limited. Frost is not one of our most widely perceptive poets, nor one of our best educated; his well-known suspicion of and distaste for systematic thought limits his understanding (as do his interests). Nevertheless, where Frost most interests himself, first, in the complex, deeply felt ambiguities and profundities of the relations between man and inhuman nature, and between one human being and another, and second, in the music of actual speech, in turn of phrase, nuance, tone of voice, few poets of this century have matched him.

In the Clearing presents no novelties to Frostians. Not since *New Hampshire* (1923) has Frost given us realistic dramatic monologues or dialogues. Moreover, in recent years his nature lyrics have been increasingly accompanied by poems that play with ideas unaccompanied by natural analogy. But even Frost's first book, *A Boy's Will* (1913), contained poems that express the same thoughts about the soul, God, or science that Frost has entertained in his most recent poetry. And *In the Clearing* contains poems, such as "Closed for Good," "Pod of the Milkweed," and the Robinsonian "Ends," which show the same sensitivity to nature and to the relations between men and women we see in *A Boy's Will*. Nor are the few weaknesses of *In the Clearing* new—with the exception of the surprising verbal infelicity of the first two stanzas of the otherwise excellence "Away!" These weaknesses are: Frost's whimsy (if you don't like it), the occasionally uncharming mixture of coy witticism and national sermonizing (as in "How Hard It Is To Keep From Being King When It's In You And In The Situation"), and the obverse side of his patriotism, a slight and infrequent tinge of contempt for foreign non-inheritors of the Western experiment (e.g., "The Bad Island—Easter," "Kitty Hawk").

Nevertheless, Frost's volumes of poetry are not very much of a piece. Each volume, in part designedly, has a very definite character of its own. Frost told Sidney Cox that when making a book of selecting poems for an anthology, he liked "to see how many poems I could find toward some one meaning it might seem absurd to have had in advance, but it would be all right to accept from fate after the fact." Not only does Frost select and arrange his poetry deliberately, but, in the past, as his bibliographers well know, he has not always printed every poem he had at his disposal. The character of *In the Clearing* does seem to be, in part, that of an epilogue to the *Complete Poems* in that it is, among other things, a commentary on and recapitulation of his ideas about life, thought, and human endeavour. *In the Clearing* contains fewer descriptions, less ambiguity, and more statements of belief than any previous book of Frost's, but, at that, Frost does not explain himself too much, nor has he lost his ability to doubt. His pithy:

> It takes all sorts of in and outdoor schooling
> To get adapted to my kind of fooling.

is both a plea not to get him wrong and a hint to the way in which he wishes his "tentatives not tenets" to be taken.

In spite of the many poems that blithely allude to the idea of God, *In the Clearing* is, as a whole, considerably less concerned with religion—theology, piety, search for extra-human justice, reason or mercy—than were the Masques. Frost here returns to the emphatic humanism of his earliest poetry. A man who offers tentatives can not properly be called either an agnostic or a believer; we ought not to feel we understand a poet only when we have made him spell out a creed. Frost has very little creed to communicate. He is, as a poet, what he is as a teacher: more concerned with educating our perception than with exploring a subject matter.

The title, *In the Clearing*, alludes to the little poem "The Pasture," which Frost prefaces to the *Complete Poems* as an invitation to his readers:

> I'm going out to clean the pasture spring;
> I'll only stop to rake the leaves away

(And wait to watch the water clear, I may):
I shan't be gone long.—You come too.

The third line appears as epigraph to *In the Clearing* and, with the dedication of these "letters" in verse to the reader, serves to make clear one of the general intentions of the book: we are invited to attend the poet as he makes a little clearing—our student-like presence is generally implied by the conversational tone of most of the poems. The first three poems and many of the later poems share, for all their differences, the common theme of human questioning, of our desire to make things clear. The prefatory excerpt from "Kitty Hawk" celebrates the splendour of our efforts; the superb last poem, "In Winter in the Woods Alone," balances the accounts: our efforts to clear against what needs to be cleared. Here, as it does throughout the volume, Frost's metaphor reminds us that a clearing is not the destruction of the forest:

I see for Nature no defeat
In one tree's overthrow
Or for myself in my retreat
For yet another blow.

Clearing, or making form (a partial "clarification of life," or a "momentary stay against confusion," as he calls it in his preface to the *Complete Poems*) has always been Frost's term for what poetry does; it has been, also, his term for all the constructive efforts of mankind. *In the Clearing* is, on the whole, a sort of hurrah for the human effort to clarify. If, as Frost reiterates, "confusion" can not be entirely vanquished, neither can man's spirit. As he quips in "Away":

And I may return
If dissatisfied
With what I learn
From having died.

---

from *The Fiddlehead* (Fall 1962)

WORKS CITED
In the Clearing. Holt, Rhinehart, and Winston, 1962.

Dream as History: Michael Ondaatje's *The Man with Seven Toes*

The poet who tackles a sizeable dramatic monologue makes a claim to artistic importance that the writer of short lyrics or unambitious anecdotes does not. Ondaatje's version of the dramatic monologue rarely uses direct speech, characterizing persons by their interior monologues rather than by their communications. The associative, dreamlike image for non-verbal states of mind comes less oddly to us, after Joyce, Eliot, and Lowell. We have learned to read a man through his sleep and through his madness. But although Ondaatje avoids dramatized-as-real speech, he also avoids ostensible dream material and the material of the characterized person's associative memory. In *The Man with Seven Toes*, we are neither *North of Boston* nor down under in Earwicker-land. Instead, as with Browning's Childe Roland, we are shown primarily the perceptual present of Ondaatje's characters: what they see and feel to be the real world. And it is their perceptions, more than their reflections, that characterize them.

The perceptive field of *The Man with Seven Toes* is intensely limited. Although a "narrator"-voice is sparingly used, it is uncharacterized, and appears more as something overheard by the chief character than as something perceiving. Rather as if the chief character dreamily saw herself in the third person. The ironic or satiric possibilities of the plot are deliberately omitted (as the historical note at the end of the poem head-clearingly underlines). The social histories of the poem's two characters are largely omitted, again focusing our attention not on things past or things hoped for, but upon the present, unintellectualized perception. By so doing, Ondaatje would have us consider that the parallels between our dreams and our histories are somewhat of our own making—that our history is to some extent the effect of our perceptions, our fears, and our behaviours—that we create the myths and circuses of our lives, that what comes to us in reality is, like our dreams, both beyond our control and created by us.

The Mrs. Fraser whose history suggested Ondaatje's fable was shipwrecked. But Ondaatje's unnamed heroine (for convenience here labeled Mrs. X) deliberately enters her nightmare: fainting with heat, she steps off a train into a fever-like desert, too tired to assert herself, or get back onto the train before it starts up again. We meet her already self-abandoned. At one level of suggestion the poem is a history of her illness; overtly, the poem is a history of the trouble she endured getting back to civilization; and at a third level, presumably intentional, the poem is her encounter with and her "escape" from her own sexual wilderness, her "shadow" self ("animus," "id," what have you).

As a history of sickness, the poem takes us from Mrs. X's initial feverish swoon, into a period of convulsions, back into a long, drawn-out fever, and finally, into a wakening release. Shortly after she loses consciousness in the heat of the desert, she enters a camp of aborigines where close-packed images of rape, goat-killing, yelling, dancing, drinking of blood (from fresh-slaughtered goats presented as analogous to the freshly raped Mrs. X) are all described through Mrs. X's perceptions as "throbbing," "thrumming," or "banging" within her. Even the food she eats is thought of as alive and as being as throbbingly sexually invasive as the savage's penis (although the food is also "like" her, the living, being eaten, victim). For Mrs. X, both swallowing and sexual intercourse involve something alien to her "alive" in her. On the level of the poem as a record of an illness, these sensations parallel the heightened sense of heartbeat, the throbbing nerves, and the nausea of a fever's delirious height. The savages are, likewise at this level, figures of a delirium, and her voiceless passivity towards them the stupor of sickness. After the delirium of the aborigines's camp the long trek city-ward is presented still as a passive struggling, a long enduring, "blood-warm" or hotter sweat, with painful hungers, nauseas and violent, ill-assuaged thirsts, and repeated swoons. The poem ends in images of cool wet, of rain, of rivers under calm ice, and in a dream lullaby of coolness, of sleep, of the city: hotel, cool bed, and civilized peoples.

But Ondaatje insists that the Australia of *The Man with Seven Toes* is as objectively real for his characters as Wessex is for Tess. Mrs. X steps off a real train, and joins real aborigines, who kindly feed her, excessively explore her, and exuberantly rape her. She meets an escaped convict named Potter, still wearing his striped prison shirt, who escorts her along the desert river back to the city. She appears to find this convict as wild, as exotic, as repelling but sexually fascinating as the aborigines. And she is glad to be rid of him. Say the townspeople, on finding the two:

Were found bathing in a river
like strange wild animals
sticking out of the water.
She when seeing us said
god has saved me.

There is no evidence before this that Mrs. X thinks or speaks of "god." Who saves her and keeps her alive, with considerable difficulty, is Potter (who got, we are given to suppose, some sexual re-compensation). Indeed, Mrs. X doesn't *think* at all. It is as if the poem is her dream and Potter, the title-hero, the chief figure of her dream. Ondaatje insists that Potter has a name and a pre-poem history (unlike Mrs. X). The insistence underlines the fact that Potter is not real for Mrs. X, and it is in her mind that we begin, endure, and conclude the poem.

The Man with Seven Toes presents not a dream so much as a history as a dream, as the creation of Mrs. X's obsessions. For when Mrs. X steps off the train, her state of soul is at once made clear and in it, both aborigines and convict are predicted:

When they stopped for water she got off
sat by the rails on the wrist thick stones.

The train shuddered, then wheeled away from her.
She too was too tired even to call.
Though, come back, she murmured to herself.
...
She woke and there was a dog
sitting on her shoulder
doing nothing, not even looking at her

but out over the land.
She lurched and it sauntered
feet away and licked its penis
as if some red flower in the desert.
She looked away but every-
    thing around her was empty.

That this common canine action should so strike her, and that she should feel her identity ignored, is appropriate to what is going to happen to her. She remains without name and almost without speech or ego until the end of the poem, where she seems to be recovering a token apprehension of herself through exploring her body with her hands, "sensing herself like a map."

The image of the red sexual flower of the wild, the animal flower, repeats itself literally and figuratively throughout the poem and is a figure for Mrs. X herself, who wears a red dress, has it stripped from her by the aborigines, gets it back, and is first identified by the convict through its redness as a non-aboriginal female. When, at the end of the poem, she sees a bird chopped redly into pieces by the hotel fan, she relaxes blissfully under the image of this living thing, this red thing, destroyed, as under a soothing rain. The reds and bruised purples of wounds, wounded animals, of sexual parts perceived as wounds, of rivers and shadows as wounds, along with the continually analogized liquids of blood, sweat, semen, undrinkable waters, and miscellaneous salty fluids, make the Australian desert riverside a sexual hell. Even the occasional healthy birds are perceived as peeing in the trees or as making hideous noises; their eyelids are like foreskins, etc. Indeed, our poor opinion of the aborigines's reception of Mrs. X must be qualified by the sex-obsessed stupor (and the red dress) in which she approached them, as we are reminded again when poor Potter encounters her:

His eyes stammering
at the sudden colour
of woman on the bank
her red dress tucked into her thighs

Don't you touch me,
he spat in the water between them
his shadow lying
in a lump at his knees.
Don't you touch me, where's the city.

I'll take you.

Mrs. X is the sick psyche, sick physically as well as spiritually. She is shown being fed, assisted, propped up, carried, sponged, grappled with—as inertly passive as a sleeper, yet as tensely horror-perceiving as the "I" in a bad dream. To her, the convict appears from the general wild sexual menace of the tribesmen, as a more individualized figure (a white man with a name), but made out of the same material as the tribesmen. He, also, is a man of the wilderness: he is tattooed with "wild" drawings, branded with a snake like a sign of the devil, striped-shirted like a fabulous wild animal, like the aborigines a hunter of considerable hunting skill (an uncivilized skill: he kills a wolf with his teeth). Furthermore, as convict, Potter is the bad Will, the thinker of bad-sexual deeds, Mrs. X's bad lover, her primitive desires escaped from jail, and thus at home in the nightmare wilderness. And Potter is he who can cope; he is the thinker of the poem; and this bad and branded male Will is going to take the passive female body back to the city. The primitive Will restores Mrs. X to her city self, the opposite of sexual wilderness, because she is not complete without him. He is an aspect of her, the male "shadow" of her subconscious.

Ondaatje's poem can thus be taken as representing a loss of the conscious self and a descent into the feared subconscious. The woman's own sexual fears (her bad, wild desires) become analogous to all that is uncivilized, hot, wounding, ugly. As the convict carries her through the nightmare, the wilderness is perceived as predominantly sexual and sick, and both the convict and the woman suffer physically. But Mrs. X is only exhausted, drained, sunburned. The man, already prison-branded and tattooed, loses three of his toes and gets his mouth badly cut (both castration analogies within the poem). Moreover, as the two walk along and through the various stinking, "blood-warm" waters, Potter and the woman are continually re-immersing themselves. When they are finally discovered in the river and Mrs. X cries out "god has saved me," it is as if Potter is, in a sense, washed away. In the last sections of the poem, she is cleansed of him. We don't know what happens to him; she doesn't care. Nor does she remember.

The concluding dream-level ballad parallels in city terms the first days of the poem. The red dress, which has recurred throughout (the bad lover achieves a red shirt from biting a wolf to death; the cocaine-stupefied birds that can be caught to be eaten have red vomit—the bitter-bitten animal aspect of Mrs. X that is at least redly destroyed, as bird, in the city hotel fan) turns up again in the first line of the lullaby ballad, along with dogs and children, now harmless and asexual, with ceremonial eating (but not blood: "silver wine" and "food in pans") and ceremonial entertainment (but not male aborigines dancing: a lady singing) and a river (but not blood-warm: under "calm ice"). It is a cool dream after long sickness. But it is not a well dream.

It is proper that, though we know Potter has a "real" existence outside of Mrs. X's dreamlike perception of him, we should not know what happens to him. For Mrs. X has sealed the door to her subconscious. To her, Potter is the savage, sexual, criminally branded Bad self. If he could cope with the nightmare, he was also part of the nightmare, and she got rid of him: "god has saved me." She has treated her history as if it were a dream. Jung wouldn't call it a happy ending.

Ondaatje's poetry is excellently rhythmed to the varieties of her neurotic sensations. His hunched condensed form with spasmodic out-reachings makes his work unrelaxing for the reader, even without the ugliness of much of his material. *The Man with Seven Toes* is a good poem, but not to be taken on a queasy stomach.

A final note. The book itself is odd-shaped. Clearly the handsome, wide pages with their glaring white spaces are meant both to suggest the long sunlit spaces of desert travel and, also, to slow down the reader's eye pace. A poet must insist that his poetry be read at blood-speed (what is poetry that we should mangle it like a bird in an electric fan?), but to do so by changing the shape of a book to the shape of a child's picture book is doubtful practice. The librarians may have to file *The Man with Seven Toes* sideways, without the title showing—a bibliophile's abomination.

from *The Fiddlehead* (Fall 1970)

WORKS CITED
The Man with Seven Toes. The Coach House Press, 1969.

The Fundamental Question about Poetry:
A Review of Ralph Gustafson's *Selected Poems* and *Theme and Variations for Sounding Brass*

The poetry of Ralph Gustafson takes seriously the fundamental question about poetry: *what is it for?* For Gustafson's is a serious poetry in the old sense, a literature distinct from prose. Traditionally the distinction between prose and poetry has lain in the greater density of textural artificiality in the poem, both prose art forms and poetic forms being equally obliged for similar demands of structural artfulness and aesthetic completeness. But in modern writing the prose of the art novel often exceeds in ornament and artificiality the prose of the modern poem, and the difference between art-prose and prose-poetry seems, now, to lie in the speed with which the author expects his work to be read, the novelist supposing a brisker reader, the poet a more ruminative one. The distinction between prose and poetry has never been absolute, but it has never been non-existent, and in these days of mounting prejudice against the conspicuously artificial in art, the distinction obligatorily phrases itself as the question: what is the artificial in art for?

In poetry there reigns at present a fastidious retreat from the grandiloquent as from the dishonest, although the plain language of our advertisements and the rococo floridity of natural beauty should give such moralism pause. But of course no art endures without artifice, and the difference between simple poetic speech and ornate language is, like the difference between a buttercup and a rose, matter for the gardener, not for the moralist.

Gustafson's best verse is ornate and artificial, and I propose to defend it as such. The artifice of his verse is adjunct to its truthfulness, the means for its matter. Nothing in us is more of the nature of ourselves and our own truth than our ability to be artificial, to be artificer, maker, poet, mini-god. Artificial speech proves the freedom of the will; pain without rhetoric is the noise of the conquered: "Ask for me tomorrow, and you shall find me a grave man."

Style makes the man. Without our own deliberated action, without our voluntary words, God is not created by man and creates not man. As Gustafson's "The Uses of Slapstick," addressed to the reader, concludes:

Without your hands
That move the hour, the hammer's action
On the string, He sits beyond
The pearly gates and twiddles thumbs.

Of course eloquence without serious matter is trivial. Had Gustafson confined himself to lovely description-by-word verses on musical or pictorial experience he would have been a lesser poet than he is. It is somewhat true, and in some moods very true, that much depends on red wheelbarrows, but as a moral convention for major verse such a statement isn't enough, nor did Williams mean it as such. It is the serious human concern at the base of great art, whether pictorial, musical, architectural, tragic, or comic, that is its distinguishing element.

The humane seriousness of Gustafson's poetry is a large part of its excellence. Of course, as in music, such seriousness may often reveal itself more as a gesture of dignity or of witty nobility than as a translatable-into-prose statement. And on these grounds, that style may be the message, I disagree slightly with Gustafson's opening poem to his *Selected Poems*, "Prefatory." "Prefatory" declares that a poem is a way of awakening perception, that a poem is a "way of happening" and that it is also a "way of concluding"; since the poem is a "way of concluding," the poem is "moral." Therefore a poem that lies is a "bad poem":

> even
> Though the music blow celestial trumpets,
> The formal Alps show thunderheads of snow.

I agree that a poem may spoil its perfection by containing a lie, but if its music makes those Alps, the poem has in its eloquence at least a portion of immortal truth and a way of "concluding" that can not be rejected. We must take our truths as partially they come. Truth is necessary, but the music of a poem is part of its truthfulness. How a poem happens is how a poem concludes.

A brief look at two Gustafson poems, "A Candle for Pasch" and "All That Is In The World," may clarify the point. Both the wistful Easter-agnostic "A Candle for Pasch" and the rowdy, anti-religious "All That Is In The World" carry their thematic point primarily through their rhythm, verse pattern, and artificial syntax. Enormously different as the rhythmic patterns of these two poems are, both reflect the sense we get throughout Gustafson's work of the crowdedly ornamented, lived-in, suffered-in, talked-in, historical, shabby, vital world that is Gustafson's universe.

In "A Candle for Pasch," the quiet grieving of the opening lines, with their echoes from Marvell and Hopkins, becomes harder, stonier, numb-veined, through their syntax, slowed rhythm, and close caught form:

> Aprils now nothing prove.
> > Not the trees'
> > > Green pieties
> Impel or mar or move.

As the poem continues, the sentences becoming increasingly elliptic, conveying by means of their over-condensation the feeling of "clogged disbelief" that fights against the Easter candle of belief. It takes a reader alert in the reading of condensed poetry to perceive that the "we" of the first sentence in the fourth verse continues to control the second sentence; but that dropped "we" by its omission not only closes in the rhythm of the verse but underlines the sense of loss and of personal numbness:

> And we are mocked. Graved,
> That gambled Love
> And lovely leave
> On Pasch, or not believed.

Those who gambled love, belief, and their leaving on Pasque (Easter) are as graved as we who can not. Both the stone at Christ's tomb and the stone of our stone-grasped philosophies remain unmoved; the last lines of the poem are rhythmically and syntactically slowed, and clogged to near paralysis:

> > Out is thieved
> > > And clogged: unmoved.
> Joy here, least: if none.

"All That Is In the World," on the contrary, is an exuberant and affirming poem, its wing-shaped stanzas expanding and contracting like hearty breaths. Each stanza opens a longer and more boisterous line, contracts towards a subduing thought, and re-expands to a medium-length line affirming, but more moderately, the basic note. The rhythm and language are Gustafson's best Browning whoopery, the right note, the right voice, the right ghost, for such affirmation:

> Such joy and jostlings nudge the elbow, anger's
>   Love damning those who roar
>   Delight and sin, equation;
>   A foot i' the grave
>   To have
>   Half goodness. Than Zion is,
>   This autumn's more persuasion,
>   This maple, more.

Gustafson's technical brilliance has always included amazing powers of recreation and a skilful use of heavy allusion and "lifted" quotation. I like the profound punning this rhetoric allows him, and am particularly grateful for the Milton, Browning, and Tennyson lines. (Hopkins, Thomas, Stevens, Williams, Marvell, and early Pound also make their appearance.) But one sometimes wonders just who it is one is admiring when stunned by such lines as:

>   he
> Doomed in that landscape but among magnificence
> By shell and seafoam tampered with, his senses
> As though by here of Aeaea used, exquisite

and:

> The world's ill-handed sorrows intervene
> And all the ornaments of clouds and trees
> And water-broken sun denounce their joy
> Roccoco to the grief.

Such lines are not derivative; they are original. Yet, as the comic books say, the Dead Speak. Indeed the vitality of these ancestral voices, and the sense of deep tradition and historical rootedness they give Gustafson's work, make one thing of Gustafson as half-shaman, true medium. It is, of course, his sense of unitedness with the world of these great ghosts that makes his voice so fully his-and-theirs; an unusual talent, but useful and enviable.

Gustafson's poetry is best when his central subject is the state of the poetic speaker's mind and when the speaker is neither a mask nor a dramatic charac-ter. Gustafson's dramatic personae are not as crankily unique, as super-real, as Browning's or Frost's; they seem sub-Poundian. And again, Gustafson's Rocky Mountain sequence, although excellent in parts, is weakened by his desire to prevent his mind from being the central experience. The poems usually limit themselves to a description of the external experience, and, worse, to the short-line rhythms of rough-country hiking, thus failing, on the whole, to convey the nobility he claims the scenery had. But the conclusion of the sequence abandons the anti-poetic for the resonant grandeur of the sonnet and the meditative imagination, and achieves in its concluding line the idea (earlier phrased as "On mountains / one does not try out metaphors") for which the sequence in general had been so simplified of poetic convention. Here poetic formality conveys the wild, inhuman natural better than the prosier, less formal, earlier verse of the sequence:

> At night, the northern lights played, great over country
> Without tapestry and coronations, kings crowned
> With weights of gold. They were green,
> Green hangings and great grandeur, over the north
> Going to what no man can hold hard in mind,
> The dredge of that gravity being without experience.

What is poetry for? The question bothers us again in Gustafson's latest work, *Theme and Variations for Sounding Brass*, his poem sequence dedicated "to the victims" of political uncharity. With these poems we not only ask the general question, but, more specifically, which artistic form is useful for what? In this latest work, which is often beautiful and deeply moving, two doubts afflict the reader: the first, was not casting this dramatic and narrative material in a primarily lyric form a formal error? And, second, does not the choice of any poetic form conflict with one of the apparent purposes of the author in presenting the material, his desire to provoke corrected political action? For in this sequence Gustafson appears to have two separate subjects with very different structural demands, and I think this dividedness of purpose injures the strength of this important and ambitious work.

In *Theme and Variations on Sounding Brass*, Gustafson has, as one of his subjects, the state of mind of the sensitive and educated man who feels an angry helplessness at the continuing news of injustice, injury, and public evil. Gustafson's second subject, indicated in his choice of news incident, is the wilfulness, the lack of inevitability, the wrongness of the incidents chosen. None of these "victims" are Hardyesque victims of fate; all are victims of man. Nor are these victims of individualized murderers—all are victims of politics. To any thinking person there is no such thing as "mere politics"—"politics" are what we live and die by. But political ideas involve criticism, experimentation, and trial; the point is action. The sermon, the editorial, the political essay are not lyric forms; they look outward not inward.

However, to agree that these evils are particularly odious because unnecessary, we require more historical material, more factual material, more dramatic material than Gustafson presents, relying, as he does in this sequence, on our pre-agreement with him. We do not agree with him, but not because of his poem, but because of what we have read elsewhere. From the point of view of drama or historical argument the "victims" of *Theme and Variations on Sounding Brass* are handled more like victims of accident than of Cain, a tendency increased by the sequence-focus upon the poetic-speaker, who is portrayed as at some distance from the incidents described, and who is responding, basically, to newspaper reportage and television. Furthermore, the diversity of the material Gustafson includes as exempla in this sequence forbids the use of dramatic or narrative form; that there are "too many" victims is one of his points. In fact, I think Gustafson's humanitarian impulse leads away from poetry altogether, because the reformer's point can not be made within the heroic fatalism of poetic conventions. (Satire may be an exception here, but Gustafson is in no mood for it in the poem sequence, and, of course, Swift, the strongest satirist, used prose.)

Artistic form almost always suggests some form of reconciliation in its iteration of moral rhythm, whether through the references to the patterns of nature, history, or myth—rhythm itself is a reconciliating force. But Gustafson is not saying something like "thasse ofereode; thisses swa maeg." On the contrary *Theme and Variations* is nearer to Mailer's essays, or James Baldwin's.

An additional artistic problem with Gustafson's political sequence derives from its point that the repetition of ill news numbs our sensibilities—the poem sequence itself becomes numbingly repetitive. *Theme and Variations* opens with five dedicatory quotations, for example; each quotation is just right, all five are too many. And the sequence concludes with the dullified statement:

> The trouble is there is too
> Much death for compassion.

In short, Gustafson contends with the ancient problem of truthfulness in communication. You can not possibly tell the whole truth in this life, and if you make half a try at it, the judge will get bored with your case. It is the artist's job to choose, to pick out of the forest of ills one Calvary.

The weakest of the poems of the sequence is the first, "Nocturne: Prague 1968," which is too general, too limp:

9

> The streets were taken in a night.
> Despite the fact that it was unexpected
>   it was incredibly efficient.
> The mild and ideologically quiet Dubcek
> was in manacles by morning.

10

> What is needed for an idea
> is a little planning,
> a few flowers.

11

> It was a period of euphoria.
> (etc.)

Whether the greater concentration in the Kent State poem, "Fantasia on Four Deaths," makes it a better poem I am not able to say, since Kent State is too "near home" for me to perceive it other than as a pain in my own bones.

The third poem, "Ricercare: And Still These Deaths Are Ours," shares with the "Coda" of the sequence a bitterly ironic speaker whose tone of emotional frustration and self-hatred denigrates himself in endeavouring to show towards these news items and photographs the type of callousness we are to suppose the sensitive newspaper reader comes to possess:

> The news shot: both
> Young, he in muck, walking,
> She in his arms, head suspended,
> Without support, her hair down
> (Her lovely hair hanging down),
> Axle-deep in thick mud
> The cart abandoned, he carrying
> Her the last three miles. It's no use
> Asking me. I don't know where.
> Poor Bengali Romeo! We,
> Too, would carry our dying wife
> Through a monsoon, if we had to.
> But we don't, do we? We know suffering
> Of course; but fleeing the army of Yahya
> Khan in East Pakistan,
> The idea, even in imaginative
> Fact, is a bit ludicrous. So far …
> … A classic.

Why "ludicrous"? The primary feeling in the poem is the poetic speaker's irritation with his own lack of hearty compassion towards each of these innumerable photographs, a lack produced by emotional fatigue, a failure of response that is, truly regarded, a health in nature, not an evil. We can't be forever crying, nor are tears all that valuable. What Gustafson eminently lacks throughout the poem sequence is the savage serenity that lets Shakespeare bring Lear out carrying the dead Cordelia. It is the artist's coldness that Gustafson lacks in these poems; he can not be showing evil, he must be making a fuss about it. Gustafson is chivvying the reader, (and, from a moral-political point of view, perhaps rightly so)—he does not want to provide a catharsis.

The fourth poem of *Theme and Variations* is the most conventional, the most cathartic, and the most successful. It is weighted as lyric, not sermon. The present with its shredded news item detail is counterpointed with the mythic and seasonal patterns of the past; the steadying touch of poetic rhythm returns towards the end of the poem like an emblem of the dignity of man, and the particularized evils of today are "coalesced" to the universal:

> As the leaf, yellow
> Strikes against the double glass,
> This winter window,
> So, man
> His splendid season,
> His certain life.
>
> May these dead
> Shock our hearts.

But Gustafson does not allow the conventionalized ending of "Aubade: Quebec" to conclude the entire sequence. In "Coda: I Think of All Soft Limbs," Gustafson returns to the recital of atrocities through the personified speaker, a somewhat duplicitous personification, because one can not believe that a man who remembers all these evils would talk smart-alec about them as Gustafson's speaker is made to do:

> They showed the corpses on
> The TV. I looked
> For genitals but they had fixed
> Up the film or else
> It was luck.
>   Then there are the children
> who must die so the others may eat.
> The worst were obviously expendable.
> You could tell: though they moved their heads
> They were no longer eager.
> The ones who got the food
> Jumped into the stream laughing,
> To show the cameras. That
> Is clear? Or should I go
> Back over it?

The photographs of unassuageable suffering seem to be a breach of the dignity of man as well as a callous gesture (as if the photographers are to be supposed only snapping for news interest, not out of any desire to provoke sympathy). The photographers, however, are not the inflictors of evil, and, as such, co-linked with the poet and editorializer: "May these dead / Shock our hearts." The speaker seems to be denigrating himself because he shares with us all (and with God) the powerlessness to redeem mankind; insofar as the anger seems to be directed towards the speaker, the "we" of the poem sequence ends in a fit of disgust is true to our psychology, but it is not useful as a stirring call to reform or as catharsis. The conclusion is a symptom of the disease it chronicles, but it is not entirely "true" to the final state of mind of the poetic speaker, who, we suspect, is a nicer type than he represents himself:

The trouble is there is too
Much death for compassion.

This compassionate poem-sequence deceives itself. Compassion wrote the poems, and neither the elegiac mildness of "Aubade" nor the self-irritation of "Coda" is the right conclusion for compassion. If the "World is such / That all we can do is send our love" is part of the problem, as Gustafson says in "Ricercare," it is also part of the answer. The answer must, however, include an admission of the impossibility of total cure and the absolute importance of still trying. The point is not one of art, but of psychology and morality, and of religion. We can sit in the Augean stables and stink, or we can sweep 'til we die. Gustafson, clearly a sweeper at heart, is trying to chronicle how it feels when we are too weary to handle a broom, but he keeps waiting to hand us one.

Gustafson's *Theme and Variations on Sounding Brass* is a distinguished failure. It fails because of the unreconciled difference between literature that stays us and literature that spurs us, the final distinction between that which is most poetry and that which is most prose. It is the distinction between art as conclusion and speech as persuasion to action. Of course the traditional answer to the dilemma is that the conventional poem, by conveying the sound of nobility, disposes the reader to act in possession of that nobility—that any assertion of good is an assertion towards good. It can also be argued that admitting injustice to be inevitable does not preclude the equal inevitability of man's struggle against it, that "victims" we have always with us, but never "too much" for compassion.

Gustafson's great poem "The Exhortation," from *Rivers Among Rocks*, in the *Selected Poems*, is a refutation of the conclusion of the political sequence, and a strong assertion of the quality of compassion that is needed, the compassion that roots itself not in an awareness of horror, but in an awareness of value, a compassion that expresses itself not in the prose of the newspapers but in the poetry of man. Its opening lines, like its closing lines, are our *answers*:

> Grief's love's origin. We cry
> For the loss, ourselves, the green rain
> In a month that has no runnels rich
> With hunger …
>
>   See,
>
> I'll unravel it: to plant a root
> You have to bury it. He who loses
> His life shall find it, etc., or
> In rusted terms: we have to love.
>
> There's a grief to it. Then, you have
> Your miracle.
>
>   Oh simple!
>
>   Grieve, Grieve.
> Pull down your usury, as old Ezra
> Bawls, meaning ourselves. Dig
> Your length in tomorrow's earth—a grief
> That will name you soon enough. Love
> And lose your profit.
>
>   Each death
>
> Is ours. John Donne said it …

and Gustafson concludes, punning gloriously (horticulturally):

> oh I would be less hortative
> As my critics ask, but less
> The man.
>
>   And what this asks is joy.
> Knowledge of sorrow is what I mean.
> By grief I mean joy. I talk
> To you flippantly in paradox.
> Understanding is lack of death.

The gardener's joy is the preacher's text. The ethics of aesthetics is confirmed through love and doubly confirmed, through grief.

Throughout Gustafson's work recur the major themes of mortality, human behaviour, religion, and our soured philosophies. Thus Gustafson's level of failure in his weaker works, such as *Theme and Variations on Sounding Brass* is still well above the minor successes of mini-concerns. Gustafson is one of our best. Any poet who wishes to write major poetry should study his work; any reader who wants a poetry strong enough to express life as we feel it when we most feel should read Gustafson.

---

from *The Fiddlehead* (Winter 1973)

WORKS CITED

Selected Poems. McClelland and Stewart Ltd., 1972
Theme and Variations for Sounding Brass. Progressive Publications, Inc., 1972.

Siwashing That All Consuming Art: Sid Marty's *Headwaters*

Sid Marty's *Headwaters* is a collection of a kind of verse written more often by Westerners than by Easterners, and more often by Canadians than by Americans. It quite possibly may be written by Australians and New Zealanders—but not by the British, for it requires, as its essential subject, a relationship to a kind of wilderness the Europeans lost before they learned to write, a wilderness with little or no history. This wilderness is no romantic Eden, no golden continent, no New Columbia to be discovered, no land of opportunity, nor is it to be conquered or civilized. It is not to be farmed, not to be archeologized, not to be bedded down in easily. Its past is Indigenous or animal; its present is hunters, loggers, miners, tourists. I call the poetry of such a wilderness "forest ranger verse." Much of Snyder's verse comes under the category; so also do Gustafson's *Rocky Mountain Poems*, J. Michael Yates' *The Great Bear Lake Meditations*, many of the poems by Patrick Lane, John Thompson, Sunyata MacLean—and certainly most of the poems published in the "forest ranger" magazine *Copperfield*.

For verse such as that of *Headwaters* can not be adequately referred to in the conventional manner as being of a particular school (with the suggestion of leader and adherents) or form (with the suggestion of metre and strophe). Rather, it is a particular kind of poetry. That there are different kinds of modern poetry nobody doubts, but most reviewers of modern verse tend either to ignore the differences of kind or to pit one kind against another. For as one may keep Chihuahuas, elkhounds, and guppies, so may one enjoy poetry of different kinds, better than as a "school." As an example of the problems raised by the term "school," Marty's inclusion in Purdy's *Storm Warning*, his dedication of *Headwaters* to Purdy, and his use of anecdotal material might arguably stamp him as a member of Purdy's "school" in spite of the fact that Marty's verse is in subject and rhythm wholly unlike Purdy's. Gary Snyder and Ernest Thompson Seton are more obvious predecessors.

Modern "forest ranger verse" must be distinguished from its relatives, the pastoral and the forest essay. Unlike the wilderness verse of Frost or Jeffers, "forest ranger verse" not only roots itself in the wilderness experience, but keeps its attention from wandering away towards direct commentary on human society. The speaker in a "forest ranger" poem is alone—or a member of a small group of people who, living with each other, think of themselves as alone—within a huge, vigorous, and physically demanding wilderness. He or they are as far from farm as from city, and unlike *Walden*'s bean-fields, the North woods require that a man sweat to survive. Atwood emphasizes the theme in *Survival*. Nature rather than society or psychology creates the survival problems in "forest ranger verse"—more Pratt than Jeffers. It is possible to write "forest ranger verse" with a tourist as speaker, as did Gustafson, as long as the tourist combines mountain sensibilities with hard work: hiking, camping—surviving. But the speaker of the typical "forest ranger" poems has a job in the woods, as axeman, ranger, monk. In part, survival itself is his work, his study:

> So I ride these mountains
> through the widowmakers
> carrying away old snags
> that catch on my leather
>
> ...
>
> Eye weeping
> hat gone
> one spur broken
> gun butt catching on limbs
> half unsaddled
> the pony mad, and
> flies would eat your socks
>
> ...
>
> Twist, dodge
> turn a useless
> half forgotten skill
> to service
>
> When the old men all are gone
> you must teach it to yourself

and siwashing
that all consuming art
was good enough
for me

       ("Siwashing")

The language of "forest ranger verse" is also definable, whether used by hard hat or by professor-turned-contemplative. This verse may use nouns exotic in specificity of mechanical, botanical, or anthropological reference. The syntax, however, is never formally complex or chattily extended; rather, it is direct, simplified, condensed. "Forest ranger verse" cultivates a sense of taciturnity, even amid metaphysical rapture, which combines well with an accurate eye for physical detail and, in Marty, a Twain-like sense of comedy. There is a comparative absence of self-drawing. Although totem figures may be named and major images may have metaphorical implications, the poems' emphases are always towards the "reality" of concrete natural detail, away from using one thing to suggest another. We confront immediate experience more than recollected emotion:

When it rained
sky's belly slashed
by sheet lightning
....
Canada geese in formation
steamed through the front yard
of my cabin, the stew pot
floated out with a load on
Swim for your dinner
said I to the mirror

       ("When It Rained")

Like the nineteenth-century transcendentalists, many of the modern "forest ranger" writers are attracted to the emphases on individual contemplation and closeness to nature of the Asian philosophies. Even non-mystic "forest ranger" writers share something of the transcendentalist-Taoist sense of the divinity of nature. There is, concomitantly, an absence of Judaic emphasis on the social conscience and human wickedness. There may be death and danger in the wilderness of these poets, but rarely anything so sordid as the visions of Isaiah (or Jeffers). Indeed history, sin, art, and the speculative intellect are largely absent from "forest ranger verse"; it thus presents a smaller world than does its majestic ancestor Walden. Nevertheless, the poetic speakers of "forest ranger verse" do dig into the concrete reality of physical experience close to wild nature in order to find out the essence of being. For not to have travelled as if to *Walden* is to have missed finding out what life *essentially* is—we do need to be alone in the woods at some time; we need this kind of experience:

> Now we have pushed those boundaries
> those edgings
> on the maps of skin
> "failings from us, vanishings"
> all out
> from the real tone
> of things
>
> And the old questions
> are still unanswered
> What is true?
> and believable, therefore
>
> Wordsworth's sexless decay,
> Sartre's black trees
> or the red wing tips
> of this flying whorehouse
> I ride in
>
> ....
>
> I have climbed mountains
> But what are they
>
> What are they
> but blue skies driven crazy cornered
> sharpened
> by the weight of heavy resolutions
> in which we played no part

("Departure")

But the love of the wilderness for its own sake, apart from what it may offer as clue to reality, is the dominant theme of *Headwaters*, and of all "forest ranger verse." Here we see as spiritual fathers: Thoreau, Jeffers, Cooper, Pratt, Grove, and the wilderness paintings of Canada's Group of Seven and of Emily Carr. (Carr's work seems to me, more than any American landscape paintings I know, to express a love for the uncivilized and vigorous wilderness, as it is, not as it might be, humanized. Traditional American landscape painters have tended to be more romantic, more humanly suggestive—so I read Wyeth— and, moreover, more often agrarian, suburban, or marine.)

With this love of the wilderness these writers combine a nostalgic love for the primitive. When, as in Snyder, the poetic speaker joins a society (rather than a group of campers or rangers) he does so as a Western outsider joining himself to a relic of the primitive past, to a pastoral Asian or ancient Indigenous society for whom ritual behaviour implying a sense of closeness to nature is still meaningful. In Marty there is an empathic sense of the wilderness, of animal nature, of Coyote the Trickster, Meschachakan the versatile, of Muskwa the black bear, or Mustahyah the grizzly. Also meaningful to Marty are the lives of the early woodsmen, the cowboys, railroadmen, siwashers. But modern Indigenous people are scarcely visible, and the modern urban tourists, unadmirable:

On the brink
stood the curious
with their cameras
their wives

("The Drowning")

Additional ancestors to this verse, along with the anthropologist resuscitators of Indigenous myth and Carr's great totem paintings, are, of course, the naturalist writers Thompson Seton and "Grey Owl."

Although the major themes of "forest ranger verse," the grandeur of nature and the dignity of man when he lives in and by it, are ancient, the typical form of this verse is modern—limpid, laconic. At least five factors dictate the typical formal qualities of "formal ranger verse." First, the strong influence of the haiku, in combination with the tradition of Zen-illumination through brief incident rather than through argument, avoids explanatory metaphor and tends to produce a verse composed of concrete detail mentioned, *felt*, but unelaborated. Second, the Williams of the shorter, earlier poems persuades most modern poets and certainly "forest ranger" poets of the value of things over ideas. (Williams said "no ideas but in things," but many modern writers have declared against ideas altogether.) And, from Williams and Olson comes the contemporary style of composing by short breath phrases, which can lead, in verse focused upon brief incidents, to brevity of expression. Fourth, the actual physical labour so often described in these poems has formal effects, forcing the poetic speaker away from armchair, feet-up rhythms into a kind of speaking-as-you-work terseness. Marty's verse tends to be much more vigorous than, say, Ammons', and this vigorousness reflects the "chunk of the grub hoe" central to Marty's themes, as opposed to Ammons' meditative relations. Lastly, the absence of chattiness mentioned above, the absence of author-to-reader commentary, condenses both line and rhythm.

Marty's verse can be distinguished from the general run of "forest ranger verse" by his two particular virtues: first, by his ability to portray animals as individual persons (not humanized but recognized); and second, by his rhythm, for Marty does not write merely sensitized prose.

Marty's ability to tell one bear from another differs both from sentimentalism and from the white-lab-coated naturalist who urges the impropriety of our interpreting animal thoughts. Marty's vision is close to Thompson Seton's or Gerald Durrell's: interpretive, realistic. Marty's animals seem to encompass a territory that includes Twain's black bawdy comedy, Thompson Seton's noble beasts, Cree divinities, Faulkner's legendary beast myths, and history's blood-and-sweat recollections. Meet two of Marty's black bears and one of his grizzlies. First, from "Too Hot to Sleep," a bear with territorial opinions:

He fell asleep, a hot june morning
above Wapta Lake, the Kicking Horse Pass
When Muskwa came down without a sound
and snuffed at his jeans

Who's this asleep on my mountain?

It's my friend Birnie asleep I said
(in my head)

I didn't hear you coming bear
I was dozing, I looked up
and there you were

You never know said Bear
just where the wind will lead me

when I'll be around
or what beat I'm hunting on

and sniffed at Birnie's collar
at his ear, which he licked tentatively
causing Birnie to moan softly

Nothing doing here he said, nothing doing

"We were just going bear," I said quietly
edging backwards

Don't move too quickly will you, said Bear
when you move, or better still
don't move at all

Are you here often, are you coming again?
he asked, flipping over a stone
licking delicately the underside
"No," I said, good he said, that's good.

Second, a smaller bear, from "Bear Again":

I tried to grab the rucksack
in the silence that followed
but bear had his paw in first
and fixed me with a red eyeball

....

"I'm hungry bear," I whispered
I was stating a fact merely
as he fished out the bags
with his dainty meathooks

Tough titty quoth he, or would have
and sooffed the whole works
wax paper and all

and, third, from "Three Bears":

a Grizzly Bear, silvertip
five, six hundred pounder
coming on so quickly
that motion would be useless

He sounds me, stops at twenty paces
to consider the next move

Speak to this bear
for he may know you,

said a voice
in my frozen senses

So I spoke softly
in his fierce hiatus
a deep and secret language
of love and claws,
a fluency I had only suspected
did make me wonder,
while he reared to his hind legs
in judgement

He swept the air once
with his claws, and hesitated
Dropping to all fours, he grunted
and moving aside
ascended the hill

Speaking to the bear is not only what the intelligent naturalist-woodsman
does, and not only the urge of our ancient Indigenous consciousness—it is
also, literally, speaking *to* the animal, rather than at it. For, as many of Marty's poems show us, these animals do know the poetic speaker—a familiar
voice-scent behaviour pattern: a comparatively harmless warden with some

territorial rights who "smell-lives" hereabouts, potentially dangerous if armed, but not attacking.

The extensive quotations above illustrate the verbal economy and precision of Marty's verse, but, analyzed, they reveal in addition to solid metrical form like a backbone that lends its own half audible dignity to these encounters. In his "Statement" for Purdy's *Storm Warning*, Marty remarks: "Poetry and the song attempt to be separate, but they keep merging into each other when I pick up a guitar." The guitar beat is audible—not over-obvious as in bad old-fashioned poetry, but not absent, as in the bad modern. Marty's basic metre is essentially Anglo-Saxon, and so natural to our tongue's plainer speech (especially when compressed, laconic, neither chatty nor lyric) that many of our modern readers trained to read poetry by eye only may not recognize it as metre at all. The metre of *Beowulf* is of weight, not syllable; you beat it out on a drum; it reflects the oar's stroke, the thumps on a harp. Two strong beats a measure, a weighted silence the equivalent of a strong beat. Very occasional use of three strong beats or a single beat measure allowed. No particular number of syllables to a strong beat, since the beats are the meaning-stress points in the sentence, not syllabic points: ("and *fixed me* with a *red eyeball*"). No particular number of weak beats. Length of stress, like a length of line, musically variable. Basic musical effect: trochaic, the two-step.

Marty tends to use the Anglo-Saxon two-beat for his physically-in-the-woods verse; he uses the iambic metre where meditative, reflective rhythms are more suitable. In "Saskatchewan Crossing Cafe," Marty intersperses his two-beat reference to nature lines with three-beat lines that refer to the café's radio music. His lyrical love poems, largely iambic, are made more musical, more dance-like than meditations regularized pentameter by irregular line lengths:

Yet you are alone with me
even in the arms of my daughters
and now, when fantasies of night
loom up
as the sharp hands of mountains

Come out
from all that ordering geometry
Unlatch the cabin door, forget

the tales of being bushed
for you
are far beyond them,
I promise you

I promise you
the cold starlight
of October

The frost on the willow
to rouse your naked foot

("Invitation and Covenant")

(Note how Marty solidifies the rhythm of the last line to reflect the cold ground.) But in "Coyote's Feast," the Anglo-Saxon rhythm reflects the poetic speaker's "tough" physical posture:

Head, hide, paunch of a cow moose
nose left on
Don't think the Crees done this
hunting at night, beer bottles
on the road for miles
Likely a whiteman poaching here
but you never know

Again, at the end of "Three Bears," the sense of danger requires the less relaxed metre:

But I am reminded
I am not at home
Here where I live
only at hazard

There is a darkness
along the bright petals

In Marty's dirge, "The Death of Mustahyah," his rhythmic abilities and his eye for realistic natural detail combine with a carefully structured multi-level symbol of great power. The grizzly of Moosehorn Lakes is the wilderness impersoned, divine, savage, Indigenous-named, a totem of the natural past. He is killed by the "rich man"—a Yankee defiler (like Eliot's Semite somehow not one of us)—but with the aid of the "poaching guide" who is one of us, whose corruption and betray of the bear for "yankee dollars" is our vice. And the spirit of Moosehorn Lakes is replaced by the divinity of corruption: the raven, carrion-eater, poacher, also Indigenous-named, and parallel to the guide:

> His terrible hide is a rag
> in a rich man's fist
> his lard sticks in the raven's craw
>
> ....
>
> Now the lake is tame, sullen
> the only thing that moves in the wind
> is Kakakew, the greasy raven

But the wilderness Bear, we are told, "killed his sons." That awesomely virile spirit of the ancient past destroyed his own seed. There can be no inheritance. What is left? The tamed lake of this "sullen land," the lake of the raven. Marty's *Headwaters* was one of the books published last year that had both something to say and the art to say it.

---

from *The Fiddlehead* (Summer 1974)

NOTES
"The use of 'siwashing' has today become a pejorative. But in the context of this review, published over four decades ago, it was meant to express a hardscrabble existence."
—Carmine Starnino

WORKS CITED
Headwaters. McClelland and Stewart, 1974.

Some Not Uncommon Myths:
A Review of Robin Skelton's *The Poet's Calling*

I do not agree with the major points of Robin Skelton's scholarly and interesting book *The Poet's Calling*. Because much of what Skelton says is widely believed, I think it important to quarrel with him at some length. These areas of disagreement come under four headings: *Form in Poetry, The Education of the Poet, What is the Poet?* and *The Survival Needs of the Poet.*

1. *Form in Poetry.* (See Skelton's Chapters Four: "Poet's Workshop," Six: "Poems in their Beginnings," and Seven: "The Many Modern Modes.")

Skelton's ideas of form are less commonly held than are his ideas about the poet. But in the literary field, where the cultured tend to see themselves as striving against the uncultured, highbrow against lowbrow, elitist against the common man, Skelton may be mistaken as a major advocate of cultured verse, and he cannot be so accepted.

Skelton speaks of poetic forms as interesting in themselves, irrespective of content. But what a poet wants to say and what he feels about it must dictate, as subject and mood, the natural flow of syntax, the basic argument of sentences and paragraphs. There is a close relationship between certain traditional forms and certain kinds of syntactic content that Skelton does not mention; he does not even seem to see the dangers of inappropriate or excessive form (e.g., the sestina) and the weakness of over-regular stress patterns. Neither our breathing nor the ocean's surf can be scanned with mechanical regularity. The rhythm of meaning is more important than any technical device for making more intricate the texture of words. A reader who overvalues devices such as rhyme, alliteration, typography, or syllable count, as Skelton tends to do, may miss the eloquence of that kind of poetry, which is exquisitely nuanced prose. There is no absolute break between poetry and prose, just a continuum. Skelton tends to mistake the Decorative for the Sublime. As consequence, the list of poets he admires and quotes is curiously uneven. Technical devices are fine feathers, but they are not the living bird.

2. *The Education of the Poet.* (See Skelton's Chapter Five: "A Learned and Difficult Art.")

Quite correctly Skelton stresses the value of wide reading and a good general education to the poet. But we all should read widely, not just those of us who are poets. Moreover, Skelton's recommendations display a disproportionate bias towards technical manuals on versification and word use, and towards those works of generalized mythology that tend to confuse the tribes in a common fairy tale, such as *The Golden Bough*, *The White Goddess*, Jung. Skelton speaks less specifically and thus less emphatically of the poet's need to read literature, and does not, to my mind, enough stress the importance of a wide reading in history. He does not mention the major political documents or any works about religious matters other than the Christian Bible—unless he includes all this under one word: "philosophy"—and to say as he does that the poet "must not be totally ignorant of the sciences or of current affairs" is hardly adequate. Whether poet or not we all need "to go to the learned astronomers"—and the mathematicians, biologists—Darwin, Cousteau, Carson, Einstein, Russell—etc., etc. And we need to be a good deal more than not "totally ignorant" about present history, current ideas, and news events.

Reading is the most efficient way of learning about life. We go to the library in order to enter the world—not because we are poets, but because we are alive, and want to live as richly as we can. Books are, of course, not the only method of education. Physical labour, exploration, seeing for ourselves—all these are part of it. But it is by words that we learn to think. Skelton's advice is directed towards people who want to increase "their bank of images, ideas, and facts" in order to serve the "high mystery" of their profession (105). But neither a fact bank nor "high mystery" of their profession is the point of education. If we read only for facts, pictures, and mysteries, we still may not learn how to think. We need to develop, through our reading and explorations, that logic which depends on a sense of moral proportion. The library itself can be a source of provincialism if we think and study too narrowly.

Too many poets of our day, whether writing as "plain guy" or as "educated fellow," write as if they knew nothing outside their own lives. The "plain guy" does not know anything that happened before he was born, the "educated fellow" does not know anything that has happened since. They have lost their sense of proportion. We can not tell the truth about ourselves if we do not know very much about the reality that surrounds us—those real ancestors, those real neighbours, those real foreigners. And it is not just poets who need the education.

Poets today veer between two failings: the trivial and the maudlin. For some reason more poets are afraid of being maudlin than of being trivial, and are, as consequence, more frequently trivial. Whether they write empty rhyme schemes or demotic ditherings they tend to avoid major subjects. Either it is: "art for art's sake," or it is: "admire my spooky nightmare!" or it is: "watch me seduce that broad!" This can be entertaining, of course. But how can poets who claim so often and so publicly to be supersensitive write only on such fiddling topics?

The maudlin sounds to us like the tears of minor nineteenth-century epitaphs or like the non-activist whimper of bleeding-heart politics. In our brutalized society vulgarity or anger are believed to be tougher, therefore more valuable. Actually, our feeling this way is cowardice, for the maudlin is the weepy edge of the painful truths. Between the deaths of Cordelia, Mimi, Little Nell, and "Daddy Dear" in the memorial column of the *Daily Gleaner* is no distinction—except in the adequacy of the expression of the single truth.

The impulse of powerful grief may often produce bad verse; more often it produces no verse. But there is no major verse that did not rise from the major, tear-jerking truths. There is nothing trivial about death, injustice, misery. A poet who never, throughout his work, risks being serious, is not worth his rattle, cap, and bells. More than any book or thesaurus, more than any fairy tale of Muse or Anima, what a poet needs for his education, what a non-poet needs for his education—is an awakened heart.

3. *What is the Poet?* (See Skelton's Chapters One: "The Speckled Bird," Two: "The Child and the Muse," Three: "A Priestlike Task," Eight: "The Problem of Poetic Authority," and Nine: "A Way of Life.")

The truth is less interesting than Skelton's answer. A poet is someone who writes poetry. Poetry is one end of the continuum of writing: there is writing with more attention to content than style; there is writing primarily intended to enrich verbally our experience; and there are all sorts of writing in between.

But the Poet is not the extra-sensitive fellow, the extra-perceptive fellow, the fellow with one less skin than anybody else, or the holy fool. His calling is not the priestlike task Skelton entitles it. Only a person who makes a point of not perceiving the people who are not poets can believe that poets are more sensitive than anybody else. (Similar people think dogs don't dream or have nightmares.) Since poets are rarely the most overworked, most impoverished, most oppressed members of our society, they are usually not society's chief sufferers. Skelton quotes with apparent approval a remark by Theodore Roethke, which condemns an academic critic as having the "sensibility of a shoe clerk." We ought not believe that a shoe clerk necessarily feels less than a real (do you dare to touch one?) poet. The inarticulate shoe clerks of this world may be as sensitive, thin-skinned, obsessed, and neurotic as anybody else; their fears, dreams, failures, hopes, and miseries, rightly observed, should reduce most poets to humility.

But the unlettered and inarticulate can only think or talk about their feelings in the clichés available to them. They are often acutely aware of the inadequacies of the expression they know to deal with the way they feel. They live in the gulf between meaning and expression. Since much verbal material is unfamiliar to their largely non-verbal lives, it can not speak for them. Instead they seek relief in the sub-verbal forms of psychological expression, drowning, or bewilderment: fast driving, loud music, speaking "in tongues," family feuds, public fights, booze, sex, ulcers, and heart attacks. Our nations seethe with unspoken agonies.

Even perception is not necessarily part of the poet's calling. The inarticulate may perceive more about some things than the articulate. Did Pound perceive the Jews? Does Layton perceive women? Sometimes it is the folly of a poet that inspires him, not his intelligence. The poet is not necessarily a prophet or a priest, or a legislator of mankind. He need not be Don Juan or Victim. He is, as poet, whatever sort of person he is as non-poet.

Skelton makes much of the poet as potential suicide. He forgets or does not know how many unhappy people there are out there, and that there are many different ways of behaving, many of them much more analogous to suicide than we admit. I agree, however, that any activity that focuses the actor's attention upon himself is more likely to produce suicide than an activity that distracts his attention, and that poetry is usually a self-centred activity. The under-exercised typewriter athlete is less likely to relieve himself in vandalism, street-fighting, or one of the self-destructive sports. A word-sensitive person may find television an inadequate drug; an intellectual may not be able to lose his sense of identity in mob emotionalism. Certainly some kinds of poor mental health increase our encounters with the numinous imagery of dreams, although our perceptions of reality or our use of words may not be thereby enriched. As a source of imagery or as subject, only, is poor mental health useful to the poet or occasionally coincidental with the production of interesting poetry.

But I think there are two main reasons for the frequency of suicide among poets, one of which Skelton mentions scantly, and the other not at all. Happiness, hopefulness, love, patience, and common sense are all directly affected by our physical well-being. Anybody who spends too much time at a sedentary job loses out on adequate physical exercise. Anybody who sticks with a poorly paying job may run out of healthy food. Anybody who overworks in order to support both family and vocation becomes physically exhausted. Intoxication releases pain, provides metaphors, but is bad for the health. Get your local poet an adequate grant of money, enough time alone to work in, good victuals, moderated intoxicants, and a daily jog and you will have more live poets grousing about how miserable they are, and fewer suicides.

Suicidal stress is undoubtedly also increased by all this piffle about the extra-special nature of the poet. Being extra-special all day would be hard on anyone. The goose who regards the gold egg as a bonus rather than as the absolute definition of her worth as goose will take the next egg, leaden, less personally.

You can always tell the dancer from the dance when the dancer stops dancing. The dancer will grow old and the poet mute but the person who once had the great honour of being the dance, the poem, that person remains. It will be easier to retire from the field of honour if we regard those who do not dance or write poetry less scornfully. If we do not condemn the inarticulate, we need not hate ourselves when we can no longer speak.

As far as the special agony of the poet goes, I must again quarrel with Skelton. I don't like the look of agony on a man who is too silly to take the tack out of his foot. The agony of some of our poets was real, incurable, perhaps inevitable. But why set up the Cowardly Lion as some kind of saint? Me, I prefer de Bergerac. Agony, showing on his long nose? Never.

4. *The Survival Needs of the Poet.* (See Skelton's last chapter, "A Way of Life," and his "Conclusion.")

I agree with Skelton that most poets need to be supported financially, that many survive by writing after work, "on the side." And that some people make life unnecessarily hard for poets—by opening closed doors, by being noisy in working areas, by interrupting their solitary concentrations, by being contemptuous of work that does not earn money. And it is also true that many people are too tired to read closely when they come home from work, so the poet is short of an audience even among the educated. Getting money to the good poets is a real problem. Since "more geese than swans now live," and they all write poetry, and since almost nobody reads it, they can't apply to the United Fund.

But this does not justify letting the baby run out into the street. Poets who claim they have to have all their time free in order to write spend a lot of it watching television, talking about hockey, drinking, and writing bad poems. They may as well have been changing the diaper. Work—in small amounts—has never injured a poet. Overwork does injure a poet—and non-poets also. So, too, do ignorance, cruelty, and self-indulgence, because the character of the human being determines what he can perceive. Truthfulness is not necessary to poetry, but it can be one of the differences between a great poetry and a trivial one. Being a poet is like being a liberated housewife—she has to demand respect for herself, but without ceasing to respect the people she lives with. The problem must be worked out at the individual level. The poet is no more justified than anybody else in being intolerant or intolerable.

How can we help? By getting more books into the schools. By encouraging public reading. By writing intensive and scholarly articles on the new writers we respect. By reading more. By proselytizing a little. By buying books for presents instead of bottles of Kung Fu Cologne or Old Joe Gin.

And by one other way—think of it as Lane's Solution—by seeing that the problems of the poet are not absolutely distinct from the problems of everybody else. Nobody, whether poet, professor, or factory worker, should have to come home from work each day exhausted. It is fatigue that ruins the poet and that decimates his audience. I would like to see every two jobs in the world spread out among three people, with no reduction in pay, but with consequent reduction in unemployment, welfare, and suicide. Just spread out the chores more thinly.

A poet is someone who moonlights as a worker in order to support his hobby. But the poet is not the only kind of person in this world who isn't given enough time or money to do the work that really matters to him. Even the very few people who are paid adequately to do what matters to them are overworked, usually, to the point that they lack the time and energy to appreciate the talents of others. We all need money, time of our own, a continuing education, and honour. We don't want a world divided into prophets, professors, and proletariat. If we feel we matter to each other, however different our talents, we may be able to help each other.

This isn't the White Goddess speaking; this is just daylight.

---

from *The Fiddlehead* (Spring 1976)

WORKS CITED
The Poet's Calling. Heinemann, 1975.

The Canadian Gardener: A Review of D.G. Jones's
Under the Thunder the Flowers Light Up the Earth

The Proserpine and Eurydice sequences in D.G. Jones's *Phrases from Orpheus* (Oxford University Press, Toronto, 1967) are among the most moving of recent Canadian poems. His new collection, *Under the Thunder the Flowers Light up the Earth*, is equally moving. Jones's themes and perceptions have not much changed over the years, but his presentation has become increasingly skilled, increasingly subtle. His latest poetry, like much of his earlier, reverently celebrates and appreciates Canadian art, Canadian artists, and Canadian nature. Even when in the West Indies, Canada is not absent, not forgot. Nature Jones loves, and next to Nature Art. And the Art he most loves is that inspired by Canadian Nature.

One of the criticism's most useful tasks is to bring its audience to an appreciation of a work of art. In this sense Jones's poetry is often a form of criticism, although as a work of art itself it runs the danger of being either much weaker than the work of art it celebrates (the poems on the painters Milne and Colville) or much stronger (the poems inspired by the poet Lampman). Jones has, over the years, paid tribute to many of Canada's artists; hence, the reader notices his omissions. Jones thus, unintentionally, arouses unreasonable expectations in his reader. The catalogue wants completion—how about those other artists, we want to ask.

All poets begin as a mixture of the poetry of others. D.G. Jones has been scrupulously honest in documenting his debts, and his tributes to writers who have affected him reflect this honesty. Jones tends to absorb his inheritance like Saint-Exupéry's python its elephant—what in the earlier verse bulges like an undigested monument is reduced in the later to a subcutaneous nuance. In Jones's new collection, William Carlos Williams's red wheelbarrow, a King Charles's head in Jones's verse, changes colour and dissolves, bolt by bolt, into a merely Williams-like affection for thing-ness, as if Jones were demonstrating for us the process of assimilation.

Jones has always been very much interested in the sensuous appreciation of minor changes. He does not tend to write about major reversals, preferring flowers to thunder. He delights in images redolent with small motions—the passing of time, the shift of a wing or a shadow, a changed nuance of emotion. At the conclusion of "Dilemmas," he speaks of "weathering" as what we "care about," rather than the eternal. He similarly concludes "Kate These Flowers … (The Lampman Poems)" with "heaven is a mortal flower." Small, and temporally vulnerable, flowers are, for Jones, the light of the earth. These are the central statements of his poetry. A generalist of the imagination would miss the point. The aesthetically indifferent cannot feel it.

Some writers today are proud of their inability to connect their emotions with the landscape, rather as one might boast of being seriously ill. Sensuous poetry, particularly love poetry, has grown extremely rare. Jones's poetry is sensuous rather than intellectual; but only senses educated by intellectual experience can fully savour Jones's sensuousness and aesthetic dexterity. Among the sensuous charms of Jones's poetic language must be mentioned his use of French. *Under the Thunder the Flowers Light up the Earth* is not a very bilingual book, for Jones's French poetry, unlike most French or French-Canadian poetry, is easy for the primarily anglophone reader. Jones seems to write French mainly for the pleasure of making sounds not possible in English. In "Words for the New Terrace," he pleases with the line "Or yellow leaves grandes feuilles d'or"—which sounds almost the same backwards as forwards. In "Pour Monique et Jean et Nicolas," he plays "woodcocks" and "galaxies" against "bécasses." One appreciates that Jones *likes* the sound of French. Jones's poetry is uncommonly directed towards the ear, and it is a pleasure to sound aloud.

I particularly liked the long lyric sequence "Kate These Flowers …(The Lampman Poems)." Here Jones takes advantage of the dramatic persona to pursue a course of poetic development without the harassing sense that the dull-witted may read it as autobiographic confession. His "Lampman" sequence is in part an appreciation of the poetry of Archibald Lampman; in part a criticism of some of the qualities of Lampman's verse or of the prevailing temper of his society; in part a criticism and appreciation of the human situation; and, primarily, a richly sensuous characterisation of two lovers whose love, like "heaven," is a "mortal flower." The sequence is a study of that love's "weathering."

Lampman, whose own title "Lyrics of Earth" might well do for Jones's whole collection, shares with Jones the tradition of poetic "high seriousness" and a romantic sensitivity to nature. Both Jones and Lampman present correspondences between the landscape and the state of the soul. But the speaker of Jones's "Lampman" poems is only occasionally Lampmanesque. Jones's "Lampman" is one of that squeamish portion of mankind who lack "the stomach to be real" and who have to learn to like the whole of Arcadian nature: its excrement and its weathering as well as its bloom. The characters "Kate" and "Archie," at times "moderate Anglicans" of our earlier, reticent tradition, are also the uneasy semi-inhibited lovers of today. The language of the last poem in the sequence, with its reference to "parachutes" and "underground resistance," puts the speaker in the modern world.

Jones's "Lampman" sequence places a change of time from early June through winter within the action of a single occasion of making love. The first lyric introduces the themes, characters, and occasion, associating the lovers and their actions with nature. Lyrics ii and vi revel in bliss, while vi comments on the sexual act. Lyrics vii and viii convey a degree of weariness and a slight uneasiness with carnality, while ix to xii modulate from sexual fatigue towards an acceptance of the seasonality of all things and a continuing sexual affection and expectation. But, hinted at the beginning of the poem, and from lyric vi on, the poetic speaker is overwhelmed with a sense of the loss of innocence, the death of the flower. The lyric sequence begins with the action of picking a dead flower and with the comparison of "Kate" to a surviving bloom, which, in turn, is compared to a star and "Kate" herself to a "day's star"—reducing both "Kate" and star to a mortal flower. Repeatedly the lover's relation to "Kate" is paralleled to mankind's often destructive relations with the earth.

> Guard yourself, Kate like the wild
> orchid, with neglect, with worse
> loneliness
>   what can escape
> destructiveness, man's damage
> emu, dodo, wild pigeon
> numerous herds and flocks

secret places of themselves invite
lovers, and new violence
                    flowers

in deep woods, beside
pools, moist rocky soil
petals twisted like brown hair

even I could not resist
ransacking the rare, delicate purse

Something is not well about the heart of Jones's Adam-Archie. The idea of sex as a destructive action is deeply rooted in many cultures, usually linked to an ideal of Edenic virginity. In Jones's "Lampman" poems, this idea seems like the taint of an inherited sense of original sin, part of the characterization of the poetic speaker. But Jones's repeated analogies with ecological sin suggest something not well about the heart of all mankind.

"Kate" was the name of Lampman's mistress, not of his wife, and this allows Jones to hint delicately of "Archie's" sense of sexual guilt without awkwardness or overemphasis, and without the Christian assertion of the sacramental nature of wedded sexual bliss. (The miracle of the Wedding at Cana makes it improper for the Christian to think of sex within marriage as destructive.) But Jones is very carefully not constructing a Christian poem, for all the references to "moderate Anglicanism," "Pentecostal bliss," or "Puritanism." The poem is sexual, and the lovers are not contractually or sacramentally bound to each other—their love is "free," "natural." The lovers do not exist "in society" but in the woods, and it is as natural creatures, rather than as social or moral creatures, that they experience the "weathering" of their love.

Most modern Canadian love poetry seems to fall into the grotesque the instant it departs from the "moderate Anglicanism" of the reformed "Archies" who write it, as if they were still not at ease with the sensuous. Jones's love sequence is thus not only one of the best but one of the few richly sensuous love sequences in our literature. The rareness of good Canadian love poetry is not irrelevant to Jones's sub-theme. For Jones's choice of a traditional Canadian poet as his speaker makes it necessary for us to consider the speaker not only as Everyman, but as the Canadian Everyman—and, of course, "Kate" as:

this land
arctic, temperate

white
like your small breasts

Thus the post-coital sadness of lyrics x and xi becomes the Canadian adjustment to Canada's temperament, society, or weather:

Gone, love's body, like a field
reclaimed by winter
all its flowers, exhausted
sick of passion, flesh itself
surrendered to the uniform
Euclidian space: blank wall
shut door, blind discreetly drawn

The speaker who, in the second lyric dreams of painting "Ottawa crimson," but comes "secretly to the fold, would find / election in your mouth," by lyric xii rejects the "rose nuances of remembered flesh" as "treacherous images," the "real / excrement of summer." And by the concluding stanza, though it is understood that spring will come again and love resist all wintering, the sense of something destroyed, something permanently lost, persists:

Who foresaw?
increasing violence accompanies
technique, the empty self

heaven is a mortal flower

Are the insights of the "Lampman" poems discoveries all mankind must make, or do they characterize a peculiarly Canadian Weltanschauung? Is Jones here, too, still writing a poetry that criticizes and appreciates the Canadian "garden?" Jones makes no affirmations beyond the value of the flower, of mortal love (sexual in the love lyrics; familial, fraternal in other poems). This is a post-Anglican poetry: beauty with change and loss is all there is. But as the liquid conclusion of Jones's "Rivière du Loup" remarks:

> mais c'est le fleuve lui-même
> qui nous assure

---

from *The Fiddlehead* (Summer 1978)

WORKS CITED

Under the Thunder the Flowers Light Up the Earth. Coach House Press, 1977.

In an Odd Way Nobler: A Review of *The Essential Don Coles*

Don Coles describes the circumstance of reading Beckett's

> own words, much quoted here, which are
> manifestly more exact and in an odd way
> nobler than the words I am normally
> exposed to ...
>
>   [as like]
> lying in a cave of wonderfully nuanced language.
>
>   ("Reading a Biography of Samuel Beckett")

For me, this is the description of how it feels to read the poetry of Don Coles. *The Essential Don Coles*, with a perceptive foreword by Robyn Sarah, is an important book, in spite of its smallness (only forty-nine pages of poetry). Naturally one wants to read more, especially the two book-length sequences, *K in Love and Little Bird*, but I can not think of a better introduction to a poet who will be increasingly recognized as one of the best of our era. The exactness, the "odd" nobility, the depth of understanding, the quietness, the tenderness, the plain but carefully nuanced style, and, above all, the beauty of Coles's work, places him, to my mind, in the company of Matthew Arnold and William Stafford.

We are not used to speaking of a "noble" style. For Matthew Arnold (see *Last Words*), nobility in writing was a product of authorial integrity, a matter of character and serious intention. By including Beckett with Arnold himself, and writers such as Coles, we arrive at a style that does not garnish itself, or show off. A writing that is modest, but not careless—that takes itself seriously, but without pomposity. Humour is permitted. Taking writing (and life) seriously does not mean avoiding being funny. And Coles can be very funny—but because he is, as well, "serious," this means that his funny poems can be deeply touching as well as amusing. "My Death as the Wren Library," an account of a dream, is tremendously funny, very beautiful—and it makes me weep. (It would take a good M.A. thesis to explain to the imperceptive how bizarrely meaningful, and how beautiful, the poem is. Read it.)

At the moment writers in English range themselves across a perhaps wider spectrum of seriousness than ever before. If, on the one hand, we have all those splendid essays by contemporary Canadian poets on Poetry and Truth, or Revelation, or our proper Relation to Nature (a recent example: Anne Simpson's beautiful *Marram Grass*), we have, on the other, the poets who win prizes and acclaim by refusing to be serious, who publish meaningless frivolities largely intended, I rather think, to make fun of the serious poets. A recent issue of *Poetry* is full of the unserious stuff, intended to be amusing, without emotional resonance, or beauty—topped by an arduously inscribed joke by Bök, a perfected example of an admirable poem nobody will ever want to memorize or weep over.

I admit that I often quite like some kinds of trivial poetry, light verse, or genial amusements. But there is a great difference between serious poetry and light verse. What makes a poem major is largely style (since a serious subject alone can't do it), but style so fused to the subject, the understanding, that the form and the subject are whole. And, if it is to be a major poem, the subject must be taken seriously, even when it is taken lightly.

One of the lightest of Coles's poems in Sarah's selection is "Kingdom," which delights in describing a Zamboni's "ignored choreography." The melodically even line lengths are mostly tipped with semi-rhymes, nothing too obvious, just enough to reflect the turnaround of the machine. The concentration of the kid "just / intent on getting it right" is reflected in the poet's concentration on getting his words right. The "odd" nobility lies in the respect for seriousness (the Zamboni operator's and the poet's) but also in the rightness of the description of skaters, the sense of balance and proportion, "rasping swiftnesses," "ampler lives," etc. The poem is just. So just that the last line is just a little bit "funny": "the perfect thing" that can and will be made again and over again. Humour, like nobility, relies on a sense of proportion:

> All along the streets the skaters
> are at supper, they've abandoned their small
> criss-crossing calls, terse celebrations, all
> those rasping swiftnesses in exchange for their
> ampler lives, and what's life is this,
> slow dance of blue light in a darkening
> space. He's going around the last bend

now. I head off. The perfect thing's
just about ready again.

("Kingdom," 52)

Coles's primary subject is not, however, "perfection," but our relationship
to time.

> In his poetry one feels the tug of the past on the present, the ever-
> present tug of the future; pathos of hindsight, pathos of aging, but
> also the consolation of memory. And one feels the vertigo of time
> —notably, in the haunting "Somewhere Far from This Comfort."
>
> (Robyn Sarah, Foreword, 7)

"Somewhere Far from This Comfort" is a long poem about a very brief moment,
a moment, when, in reverie, the poet has a glimpse of his childhood—just
a glimpse, compared, by Coles, to the temporary lighting up of fields by a
swivelling lighthouse beam:

> there I am there, right there
> for a moment in the light
> oh, I am sure it was I
> as the light ran over me
>
> what was I doing, doing
> I seemed to be reading, or
> talking, perhaps, talking
> yes, words and light together
>
> the words seemed like fields
> fields, but the dark entered them
> almost at once, those words
> they filled up with darkness instead ...
>
> [and the light]
>
> ran ahead over the fields
> they are empty of me now, they are only fields
> though the light ran over them
> anxious and swift as a childhood.

("Somewhere Far ..." 40-1)

Another of my favourite Cole poems is "Not Just Words but World," written from the viewpoint of a dying woman:

> Now it's just a straight dash
> for the dark, so late the wasteful agendas
> of expectation laid by.
>
> Only the small ones, perpetual, remain. Now
> she's sure she should have sat, chin in hand,
> watching her son's new eyes move, the sunlight
> on the floor ...
>   Does it matter?
> Yes. Her daughter on the favourite roan pony,
> cantering past, straight-backed and intent—
> for that one, never such rapture since. Nothing
> even close. Leave him, she should have told her,
> all those bleak years. Of course she should,
>
> and was so near to it so often. But
> were all those nights like this one,
> through her bedroom window slow field of stars?
> Those too. Those too.
>   ("Not Just Words but World," 18)

I have read many novels that have said less.

Another tour de force is the long sequence "Landslides, *Visits to the Gericare Centre*." The speaker is visiting his mother, who has gone beyond the ability to speak or clearly respond:

> Words like "worth," "dignity," etc.
> circle this ward like planets.
> If these words are not dead, if
> those planets are reachable, they are for
> moated and convoyed travellers.
> Over the car radio, report of
> a white bear sighted forty miles off
> Baffin, swimming away from land.
> tonight, driving towards you,
> away from land.
>
>   (X from "Landslides," 37)

The bear, swimming away from land, will die. To watch over the slowly dying, their effortful "swimming away from land," is to feel oneself advancing on that dark and shoreless voyage ourselves. The selection concludes with the speaker imagining the "hiding place" of his mother's long past youth:

> Who is here now to find you
> as you were,
>
> who is here to find you before
> the roaming into womanhood,
> to find you among the leaves?
> Press my hand if you know.
> Press it anyway.

(XI from "Landslides," 37)

To borrow again from Matthew Arnold, I would have to say that Coles writes "touchstone" poetry. Touchstone (see Arnold, "The Study of Poetry") is a line from poetry we remember easily and quote often, a line that says for us something at once meaningful and beautifully expressed. It is the nuance that does it. As in the above passage, the acknowledgement that the mother addressed may no longer understand what he is saying, or for what he is grieving. She will respond with the last remnant of her failing abilities. Perhaps.

My favourite Coles touchstone is from "Self-Portrait at 3:15 a.m.": "an hour's immortal, even if a life isn't" (50).

Yes, we know that is true, and it is poems like Coles's that make us realize, for all our mortalities, "the perfect thing's / just about ready again." We have to be grateful.

---

from *The Fiddlehead* (Spring 2010)

WORKS CITED

The Essential Don Coles. ed. Robyn Sarah. The Porcupine's Quill, 2009.

SIX:

Closing Arguments

Alternatives to Narrative: The Structuring Concept

Are there alternatives to narrative? We live in history—or herstory—the story that is telling itself, and any utterance of ours makes part of that unfinished narrative. Time is the grammar of our perceptions. Our desires, our memories, and our sentence shapes have chronology and the assumptions of causality. Narrative assumes and implies chronology and causality, with their structural implications. And the beginning and the end of a narrative are defined by the choice of a subject. The hero dies, or the war is over, what comes next is a different story.

It is easy to think of narrative as being the essential form of all writing, the urtext of all poetry. Yet some of our oldest poems are not narrative: praise, prayer, tirade, persuasion, argument, instruction, description, riddle, and rune. Non-narrative forms of poetry differ from narrative poetry in a very significant way: their ends are not primarily selected and defined by the choice of subject. And in a few kinds of non-narrative poetry, chronology and causality are very differently, very non-narratively, very un-historically viewed.

What chooses the end in a non-narrative poem? Certainly a sense of an imagined audience, who must not be bored, insists on a stopping point of some sort. In some kinds of non-narrative poetry, the relationship between the writer and the imagined audience directs the poetic structure, as, for example, in poems of argument or persuasion. For, as an example, to keep on talking much after one has made one's point or request is tactically an error.

But there are also non-narrative poems which are not structured by an imagined author-reader relationship, whose ends are arbitrary, even unnatural. There are interesting reasons for this, and I would like to look at the long, non-narrative poem with you primarily in terms of what governs the structures, and especially the endings, of such non-narrative poems.

Let us start by visualizing the structures of the more ordinary sorts of long poem. The narrative, regardless of the order in which it is presented, regardless of the use of alternative or contradictory elements, is essentially a linear, a chronological segment. That Ondaatje's *The Collected Works of Billy the Kid* is about a myth rather than about a person does not make this many-leveled work less linear, or less chronological.

The poem that argues or demonstrates its point is essentially circular: thesis, illustrations, and concluding summary or exhortation. Such a circular structure may include a considerable deepening and subtilization of the initial thesis, but it does not offer a change of direction. It directs and shapes itself towards its audience and concludes by stating explicitly the point implicit or explicit in its opening. Examples of this sort of poem are Anne Marriott's "The Wind Our Enemy," and Dorothy Farmiloe's "Blue is the Colour of Death: A Short History of Southern Ontario."

The poem of persuasion, on the other hand, does not initially announce its intentions, but leads the reader indirectly toward its point or points. Such a poem may be as full of divagations as the notoriously wayward essay poems of Robert Frost. Or it may be as seductively lyrical and anecdotal as Tom Wayman's "Asphalt Hours, Asphalt Air," which becomes openly hortatory only at its end. The shape of the poem of persuasion is, to my mind, estuarine—it takes a winding path to its delta.

Another kind of poem often thought of as non-narrative, but which for me is narrative, is the poem that chronicles the progression of a thought. Its ending is defined by the intention of the poem. Instead of conveying to the reader a point that the poet, by implication, has already made clear to herself, the narrative of thought primarily conveys the processes of, the experiencing of, thinking that thought. And in fact, as opposed to theory, it is not possible for living creatures to think without emotion or to feel without thinking. It is false to equate "thought" with "verbalization." (Musicians, painters, babies think.) But it is possible to feel tepidly or to think shallowly. A cartoon shows a cat sitting in and staring at a corner; the cartoonist's balloon shows the cat as thinking "corner" in a comfortable, feline way. For most of us the process of thinking proceeds by just such small, sensuous steps. We don't pounce, catch, nibble at first scent. We do not think of everything all at once, or, if someone can, they can not prove it to me all at once. Thus the narrative of thought is chronological, and linear.

But thoughts, particular concerns, do not necessarily come easily to a resolution. Some thoughts nag. Some thoughts, some concerns, are sooner tired of than settled. And the nagging, repetitive quality of concern may structure itself into the poem that chronicles it. Dennis Lee's "The Death of Harold Ladoo," and Phyllis Webb's "Failed Poems," and "A Question of

Questions," have, all three, the nagging, obsessional quality we recognize from serious thought.

But these two poets reach their poems' endings by very different routes. Lee gets to the end of his poem by exploring and defining for himself the fullest range of his feelings; in doing so he educates himself. The end of "The Death of Harold Ladoo" achieves the sense of exhaustion and release psychiatrists seem to desire when they encourage their patients to "talk it out." Webb, on the other hand, does not chronicle dogged self-exploration. She describes, instead, the sense of rational, imaginative, emotional impasse. And, invoking an equally valid but different mode of psychological release, she forces her protagonist, the thinking mind, out of the trap of the obsessive concern through a strong break, or disjunction, of thought and attention. Her poems, "Failed Poems," and "A Question of Questions," are Zen poems. Her point in them, if you recall the Zen anecdote, is that the goose does not *have* to be stuck in that glass bottle.

To summarize, poems that chronicle an event, argue a point, or endeavour persuasion, all have endings contained, in some fashion in either their subjects or their intentions. They are structured like the child's game: the child says "Guess what!" You say, "What?" the child says, "That's what!"

But there are kinds of long non-narrative poems that do not have a point to say "That's what!" about, that do not contain their endings in their intentions or subjects. For my present purposes I'd like to speak of these sorts of poems under four headings: First, the game poem. Second, the global poem. Third, the poem that is a journal of an itinerant mind. And, fourth, the shards poem. Each of these headings refers in some fashion to the world view of the poet making such a poem. By world view I mean what we posit as the nature of existence as we order, or disorder, our art. Constructing narrative, for example, we posit time, and some sort of causality. In an address to an audience, we must posit an audience.

The game poem supposes poem-making a game. Short or long, the game poem exists as such only during its making. Once written down, it has become something else. Indifferent to passion, the game poem is provoked by a spirit of play. It is to be made by one or more people under conditions they invent. And the rules according to which it ends exist only because we enjoy playing within a pattern.

At Koraku-En, in Japan, there was a garden house built over a stream. Gentlemen would amuse themselves by composing poems according to rule while a cup of sake drifted from one end of the house to the other. Similar games exist today, most frequently at poetry workshops. And of course there is poetry writing as it is often taught in our schools, where students are taught to write poems, although unmoved by any thought, uncharmed by any verbal discovery, on the schoolteacherish principle that what matters is not to win but how to play the game. And there is, also, game criticism.

Automatic writing, too, begins as game poetry. But there is that in our nature that resists triviality. Our dreams strive toward significance. The kitten plays at reality; so do we. And we learn that to catch something that wriggles on its own is a better hunt.

Yet for a person who is more interested in the moment of making than in the thing made, or in the processes which connect to the making, to a person who resists narrative causality or temporal finality, the games approach to poem-making promises excitement, immediacy, and challenge. And, in addition, it represents a philosophic truth. "*Now*," such a poet can argue, "is only the time we have. *Now* is our only poem. The sentence I have just spoken is dead." Such poets may not make good gardeners or historians. Theirs is the world view of the mayfly. But they are not wholly wrong.

The global poem is created upon a vision of the absolute connectedness of all things, all nature, all humanity, all time. In this world view, the human mind is not imaginable or distinguishable apart from its context. And there is no single point in a linear vision of time. Rather, the present moment is knitted into the movement of all being, past and future together: this hand, and all those galaxies. For example, in Phyllis Gotlieb's "Ordinary, Moving," the voices of the child of the time of the Pharaohs and of the non-anthropoid child of a silicon-based planet may be supposed singing together with the child victim of the Holocaust. Daphne Marlatt's *Steveston* is also a global poem, in which an enormous range of time and experience is perceived as fluidly knitted together, interconnected, organic, and whole.

Both Gotlieb and Marlatt emphasize the uniqueness of the individual, the accidental, and the wilful. Yet, for both poems, the individual, the wilful, the accidental is but the flick of a fish's tail in the ocean of the universe. The general tenor of the global poem emphasizes the oceanic nature of all being:

its flux, its continuities, its generalities, its seasonal patterns.

The global poem must end where it begins, for there is no seam on a globe, no beginning, where all is connected. And no single point in the globe can take priority. Yet we can not say that where such a poem begins or ends does not matter. For we do not experience a poem in one lump; we experience a poem in temporal order. Thus, whatever we read first colours what we read next. What we read last has the resonance of resolution.

Both Gotlieb and Marlatt use as refrain and as ending for their global poems the base image of their "territory": in Gotlieb the playground, in Marlatt the river going into the sea. That their poems are the lengths they are is largely a matter of kinesthetic tact, of knowing how long the melodies should go on.

But the lining up of a global poem in an order to be read or experienced chronologically can force an interpretation or a point upon a poem which might not have that interpretation or point as it was conceived globally. For example, in my poem "The Seasons," I saw that whichever season I chose to end the cycle—summer, fall, winter, spring—would effect differently the general tenor and effect of the poem. Yet we can no more experience all seasons together than we can hear all humanity singing. Our temporalities impose themselves upon the vast, and thus distort.

The conscious awareness of, and the admission of, such temporal distortions or partialities of thought and of the records of thought define the journal of the itinerant mind. There are, of course, other kinds of journal poems. A journal kept of a particular event, for example, chooses its beginning and its end; it is narrative. But the journal of the itinerant mind chronicles without an ordering focus. And its subjects and intentions demand no particular end. Louis Dudek's *Atlantis* is such a poem. So, too, is Daphne Marlatt's *What Matters*. In both poems the mind, thinking, may make connections. But things do not necessarily seem to connect. As Dudek says, "there is more than one road."

Where should the journal of a mind begin? Some male poets seem to think of themselves as beginning as energetic sperm. But female poets rarely think of themselves as beginning as rational ova. We began, of course, when the universe began. But we begin in print with whatever we've got that is good enough to begin with, somewhere in the middle of our life. And we go on until, like Thoreau at Walden, we discover a path where we have walked too often.

How do we pick out a chunk of journal to present to the not-very-patient reader? Most journal poems seek some sort of narrative remnant, time frame, or referential continuity for the portion of journal they publish. Since the last stanzas of any published portion will have positional resonance, the journal poets are careful to end with passages that can carry the weight of such interpretation. But the journal of the itinerant mind can not end with a full stop, with a grand resolution. Nor can it end with a seamless glide back into its beginning. It is a journal of experience: and therefore partial, linear and open—at both ends.

The journal of the itinerant mind, then, does not suppose the connect-edness of all things. But it does insist upon the partial continuities of the thinking mind, the identity that, in the act of thinking, defines itself. Shards poems do not assume even that continuity. Shard poems arise from a world view, a perception, that patterns, forms, meanings, values—are the arbitrary invention of the mind. Causality, chronology, even reason may be rejected. What exists is pain, mess, perhaps beauty, perhaps heroism. Perhaps not those. Shards poetry is not non-narrative, but anti-narrative.

But it is very difficult to maintain the shards vision. For, as I have already said, the human mind, the human sentence, moves toward the imposition of order. Andrew Suknaski's "Montage for an Interstellar Cry" and Roo Borson's "Rain" are both, to some extent, presentations of the shards vision. But both poems retain affirmations of humane values or an expression of human pain. Meaning retains its foothold in their visions. For to represent meaningless-ness by reproducing meaninglessness is to produce a dead poem. J. Michael Yates, who has written some fascinating poems, has over the years increas-ingly injured his poetry, using words against their denotation and context, and sometimes writing wholly outside of emotional experience, as if holding a mirror to a dead mouth. The attempt is philosophically honourable, but an occasion for grief.

If a poet removes all organic and traditional pattern, all causal and com-municative reference, all the grammar of perception and the tact of reader/author relationship, the material left may represent an essential truth, but it has become duller to read than a tooth chart. Fortunately, few poets succeed so far. Breaking the sentence into picturesque verbal debris, we are tempted to recombine it with music, mime, or sculpture, where it regains human con-notations, as in o-huigin or bpNichol.

In fact, the emotion we have of the disconnectedness and meaningless-ness of all things, of the "absurd," is based, as we know, on our ignorance, and on our very considerable vanity. We insist upon being the measure of all things. We dislike being regarded as unimportant by viruses, astronomers, or prime ministers.

But the anguish we feel at the gulf between the mathematical order of the universe and our preferential order of values is itself part of the order of the universe, as is our frequent stupidity, our occasional nobility, and our abid-ing ability to act, or to choose not to act. All courage, cowardice, all play, connect to, affect, and are affected by all things—but only as the pulsings of a dust. It is not our lack of freedom that makes us feel this life absurd, but our inability to control the free choices of others, the free falls of the atom, the mathematical tides of gravity. (Parenthetically, I could add that I do not believe that God can erase Herself by subverting the mathematical conditions that make it possible for me to imagine Her.) What we do know is precisely this: The world is organic. The world is whole. But it is not ours.

Nor do we really believe in chaos. We believe in our arthritis; we believe in the stars; we believe in the mess of our experience. We believe in what we use—our language, each other. We keep on talking. We may continually change our minds about what patterns we think we can see, but, as Robert Frost says, "We can't say nothing is clear."

Remembering Frost, I remind myself that a poem is always a clarification, a pattern—not The Clarification, The Pattern. A poem is a small candle, and will not last long against our darknesses, but we read our lives by these short flames. In any poem that goes on long enough, the mind will start rearranging the furniture of experience, for the sake of the pattern. We housekeep in eternity.

Our inventions against patterning are only a twist of the kaleidoscope. We tell lies for the sake of their patterns. We almost believe in the lies—the polarizing myths, the generalizations, the conventions—for the sake of such patterns. We take time to reason against time and reason—for the sake of the patterns of thought. Time, pattern, for the sake of—chronology, causal-ity—these are the germs of narrative. *Are* there alternatives to narrative? I am back to where I started. You can see this is a circular paper.

But I have one thing more to say. We must remember the difference between the two lives of a work of art. When a poem is in the process of being created it is alive in the same sense that a wet clay pot is alive on the potter's turning wheel. The thing-being-made lives within the hands of the artist. But when the pot is fired, the poem printed, the artist dies to the work of art. All poets are dead. The poet existed only while she was making the poem. I have left the time where I made that poem and that poem has entered into its other life, its own life, out of my control, and beyond my making. It has entered the time of others. It has gained, not immortality, which means experiencing time forever, but the petty eternity of art. As long as the recorded poem lasts, only its readers change.

from *Open Letter* (1993)

A Reader's Deductions

Theory operates according to the principle of indeterminacy: what furnishes one perception obscures another.

We can not construct the questions for the answers we think we want.

The axiom can not disprove itself. Nor God undo math. Forgive necessity.

Most communication is non-verbal; all communication is partial. Half-truths are not lies.

We only bear witness to our own imagination. Rumour shapes experience.

Meaning precedes the word. Perception is narrative. The bee, too, has patterns.

Enigma is the conflux of patterns.

As record of time, a poem is narrative. Image is submerged narrative. Nouns are verbs.

Imagery is not necessary to a poem. Musicality is not necessary to a poem. Ideas are not necessary to a poem. A poem says how its words feel.

The associations of poetry work through convention. Distrust the subconscious; it furnishes clichés.

Disruption, too, is a convention.

Today is new to the old; yesterday is new to the young. What is wholly familiar no longer is true.

I am the story I tell. You are my different story.

To resist the sentence is to resist fellowship.

It is not the poem which closes, but the reader who is let go.

---

from *Keeping Afloat* (2001)

Truth or Beauty: A Manifesto

I. *The Urn's* "Pain Face"[1]

Occasionally we find ourselves experiencing Beauty so intensely we almost lose our sense of being embedded in time. At such rapturous moments, Beauty seems to be enough: all we need and can know, as Keats's urn insists. Time, passing, drags us back to the diurnal drudge and we begin to believe that those joy-filled moments of aesthetic ecstasy are irrelevant: not "all we need to know," but instead a soothing prettification of or disguise for the normal, disagreeable, unbeautiful Truth. Beauty, we are told, reconciles. Beauty urges us to accept what we should resist, or change. We are quite sure we need to know Truth; we are generally sure Truth is not beautiful.

But what is Truth? To an observant eye, or an emotionally impervious eye, the laws of nature are beautiful not only as theory but as perceived in phenomenological change: maturation, dissolution. The Beauty of nature is Truth—but it is inhuman. We, who watching leaves fade grieve for our own fading (see G.M. Hopkins's "Spring and Fall": "it is Margaret you mourn for"), are too emotionally identified with nature's creatures and victims to find Beauty where we find no joy. Suffering, we say, is not beautiful. But Katisha (in Gilbert and Sullivan's *The Mikado*) finds beauty in the roaring of a tiger and is right to do so. Beauty can be terrifying, horrifying, unbearable. *King Lear* is beautiful.

We early learn to distrust Beauty. "Don't touch the flame! Don't pat the snake!" We learn to think beyond the appreciation of Beauty, and ask ourselves, what is the Truth? The Beauty of art can disguise the whole Truth of its ostensible subject. Consider those briskly patriotic marches (whether or not sung by Nanki-Poo) or the relentless sadness of "The Ballad of Chevy Chase" ("I'll just lie down and bleed a while, and then I'll fight again"). In each, the Beauty of bravery disguises from us the moral repulsiveness of slaughter. But bravery is part of the truth, just not the Whole Truth. We cannot perceive, imagine, or tell the "Whole Truth." As an answer to the ultimate question of Pilate's ("What is the truth?" in John 18:38), Douglas Adams's "42" from *The Hitchhiker's Guide to the Galaxy* remains as good as any other.

Contenting ourselves as best we can with what truths we do know, we tend to identify Beauty with the not-true because we find so much of our experience boring, painful, or morally repulsive. Therefore we suppose that a true description of ordinary life must not be beautiful, and that a beautiful description cannot be true. *Truth is not Beauty*, we assert. The truths we know do not seem to us beautiful, and attention to Beauty can prevent us from perceiving some truths. We are normally surrounded by beauty, which we tend to ignore, and to which art can draw our attention. We sympathize with St. Bernard, who is said to have taken long walks while pondering Truth during which he would from time to time strike off the heads of flowers at the side of his path. Their beauty interrupted his spiritual meditations—it was irrelevant, distracting—and, because Beauty can be distracting or irrelevant to our intentions, we reject the urn's assertion that Beauty is Truth.

Truth, we say, is a matter of survival—and thus to know or say the Truth is more important than to recognize or make Beauty. Thus we tend to believe that by rejecting Beauty we come closer to the Truth. But many truths cannot be told without Beauty. Was Matthew Brady, the American Civil War photographer, telling falsehoods when, it is rumoured, he rearranged corpses for the purpose of making more effective photographs? His beautiful (and horrifying) photographs tell us more about the war than do less skilled photographs of the same scenes. And who has told us more Truth about war than Goya? But we can't claim that Goya's etchings are not beautiful.

Consider the artless accounts of reporters, diarists, letter writers—people who go out of the way to report "just the facts" (as if dullness were always more truthful than the well-written.) These do not tell us as much about the world we inhabit as can the beauty of a work of art. Art can make Truth more visible, more powerful—and more inhabitable. Art can tell us where we are in the universe, how we feel, how things happen—art explains, it demonstrates—as the cliché goes: "it brings alive."

Art, making Beauty, informs us.

Keats's urn shows us its joy face, showing Beauty as a pause in time, immortal because out of time. But an urn, a work of art, might as easily show us its pain face, showing us Beauty within time, mortal, temporary—and as overwhelmingly beautiful as the urn's joy face, but showing instead suffering, passion, madness, grief, terror. This Beauty, this Truth, may also be all we know or need to know. It does not reconcile. If we want to know the truth about what it is to be human, we need art to tell us. We need both faces of Keats's urn.

II. *The Urn's Joy Face*

Poetry that shows us the urn's "pain face" continues to be written. But to judge by awards, reviews, grants, praise, publishers' choices—serious poetry is out of fashion. Most art, and, nowadays I think, most poetry, is intended to amuse, much like Walt Disney's Mary Poppins, who provides "a spoonful of sugar" to "make the medicine go down"—but without any "medicine." Of course we don't need "medicine" all the time—people "mutht be amuthed," as Dickens's Sleary (see *Hard Times*) reminds us. The "joy face" of the urn is as valuable as the "pain face," but I have come to believe that in today's poetry and writing about poetry there is too much sugar.

Six indications of the present bias in favour of sugar:

1) During the Poetry Weekend at the University of New Brunswick there have often been readers who, before presenting their poems, apologize to their audience of fellow poets because the poems they are about to read are not amusing. They apologize for writing about sadness, death, illness; they apologize for "negative" emotions. The majority of the Poetry Weekend readers, however, stick to presenting material that will not distress the audience. (No university audience is distressed by "bad" language, only by serious topics or emotional presentations.)

2) One of Canada's best poets, editing an anthology of contemporary poems, wrote in her introduction that she felt such an anthology was and should be like entering a party: genial conversation, good music, great food and drink—everyone having a wonderfully convivial time. Yet almost all of the major poets have written at one time or another dark, distressing poems—do we make them empty their pockets before they can come in? Granted, some poets (such as G. K. Chesterton) would be good party poets, but … Hopkins? Dickinson? Hardy? By preferring party poems as much as she could, the editor skewed the anthology. (Of course the poems submitted to her were probably selected by editors who shared her bias.)

3) Recently a new literary magazine, whose name I omitted to write down, declared that it would "eschew" publishing the "overly personal." But the personal is where all poetry begins. There are, I agree, some subjects not suitable for public chatter, but poetry and prose fiction, demanding as artworks more of our private attention, should not be so confined. Should we censor the musings of Leopold Bloom? (Perhaps what the magazine meant by "overly personal" were "feminist subjects" like menstruation?) There are no subjects and no emotions unsuitable for poetry. There are only two kinds of poetry: poetry that seems to have been written with ink, and can be intelligent, charming, serious or cozy—but always cool, and poetry which seems to have been written in blood: passionate, personal, and sometimes uncomfortable. As Walt Whitman writes in Leaves of Grass, "Who touches this, touches a man."

4) At present, critics, editors, judges, and teachers of creative writing overvalue "innovative" form—not original insight, not re-examination of language use (as the first postmodernists recommended)—but innovative form, which is a mechanical skill. There are at least two aspects of the "innovative" that affect the sugar content of contemporary verse: first, the contention that verbal disarray reflects or represents the chaos or disorder of nature and the inadequacy of language to convey much "meaning." This leads to a rejection of narrative, argument, or symbolic representation, and, with its emphasis on disruption of "meaning" leads to a refusal to deal with the distressing—a cop-out I think. Second, "innovative" carries with it a rejection of the supposed formalities and emotional seriousness of the past, perhaps especially a rejection of the extremely personal, highly emotional, embarrassing poetry of the great poets who immediately preceded us. Plaths don't party. They embarrass us. (There is no prejudice against poems vehemently expressing opinions and attitudes the audience already has, and is comfortable with possessing.)

5) Even the least "innovative" of our poets are affected by our desire to be amused and pleased. Our nature-loving poets nearly all produce poems describing the natural beauty of forests, fields, beaches, backyards as being unsullied, un-endangered places where one can serenely meditate Beauty (or at least prettiness.) The most popular poets, such as Mary Oliver, produce poems as accessible and as sugary as the paintings of Norman Rockwell. The best

Canadian poetry, we are led to suppose, has a "positive" attitude—rather like the Monty Python song, sung by Brian while being crucified (see *Life of Brian*): "Always Look on the Bright Side."

6) The peddling of literary artifacts as amusements, or "play," seems to me a sign of the current degeneration of postmodernism from its original emphasis on thoughtful inquiry to a mere display of disconnection. A major Canadian publisher is currently promoting a sequence of titbit texts by Molly Peacock as "delish"—like tiny chocolates. This material, a not uncharming variation on the parlour game "I Love My Love With an A Because Her Name is Amanda," does without the narrative force or semantic interest of, say, "The Young Lady From Twickenham," and is accompanied by pictures that rarely refer to the text nor suggest possible alternate narrative. Pure innovation. Purely postmodernist. Sugar.

❦

There is no harm and indeed much pleasure in sugar now and then. But if this is what we mostly ingest, we will die of spiritual malnutrition. We need to value the "pain face" of the urn. Pleasure without pain is not Truth—and playfulness is not Beauty. Yet there is still much beautiful pain poetry being written, which we should value more than we apparently do. Instead of ending this essay with a lengthy but necessarily partial list of Canadian poets who have written eloquently of the "pain face," I will conclude by quoting two powerful, beautiful, and dissimilar, pain poems. Neither "delish."

> Latimer's Statement to the Police
> by Dave Margoshes
>
> Let me be clear about one thing:
> I killed my daughter.
> After the wife and the other kids
> went to church, I put her in the half-ton,
> turned on the engine, and we sat there
> for a while, radio on, the C&W station
> from Saskatoon, the heater rumbling

like a cat on your chest, the stars
twinkling in the sky above us
except that it was daylight and
we couldn't see them. she took my hand
and said *Daddy*, not that she could, but I knew
that's what she meant.

                             After a while
I got out, told her *be right back, ain't*
I always? and went into the machine
shed, the hose right there on the bench
where I left it, a black snake in my hand
except hollow and cold, all the poison
already in my heart. It only took
a few minutes. she didn't cry,
and me neither. I stood in the barnyard
in the snow, my boots open, no gloves,
my hands cold, looking
up at those damned stars.

                 Through
           by Sharon McCartney

Remember the night I completely lost it?
Pouring shots in the kitchen. To irony!
Then dancing into bookshelves. Wasn't
it obvious I was desperate. Unhappiness
a conflagration I was attempting to douse
with thimblefuls of alcohol. Nothing gets
easier. Nothing. Winter-stunned denizens
of this hateful municipality, boot-tongues
flapping, wandering the Superstore aisles
brokenly, mouths open. No, dear 84-year old
Margaret greeting me at the pool, no, it isn't
a fresh, crisp day. It's a truly fucked-up day,
my marriage moribund, thoughts a mutinous
rabble. Your small town pride, morality,
just more ways to get suckered, hoodwinked,
hand over your taxes. Peace, charity, warmth

like the dog's favourite ball lost under snow
until April, or the cold lump of flesh incised,
the wound cauterized with the iron of desire,
blind passion—when he wants to slap me,
but gently, I let him. My life like a party
I'm dying to leave—the wrong people came.

---

from Anstruther Press chapbook (2015)

NOTES

[1] Title and subject of this essay suggested by the poem "The Pain Face" by Shane Neilson, and by his chapbook Able Physiologists Discuss Grief Musculatures.

[2] The lyric contains the line, "whose shoes were too tight to walk quick in 'em."

WORKS CITED

Adams, Douglas. *The Hitchhiker's Guide to the Galaxy, a trilogy in five parts*, Heinemann: London, 1995: 128

Margoshes, Dave. *Purity of Absence*. Vancouver: Porcepic Press, 2001: 88.

McCartney, Sharon. *for and against*. Fredericton: Goose Lane Editions, 2010: 20.

Peacock, Molly. *Alphabetique: Twenty-six Characteristic Fictions*. Toronto: McClelland and Stewart, 2014.

Whitman, Walt. "So Long." *Leaves of Grass*. (Critical Edition.) New York: Norton, 1973: 505.

Acknowledgements

SHANE NEILSON

I thank Carmine Starnino and Aimee Parent Dunn at Palimpsest Press for immediately seeing the value in this project. I also thank Elizabeth Diemanuele for acting as a transcriptionist for many of Lane's pieces, and also for Elizabeth's recommendation of including the Sid Marty review in *Heart on Fist* that otherwise would have been uncollected. Finally, I thank the old fern itself for investing in Lane over fifty years ago. It is not hyperbolic to state that Maritime writers owe much of their writing lives to *The Fiddlehead* as institution and patron. One of the *Fiddlehead* people that I insist on singing praise to specifically is *Fiddlehead* reviews editor Sabine Campbell, who has worked with Travis for many years. But I also sing praise to all the other periodicals Lane appeared in, including *The Antigonish Review*, *A.R.I.E.L.*, *Canadian Literature*, *Canadian Poetry*, *Essays on Canadian Writing*, *The Humanities Association Bulletin*, *The Malahat Review*, *Open Letter*, and the *University of Toronto Quarterly*. I salute the editors of same.

TRAVIS LANE

I wish to thank my editors, advisors, and friends in poetry—especially Shane Neilson, without whose efforts and advice this collection would not have been made.

Sources

I.

"Contemporary Canadian Verse: The View from Here." *University of Toronto Quarterly*, 52.2 (Winter 1982/83): 179-90.

II.

"Roads Round about Here: The Poetry of Robert Gibbs." *The Humanities Association Bulletin*, Vol. XXIII #4 (Fall 1972): 47-54.

"The Muskrat in His Brook: The Poetry of A. G. Bailey." *The Fiddlehead*, 100 (Winter 1974): 95-101.

"A Sense of the Medium: The Poetry of A. G. Bailey." *Canadian Poetry*, 19 (Fall-Winter 1986): 1-10.

"An Unimpoverished Style: The Poetry of George Elliott Clarke." *Canadian Poetry*, 16 (Spring-Summer 1985): 47-54.

"Maximalist Poetry: A Review of Whylah Falls by George Elliott Clarke." *The Fiddlehead*, 172 (Summer 1992): 140-3.

"Say What You Can: A Review of Milton Acorn's Whiskey Jack and The Uncollected Acorn and James Deahl and Milton Acorn's A Stand of Jackpine: Two Dozen Canadian Sonnets." *The Fiddlehead*, 155 (Spring 1988): 99-101.

"Summoning All That's There: A Review of Anne Simpson's Loop." *The Fiddlehead*, 220 (Summer 2004): 161-6.

"Haligonian Charm: Sue Goyette's Outskirts and David Hickey's Open Air Bindery." *The Fiddlehead*, 251 (Spring 2012): 103-6.

"Review of For and Against by Sharon McCartney." *The Antigonish Review*, 171 (Fall 2012): 49-52.

III.

"Rare Mountain Air: A Review of Phyllis Webb's Selected Poems 1954–1965." *The Fiddlehead*, 92 (Winter 1972): 110-4.

"Travelling with St. Theresa: The Poetry of Paulette Jiles." *Essays on Canadian Writing*, 10 (Spring 1978): 61-72.

"Self-Conscious Art: A Review of Daphne Marlatt's How Hug A Stone, Andrew Suknaski's Montage for an Interstellar Cry, E.F. Dyck's The Mossbank Canon, and Geoffrey

Ursell's Trap Lines." *The Fiddlehead*, 142 (Winter 1984): 96-101

"Imagining a Hero: A Review of John Barton's West of Darkness: A Portrait of Emily Carr and Douglas LePan's Weathering It: Complete Poems 1948–1987." *The Fiddlehead*, 159 (Spring 1989): 104-10.

"Other Tastes: A Review of R. M. Vaughan's Invisible to Predators, Margaret Christakos's wipe.under.a.love, and Elizabeth Philips's A Blue with Blood in It." *The Fiddlehead*, 207 (Spring 2001): 111-116.

"Poetry for the Ear: A Review of Jeanette Lynes's Left Fields and The Aging Cheerleader's Alphabet." *The Fiddlehead*, 223 (Spring 2005): 115-7.

"A Rare Originality: A Review of Hannah Main-Van der Kamp's According to Loon Bay." *The Fiddlehead*, 227 (Spring 2006): 106-9.

"What She Saw: A Review of Karen Solie's Pigeon." *The Antigonish Review*, 175 (Autumn 2008): 81-5.

"The Necessity of Re-vision: A Review of Al Moritz's The New Measures." *The Fiddlehead*, 257 (Autumn 2013): 111-5.

IV.

"Two Translations: A Review of Marie-Claire Blais's Veiled Countries/Lives and Eugenio Montale's The Bones of Cuttlefish." *The Fiddlehead*, 144. (Summer 1985): 100-3.

"Heart on Fist: Three Translations. A Review of Anne Hébert's Selected Poems, Knut Ødegård's Bee-Buzz, Salmon Leap, and Tarjei Vesaas's Selected Poems." *The Fiddlehead*, 164 (Summer 1990): 97-103.

"Death-in-Life/Life-in-Death: A Review of Tomas Tranströmer's For the Living and the Dead. Trans. Don Coles." *The Fiddlehead*, 191 (Spring 1997): 119-21.

"Speech as Machination: A Review of Nicole Brossard's Installations. Trans. Erin Mouré and Robert Majzels." *The Fiddlehead*, 209 (Autumn 2001): 108-10.

"Deep Time: A Review of Hélène Dorion's No End to the World. Trans. Daniel Sloate." *The Fiddlehead*, 230 (Winter 2007): 96-101.

"Identifying Greatness: A Review of Nichita Stănescu's Occupational Sickness. Trans. by Oana Avasilichioaei." *The Fiddlehead*, 244 (Summer 2010): 197-201.

Seul on est: A Review of Serge Patrice Thibodeau's One. Trans. Jo-Anne Elder." *The Fiddlehead*, 243 (Spring 2010): 109-12.

V.

"Review of Robert Frost's In the Clearing." *The Fiddlehead*, 54 (Fall 1962): 56-60.

"Dream as History: Michael Ondaatje's The Man with Seven Toes." *The Fiddlehead*, 86 (Fall 1970): 158-62.

"The Fundamental Question about Poetry: A Review of Ralph Gustafson's Selected Poems and Theme and Variations for Sounding Brass." *The Fiddlehead*, 96 (Winter 1973): 106-14.

"Siwashing That All Consuming Art: Sid Marty's Headwaters." *The Fiddlehead*, 102 (Summer 1974): 125-33.

"Some Not Uncommon Myths: A Review of Robin Skelton's The Poet's Calling." *The Fiddlehead*, 109 (Spring 1976): 114-8.

"The Canadian Gardener: A Review of D.G. Jones's Under the Thunder the Flowers Light Up the Earth." *The Fiddlehead*, 118 (Summer 1978): 152-6.

"In an Odd Way Nobler: A Review of The Essential Don Coles. Ed. Robyn Sarah." *The Fiddlehead*, 243 (Spring 2010): 101-5.

VI.

"Alternatives to Narrative: The Structuring Concept." *Open Letter* 6, nos. 2-3 (Summer-Fall 1985).

"A Reader's Deductions." *Keeping Afloat*. Toronto: Guernica, 2001. "A Reader's Deductions" was reprinted courtesy Guernica Editions.

"Truth or Beauty: A Manifesto." Toronto: Anstruther Press, 2015.